1991

Pills and the Public Purse

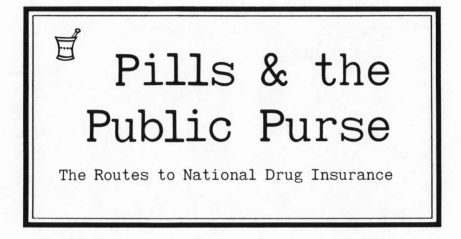

Pills & the Public Purse

The Routes to National Drug Insurance

Milton Silverman
Philip R. Lee
Mia Lydecker

University of California Press
Berkeley • Los Angeles • London

Library of Congress Cataloging in Publication Data

Silverman, Milton Morris, 1910-
  Pills and the public purse.

  Bibliography: p.
  Includes index.
  1. Insurance, Pharmaceutical services—United
States.   2. Drug trade—United States.   I. Lee,
Philip R., joint author.   II. Lydecker, Mia,
1926-   joint author.   III. Title.
HD7103.5.U5S57   368.4′2   80-6058
ISBN 0-520-04381-2

University of California Press
Berkeley and Los Angeles, California

University of California Press, Ltd.
London, England

Printed in the United States of America

1 2 3 4 5 6 7 8 9

Contents

List of Tables

Foreword

This year Americans will pay nearly $700 apiece for health care, and our nation's total medical bill will amount to nearly 10 percent of the gross national product. During a time in which inflation has been our most important domestic political headache, the skyrocketing cost of health care has become a troubling preoccupation—especially for older Americans who live on fixed and often inadequate incomes. Although pharmaceuticals account for only 10 percent of our total expenditure on health, it is often the critical fraction for the chronically ill and the elderly. And there is scarcely an enterprise in our contemporary economy as complex, and as full of challenging policy problems, as the marketing of prescription drugs. These compounds are full of potential for medical benefit; indeed, we depend almost entirely upon them for the management of a number of important conditions. Yet they are also sometimes capable of producing damaging side effects, or of being so inappropriately used that they carry significant risks without compensating benefits. They are heavily promoted through a system whose cost adds up to over three thousand dollars per year for each practicing American physician—yet the people who order them, and at whom all the advertising is aimed, neither take the drugs nor pay for them. There is no business quite like it.

It is small wonder that in an environment so complex, the determination of price is subject to a variety of influences. In my own term as Commissioner of the Food and Drug Administration, I was subjected to strong views of industry, professional and interest groups, and other government agencies on a wide range of price-regulated questions, including these:

- Should States require that prescription forms be written so that the physician must indicate specifically that the patient is to receive a brand-name drug instead of the lower-priced generic equivalent?
- Should Federal law require that generic names of drugs be simpler and easier to remember than the brand names, instead of the other way around as it is now?
- Should it be required that drug prices be posted in pharmacies?
- Should the government limit the amount it will reimburse Medicare and Medicaid patients for particular drugs, so as to encourage the selection of lower-priced alternatives among equivalent drugs?

These questions are more important today than ever. An increasing fraction of the prescriptions are being written not for such episodic illnesses as an infection or acute disease, but for use in a continuing effort to change the patient in some way. The middle-aged man with high blood pressure who takes antihypertensive medication; the woman who takes birth control pills in order not to conceive a child; the sufferer from chronic muscle spasms who takes a minor tranquilizer; all these are examples of a new pattern of drug usage. Because the medication is taken month after month, year after year, we have grown more concerned about the possible accumulation of side effects. And we have also become more conscious of cost.

For all these reasons, drug prices are the focus of this comprehensive thought-provoking, and sometimes justifiably angry book. The authors bring a remarkable array of experience to their task. Dr. Philip R. Lee, now Director of the Health Policy Program at the University of California Medical School in San Francisco, is a former Chancellor of that campus and earlier served as Assistant Secretary for Health. He and Dr. Milton Silverman, a scientist and science writer, collaborated on an earlier book about the drug industry, *Pills, Profits, and Politics*. Mia Lydecker, a longtime research associate of Dr. Silverman, is a staff editor of the Health Policy Program.

The subject of drug prices—and its inseparable companion issue, drug quality—is, like many aspects of modern health technology, a complex and controversial one. We are all familiar with the capacity of modern pharmaceuticals to bring us extraordinary medical benefits. Increasingly, however, we are finding that they can also do harm—and that they often cost more than they should. This book explores the sources of the latter problem, and will help in the effort to find ways of solving it.

DONALD KENNEDY
President
Stanford University

Preface

For close to half a century, a national health insurance program for the United States was considered—like "prosperity"—to be just around the corner. Now, as we enter the 1980s, the advent of such a program for this country—the only industrialized nation in the world without one—remains elusive.

The atmosphere in the 1980s, however, is far different from that in the 1930s and 1940s. To a considerable extent, at least where the more than forty million beneficiaries of Medicare and Medicaid are concerned, we do have a national program. Where medical leaders once denounced any federal health insurance program as socialistic or communistic, if not a step to total anarchy, most physicians have now found that they can live with a national insurance system—if not exuberantly, at least comfortably. And profitably. Where drug industry leaders once feared that any coverage of drugs in a national program would wreak havoc on their sales, their research, and their profits, most industry leaders have found that they, too, can live comfortably —and profitably—with the restrictions that any governmental program inevitably entails. Pharmacists—and patients—have discovered that they can cope with the restrictions and the paperwork that is involved. And, within government, bureaucrats have come to understand that, where health is concerned, there will be times when governmental efficiency must take second place to the quality of health care. These lessons, acquired over many decades, have often been painful. But they have also been valuable.

It is our tentative opinion that, barring an all-out depression or a nuclear war (which we may or may not survive), the expansion of national health insurance in this country is inevitable, perhaps as early as the middle or late 1980s. We hope that this expansion will come gradually, with a few more groups of beneficiaries added here and a few more services added there. Which new beneficiaries and which new services are, of course, matters that will be invitations to controversy. Any such controversy should not create dismay. That is the nature of the beast.

As one of the more tempting incremental expansions of national health insurance, the coverage of prescription drugs deserves particular attention. In comparison with the coverage of all or most physician services or hospital services, the amount of federal funds involved would be relatively small, yet the cost and health benefits could be relatively large.

If national drug insurance is to be developed, either as a part of national health insurance or as a freestanding program on its own, consideration of the key policy options must not be postponed until the necessary legislation is considered by Congress. Physicians, pharmacists, health economists, and the drug industry must start this consideration now. And the public, as patients, premium-payers, and taxpayers, must be involved from the outset. As we have said before, the objective is not cheap drugs or cheap health care but good health.

Although this book is directed primarily toward policy issues concerning drug insurance, the presentation of some background material may be helpful. Thus, Part I reviews the complex but fascinating situation concerning drugs, the drug industry, and drug regulation. To some extent, this section updates data which we presented in 1974 in our *Pills, Profits, and Politics*. The equally complex interrelationships among patients, physicians, and pharmacists are discussed in Part II. In Part III we consider some of the major approaches toward cost-containment and toward the improvement of drug therapy. In Part IV we describe some of the drug insurance programs already functioning in this country and in several foreign countries, and we present our recommendations for a future drug program in the United States. These recommendations—and perhaps others—must not be analyzed in isolation. What must be evolved is a package or combination of approaches. And, as shocking as this may seem to some special interest groups, there may be a need for compromise.

In 1980, while this book was in preparation, the U.S. Department of Health, Education, and Welfare (HEW) was changed through a governmental reorganization to the Department of Health and Human Services (HHS). In an attempt to minimize confusion—to ourselves as well as our readers—we are continuing here to refer to the Department as HEW. After the many years we worked with and within HEW, we find it difficult for old dogs to learn new names.

During the preparation of this work, we called on many old friends and some new ones for guidance, counsel, information, and advice (which we did not always accept). They deserve to share in any commendation which this volume may receive, but they bear no responsibility for any sins of omission or commission, and particularly for our recommendations. Particular thanks go to the following:

- Jere Goyan, then Commissioner, and Mark Novitch of the Food and Drug Administration.
- Michael Riddiough of the U.S. Congress Office of Technology Assessment.
- Thomas Fulda of the Health Care Financing Administration, and Vincent Gardner, formerly of HCFA and now of the National Association of Chain Drug Stores.
- Robert Ball of the National Academy of Sciences/Institute of Medicine.
- Gerald Rosenthal and his colleagues at the National Center for Health Services Research.
- Robert Levy of the National Heart, Lung, and Blood Institute.
- Graham Dukes of the Dutch Ministry of Public Health and Environment.
- The administrators of the many American and foreign third-party drug programs who shared with us the background and current status of their operations.
- T. Donald Rucker of Ohio State University.
- John Yudkin of the University of London School of Medicine.
- Robert Maronde of the Los Angeles County-University of Southern California Medical Center.
- Wilbur Cohen of the University of Texas.
- Leo Hollister of the Palo Alto, California, Veterans Administration Hospital.

- Philip Hopewell of San Francisco General Hospital.
- Paul Reinhardt and Michael Trollope of the Palo Alto Medical Clinic.
- William Apple and his associates at the American Pharmaceutical Association.
- Robert Johnson, John Skhal, and Pierre del Prado of the California Pharmacists Association.
- Aida LeRoy and M. Lee Morse of Drug Information Systems, Washington, D.C.
- Donald Roden of Pracon, Inc.
- James Russo, Michael Philippe, and Thomas Collins of Smith Kline & French.
- Irwin Lerner and Kwang Lee of Roche Laboratories.
- Duffy Miller, Alex Michailevsky, and their colleagues at the Pharmaceutical Manufacturers Association.
- Our co-workers at the University of California, San Francisco, including especially Donald Beste, Helene Lipton, Anne Scitovsky, Sharon Solkowitz, and Chester Yee.
- Our assistants Penny Shanks and Sharon Lydecker.

Our work was supported in part by a grant from the Commonwealth Foundation. We deeply appreciate the Foundation's continuing confidence in our studies and its willingness to provide financial assistance without attempting in any way to influence our findings or recommendations.

We would also like to acknowledge the generous support of the Robert Wood Johnson Foundation of Princeton, New Jersey, and the National Center for Health Services Research, Department of Health and Human Services (Grant No. HSO 2975).

Finally, our thanks to Grant Barnes and his colleagues at the University of California Press. For more than seven years, they have given us not merely their confidence, their encouragement, their courageous support (at a time when supporting us took courage), and the benefits of their great editorial skills—especially those of Paul Weisser, our manuscript editor—but also their warm friendship. We are truly grateful.

San Francisco   MILTON SILVERMAN
September 1980   PHILIP R. LEE
                                         MIA LYDECKER

Milton Silverman, Ph.D., born in San Francisco in 1910, was trained in biochemistry and pharmacology at Stanford University and the University of California School of Medicine.

From 1934 to 1959, he won national recognition as the science editor of the San Francisco *Chronicle*, and later as a science writer for the *Saturday Evening Post, Collier's, Reader's Digest*, and other magazines. He is the author of *Magic in a Bottle*, a history of drug discovery, and he is a past president of the National Association of Science Writers, and a winner of the Lasker Award for distinguished medical reporting.

His own research has included studies on synthetic sugars, anesthetics, the pharmacology of alcoholic beverages, and cultural drinking patterns in Italy, Brazil, France, Sweden, and the United States.

He served as a special assistant to Dr. Lee in Washington from 1966 to 1969, and again at the University of California, San Francisco, from 1969 to 1972. He is now a research pharmacologist at UCSF's School of Medicine, a lecturer at the Stanford University School of Medicine, and a consultant to the Food and Drug Administration.

Philip R. Lee, M.D., a member of a noted California medical family, was born in San Francisco in 1924. He was trained at Stanford University, the New York University-Bellevue Medical Center, and the Mayo Clinic.

He joined the staff of the Palo Alto Medical Clinic in 1956, working primarily as a family physician. From 1963 to 1965, he was the director of health services in the Agency for International Development; and from 1965 to 1969, he was the Assistant Secretary for Health and Scientific Affairs in the U.S. Department of Health, Education, and Welfare.

He served as chancellor of the University of California, San Francisco, from 1969 to 1972, and has been a professor of social medicine there since 1969.

His own studies have involved him in such fields as health manpower, health care for the elderly, bioethics, drug regulatory policies, and governmental health policies in general.

Mia Lydecker, born in The Hague, Holland, in 1926, was trained at the University of Utrecht, Louvain University, and the Sorbonne before coming to the United States. She began her career as a research associate with Dr. Silverman in 1962. During the past few years, she has worked with him in studying drug promotion and national drug insurance programs in Japan, Australia, New Zealand, Canada, and more than a score of other countries in Europe, Asia, and Africa.

During their years in Washington, Dr. Lee acted as chairman and Dr. Silverman as executive secretary and staff director of the HEW Task Force on Prescription Drugs. Ms. Lydecker served briefly as a consultant to the Task Force. The reports of this group in 1968 and 1969 led to significant changes in federal drug policies. That work also led to the publication in 1974 of *Pills, Profits, and Politics* by Drs. Silverman and Lee, which focused public attention on drug company policies and profits, as well as on the irrational prescribing and use of drugs. In turn, this led Drs. Silverman and Lee and Ms. Lydecker to the investigation of multinational drug company promotion in Latin America and the publication in 1976 of *The Drugging of the Americas*.

Dr. Lee is now director, Dr. Silverman a senior faculty member, and Ms. Lydecker a staff editor of UCSF's Health Policy Program.

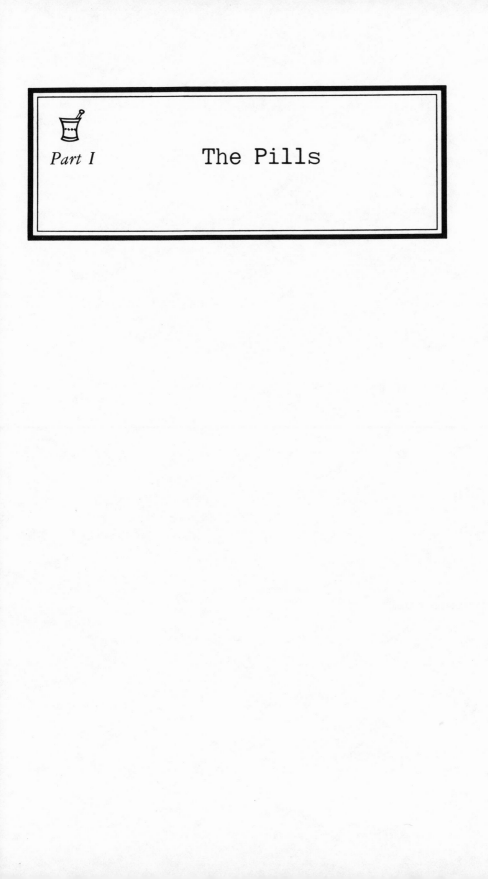

Part I The Pills

Since the end of World War II in 1945, and certainly since 1955, there has been growing evidence that appropriate treatment with drugs represents probably the most widely applied and most cost-effective form of medical treatment. There has been mounting proof that drugs can control most bacterial infections and now some viral infections, speed recovery, minimize crippling and other disabilities, make feasible surgical feats that were once impractical or impossible, and reduce the financial burdens of illness on society. Such developments as the introduction of sulfa drugs in the 1930s, penicillin and the other antibiotics beginning in the 1940s, the antihypertension drugs, the diuretics, the major tranquilizers, and cortisone and its relatives in the 1950s, the drugs against depression in the 1960s, and the beta-blockers for use against hypertension, heart arrhythmias, and angina, and the histamine-blockers against duodenal ulcer in the 1970s have come close to revolutionizing the practice of medicine.

Much of the credit clearly belongs to the drug industry in general and the American drug industry in particular. During the past decade, pharmaceutical firms have continued to produce drug products of remarkably high quality—though not of invariably perfect quality. They have introduced a myriad of drugs, all of them by definition new and some of them important. They have raised their prices, but these raises must be considered modest in comparison with the astronomical increases in physician fees and hospital bills. Some of the compan-

3

ies have continued to rail at the Food and Drug Administration, and especially at FDA's enforcement of the 1962 Kefauver-Harris Amendments. These amendments stipulated for the first time that a new drug could not win FDA approval without substantial scientific evidence of not only its relative safety but also its efficacy. Nevertheless, most industry leaders who once denounced Kefauver-Harris as an unmitigated disaster have found that they can live with the law in reasonable comfort. And profitably.

Much credit, too, belongs to physicians who prescribe or administer drugs. There appears to be a growing awareness among them that practically no drug is absolutely safe; any drug product sufficiently potent to alleviate a symptom or control a disease is also able under some conditions to cause injury, tissue damage, or even death. Fewer physicians seem to accept the rationalization that "the prescription may not help but it won't hurt."

Credit for a portion of the new attitudes toward drugs must go to clinical pharmacists, who are probably more knowledgeable about drugs than are most physicians. Once a diagnosis has been reached, physicians are increasingly turning to clinically trained pharmacists to suggest which drug and which form of that drug might be most useful for a particular patient.

As remarkable as this drug revolution may be, it has one distressing flaw: *many patients cannot afford to pay for the drugs they need.*

At this point, we must emphasize that we are concerned in this book almost exclusively with prescription drugs (plus insulin). Nonprescription or over-the-counter (OTC) drugs also have a role in health care, but in most instances their cost is not burdensome, and few if any insurance programs, governmental or private, provide reimbursement for their purchase.

Under the present system of health care delivery in the United States, there is no national program to cover drug costs under a national health insurance plan. This country is probably the last industrialized nation in the world without such a program.

There are, of course, some groups who have more or less adequate protection against drug costs. Drug coverage is provided under the Veterans Administration (VA) medical care program for veterans with service-connected disabilities, and by the Department of Defense for military personnel and their dependents. Similar benefits are furnished under many union health programs and some private insurance plans. There are, however, three groups whose protection is glaringly deficient:

Under Medicare, the elderly—those aged 65 or more—have most of their prescription drug expenses covered, but only when they are hospitalized; to purchase drugs from a community pharmacy, they must pay out of pocket or purchase supplemental private insurance, which few of them can afford. Among the elderly, pockets are notoriously empty. They represent only about 11 percent of the population, but they account for 25 percent of all out-of-hospital prescription drug expenditures.

For the medically indigent and those on welfare, drug coverage is provided in nearly all states under a Medicaid program for both in-hospital and out-of-hospital drug costs, but unfortunately only as an optional benefit. Coverage is usually determined by state formularies specifying those drug products for which reimbursement is allowed. In twenty-one states, only the medically indigent are covered; in most others, the medically indigent and the medically needy are beneficiaries; and in three, there is no Medicaid drug coverage at all. In many states with drug programs, shrinking budgets have reduced such coverage to distressingly low levels. Like the elderly, the poor suffer from an inordinately high amount of sickness.

Finally, there are those persons of any age who are victims of serious, chronic, disabling diseases and who could benefit greatly from drug treatment. Many of these patients have no job, no insurance protection, no membership in any health plan, and rapidly dwindling assets. As a group, they have no strong voice to speak for them in the halls of Congress.

To some people, the very idea of setting up a government program to deliver adequate help to these groups, and perhaps others, is anathema. They have reacted by using bumper strips and other signs asking, "Do you want health care controlled by the people who gave you the Postal Service?"

This is an intriguing question. It might be countered by such equally simplistic queries as "Do you want health care controlled by the people in the private sector who gave you polluted air, soil, rivers, and lakes? Or who were responsible for destructive oil spills? Or who marketed poisonous soups and drugs whose toxic properties were long concealed? Or who produced flammable nightwear for children? Or whose automobiles had to be recalled as defective by the tens or hundreds of thousands? Or who have been largely responsible for the rapid increase in the cost of health care during the last fifteen years?"

All of these questions—and the list could be expanded many times—must be dismissed as irrelevant. The vital problems concern how to devise the best possible system, with the maximum benefits, the minimum defects, and the greatest help for those who desperately need it.

Intimately related here is the issue of what is termed distributive justice. Unless the coverage is provided on all drugs for all people—an approach that seems totally impossible for the foreseeable future because of unacceptably high costs—the benefits must necessarily be rationed. But in what way? Should the program be designed to help primarily those who have paid their taxes and thus *earned* the coverage? Or those who have been economically and culturally deprived and may be thought to *deserve* it? Or those who are seriously ill and *need* it?

MODERN DRUG USE

Any rational decisions in this complex and often emotion-charged field must be based on reasonably complete knowledge of the clinical and economic facts involved. Unfortunately, this knowledge is not readily available. Many of the so-called facts are based on data that are often outdated, incomplete, and of questionable reliability.

There is, for example, no agreement on how to answer what should be the simplest of questions: What is the current prescription drug bill at the retail level? At a 1977 conference, it was stated that recent estimates ranged from $10 billion a year or less to $14 billion or more.[1] Using the latest available information on sales at the manufacturers' level[2] together with an old and possibly useful rule of thumb that total retail drug sales are roughly double total manufacturers' sales, it may be suggested that the nation's prescription drug bill was in the neighborhood of $18 billion in 1978 and $20 billion in 1979.

Included in these figures are prescription drugs dispensed not only by independent and chain pharmacies in the community but also by mail-order pharmacies, dispensing physicians, discount pharmacies, nursing homes, hospital pharmacies serving both inpatients and outpatients, and governmental institutions.

These figures may appear large, but they represent only a small fraction of the nation's bill for all health care services and supplies: $163 billion in fiscal 1977, and $200 billion in fiscal 1979.

Roughly 35 percent of hospital drugs and 9 percent of prescription drugs dispensed outside of hospitals are paid for under the Medicare and Medicaid programs.[3] Paying for drugs in such quantities makes the United States government one of the largest single drug purchasers in the world. For that reason, if for no other, the government now has a more-than-passing interest in drug prices.

There is similar confusion over the matter of total numbers of prescriptions dispensed each year. One reason for this is the fact that a prescription filled for a hospitalized patient may be substantially different in nature, size, and cost from one filled in a neighborhood pharmacy. Another reason is that the figures obtained by various marketing survey groups are derived by different methods for different purposes, and their various findings are not readily comparable.

According to one survey, the number of prescriptions dispensed annually by retail pharmacies rose steadily to a peak of 1.52 billion in 1973 and then dropped slowly each year thereafter: 1.50 billion in 1974, 1.49 billion in 1975, 1.46 billion in 1976, 1.41 billion in 1977, 1.40 billion in 1978 and 1.37 billion in 1979.[4] One proposed explanation for this decrease, especially in the face of steadily rising total annual expenditures, is that, since 1973, American physicians have been writing fewer prescriptions but each prescription calls for a larger quantity of the drug product. Other explanations include the possibility that, during the recent recession, some patients postponed obtaining refills. Recent regulations of the Drug Enforcement Administration (DEA) make it somewhat more difficult to obtain refills of certain classes of drugs—for example, barbiturates and other sedatives—and hospital pharmacies rather than community pharmacies are filling more prescriptions for outpatients. Perhaps some physicians are responding to pressures to cut down on their prescribing.

Among these billions of prescriptions, drug experts are struck— and some of them seriously alarmed—by the continuing high proportions represented by two classes of drugs: antibiotics and other antibacterial agents on the one hand, and such psychoactive drugs as stimulants, sedatives, and tranquilizers on the other.

Antibiotics and other anti-infectives account for about 14 percent of all prescriptions and for 15 to 20 percent of those dispensed to hospitalized patients.[5] Many of these drugs are ordered for the treatment of the common cold, the "flu," and other upper-respiratory viral infections for which there is no evidence that they possess any value. Often, especially for patients about to undergo surgery, these drugs are ordered as prophylactics to prevent postsurgical infection, but in situations or in amounts which are open to question.

In the case of psychoactive drugs, there has been much controversy. They account for about 12 percent of all prescriptions. Their use more than doubled between 1958 and 1973, soaring from roughly 90 million to 223 million prescriptions annually.[6] Studies have shown that 67 percent of all psychoactive drugs, 74 percent of antidepressants, and 82 percent of stimulants were prescribed for women. Women between the ages of 40 and 59 were the largest consumers.

The significance of such prescribing is discussed in more detail in Chapters 2 and 3.

A recent report[7] also shows the following:

- The average price of a retail pharmacy prescription rose from $2.00 in 1950 to $3.62 in 1960, $3.72 in 1970, $5.60 in 1976, $5.98 in 1977, $6.44 in 1978, and $7.03 in 1979. In 1979, the average price for a prescription calling for a brand-name product was $7.35, while one calling for a generic-name product was $5.03.
- At least some physicians are more inclined to prescribe generically, allowing a pharmacist to dispense a low-cost product instead of a more costly brand-name version. Generic prescribing, at least as seen in retail pharmacy records, increased from 6.4 percent of all new prescriptions in 1966 to 14.1 percent in 1979.
- The average number of retail store prescriptions dispensed per capita, which had risen steadily from about 2.4 annually in 1950 to 3.6 in 1960, 5.4 in 1970, and 7.3 in 1973, dropped to 6.5 by 1977 and to 6.2 by 1979.

"The word is getting through," says one of our clinical colleagues. "We've been prescribing too much. We've been prescribing when a drug wasn't really needed for medical reasons. And we've been prescribing needlessly expensive products. We hear it from drug experts. We hear it from our professional colleagues. We hear it from the insurance companies, and the people at Medicare and Medicaid. Hell, we're even hearing it now from patients."

Whether this downward trend is a reflection of changing patterns of prescribing, better patient information about drugs—especially about their potential risks—or economic conditions remains to be seen.

In general, it may be expected that either drug use or drug expenditures or both will grow for many years to come. This will be due to a number of factors:

- The slowing but still continuing growth of the total population.
- The increasing proportion of elderly people in the pop-

ulation. (The elderly on the average use three times as many prescriptions as do those aged up to 65.)[8]

- The increasing proportion of women in the population. (Women use about 50 percent more drugs than do men.)[9]
- The increasing number of people with health insurance and the related increase in the number of physician visits. (Recent studies have indicated that almost two-thirds of all physician visits result in the prescription or recommendation of a drug. The number of prescriptions written averages about 1.7 per visit.)[10]
- The growing use of hospitalization. (On the average, one new prescription is written for each day in a hospital, or roughly eight prescriptions for a typical hospital stay.[11] On the other hand, present efforts to contain hospital costs may eventually result in less or shorter hospitalization.)
- The possible or probable introduction of new, innovative, "breakthrough" drugs that can be used to control conditions that cannot be controlled by any drugs now available.
- With the implementation of national health insurance, it is our estimate that drug use, especially out of hospitals, would increase by about 10 to 15 percent the first year, with small annual increments thereafter, for the particular population group covered. Some observers predict that the increase would be only 5 percent, while others put the figure closer to 25 percent.[12]

Finally, it must be noted, the approximately 1.4 billion community pharmacy prescriptions, carrying a retail price tag of roughly $9.8 billion, do not give the total drug bill for the United States. We estimate that there should be added about 0.3 billion prescriptions filled by discount stores and other miscellaneous outlets and by dispensing physicians, 1.2 billion filled for nongovernmental hospital inpatients and outpatients, and 0.1 billion dispensed by VA hospitals and pharmacies and other governmental institutions. That gives a total of about 3.0 billion prescriptions and a total annual expenditure of $18.0 billion. There may also be added nearly $5.0 billion for over-the-counter products.

Who pays this drug bill? The public does, through out-of-pocket expenditures, taxes, insurance premiums, and increased prices of all kinds of goods—from automobiles and canned foods to television sets and paper clips—produced by companies that pay health insurance premiums for their employees.

It all comes out of the public purse.

So far as prescription drug expenditures are concerned, at least as of 1978, only about 14 percent of the costs outside of hospitals were covered by any form of insurance. In striking contrast, insurance covered 66 percent of physicians' services and 90 percent of hospital care costs.[13]

THE DRUG INDUSTRY

Five years ago, we portrayed the drug industry—the American drug industry in particular—as big, profitable, and powerful. It seemed to be remarkably productive—far more so than some of its critics proclaimed, but perhaps less so than some industry spokesmen declared.[14] Its innovative discoveries of important new products had contributed significantly to the control of disease.

Since that time, even during the recession of the mid-1970s, the American drug industry has continued to be big, profitable, powerful, and productive.

Ironically, starting as far back as the early 1900s, the industry has often greeted proposed changes with a the-sky-is-falling attitude. Each time a governmental law or regulation was proposed to improve the safety, efficacy, and even cleanliness of drug products, or to limit drug expenditures, many industry representatives warned that the proposed controls would inevitably force them to curtail their vital research designed to develop better drugs for the future. Yet, although new controls were put into effect, the industry has continued to remain productive and to prosper. (It is conceivable, of course, that some future action by the government may actually bring the sky tumbling down upon the drug companies. That would not only be sad for the companies but an absolute disaster for patients.)

There are several yardsticks by which to measure the productivity of the American drug industry. From 1940 to 1975, of the 971 new single drug entities introduced (not counting new combination products or new dosage forms), 662, or 64 percent, were developed in the United States.[15] U.S. sources—mainly industrial but also university and governmental—developed approximately twice as many new products as the rest of the world combined.

Drug sales in this country have continued to mount year after year. As shown in Table 1, domestic sales in actual dollars rose fivefold from $1.9 billion to an estimated $10.1 billion between 1961 and 1979.[16] Much of the increase during the past decade was the result of inflation, but the figures given in constant 1967 dollars, to account for inflation, show a fourfold rise from about $1.8 billion in 1961 to $7.2 billion in 1979.

Many industry spokesmen have long warned about the riskiness of the drug business. There is no question that the discovery of an unanticipated side effect may demolish the prospects of a new drug which took many years and many millions of dollars to develop, but

TABLE 1. *The American Drug Industry: Worldwide and U.S. Sales*

Year	Worldwide (actual dollars, in millions)	U.S. (actual dollars, in millions)	U.S. (constant dollars, in millions)	Deflator Index
1961	2,685	1,934	1,787	1.082
1962	2,932	2,199	2,082	1.056
1963	3,152	2,317	2,224	1.042
1964	3,405	2,479	2,386	1.039
1965	3,841	2,779	2,693	1.032
1966	4,256	3,011	2,935	1.026
1967	4,707	3,226	3,226	1.000
1968	5,280	3,655	3,692	0.990
1969	5,832	4,008	4,028	0.995
1970	6,442	4,322	4,352	0.993
1971	7,020	4,667	4,714	0.990
1972	7,827	5,018	5,023	0.991
1973	8,755	5,507	5,513	0.999
1974	10,120	6,083	5,838	1.042
1975	11,543	6,895	6,091	1.132
1976	12,832	7,669	6,375	1.203
1977	13,896	8,233	6,565	1.254
1978	16,840	9,156	6,542	1.319
1979 (est.)	n.a.	10,154	7,191	1.412

SOURCE: Pharmaceutical Manufacturers Association, *Annual Survey Reports*, Washington, D.C.

Worldwide Sales: Data shown for human and veterinary products, dosage forms only.

U.S. Sales: Data shown for human products, dosage forms only.

Constant Dollars: 1967 = 100.

TABLE 2. *Net Drug Industry Profits After Taxes,*
as Based on Percentage of Investment

Year	All Manufacturing Industries (%)	Drug Industry (%)
1964	11.6	18.2
1965	13.0	20.3
1966	13.5	20.3
1967	11.7	18.7
1968	12.1	18.3
1969	11.5	18.3
1970	9.3	17.6
1971	9.7	17.9
1972	10.6	18.6
1973	13.1	19.2
1974	14.9	18.8
1975	11.5	17.5
1976	13.9	18.0
1977	14.2	18.2
1978	15.0	18.8
1979	16.5	19.5

SOURCE: Federal Trade Commission, *Quarterly Financial Reports*, various issues.

the drug industry remains one of the most profitable of all manufacturing industries in the country. As indicated in Table 2, net profits after taxes, as based on equity or investment, have continued to be remarkably steady and high.

In other nations, notably West Germany and Great Britain, drug profits have been considered to be so high that the governments felt obliged to take corrective action. In Great Britain, for example, an agreement was hammered out between the industry and the Department of Health and Social Security to reduce profits after taxes as based on investment from 21 percent in 1969 to 15 percent in 1975.[17]

Some economists, both in and out of the industry, have charged that the accounting system on which such profits are calculated is unfair. The present system treats the industry's substantial investment in research as an ordinary business expense like salaries, supplies, and rent. Instead, it has been held, research expenditures should be treated as if they were a capital investment. Such an approach would reduce the industry's net profit rate, but that rate would still be significantly above average.

Beyond any doubt, the annual research investment of the American drug industry has been substantial, rising from $245 million in 1961 to $1.4 billion in 1978 and an estimated $1.6 billion in 1978 (see Table 3). These amounts, given in actual dollars, cover all research conducted worldwide on both human and veterinary products by U.S. firms and all research conducted in the U.S. by U.S.-based subsidiaries of foreign-owned companies. In practically every year, research expenditures have represented between 9.1 and 9.8 percent of sales. It is not known what portion of these sums actually covers physician education, promotional activities, and the like.

Increasingly, especially in the last decade, American firms are moving the scene of much of their research to foreign countries—not to escape high labor costs but because competent investigators are available in many foreign medical centers and can work under some-

TABLE 3. The American Drug Industry:
Worldwide Sales and Research
(in millions of dollars)

Year	Sales	Research	Percentage (Research/Sales)
1961	2,685	245	9.1
1962	2,932	259	8.8
1963	3,152	292	9.3
1964	3,405	310	9.1
1965	3,841	365	9.5
1966	4,256	416	9.8
1967	4,707	461	9.8
1968	5,280	495	9.4
1969	5,832	550	9.4
1970	6,442	619	9.6
1971	7,020	684	9.7
1972	7,827	726	9.3
1973	8,755	825	9.4
1974	10,120	942	9.3
1975	11,543	1,062	9.2
1976	12,832	1,164	9.1
1977	13,896	1,266	9.1
1978	16,840	1,397	8.2
1979 (est.)	n.a.	1,593	--

SOURCE: Pharmaceutical Manufacturers Association, Annual Survey Reports, Washington, D.C.

what less rigid controls than those enforced by the U.S. Food and Drug Administration. Such a step has clearly helped U.S. firms to get their products on the market quickly in such countries as Great Britain, France, and West Germany, and in scores of Third World nations. It has not, however, enhanced the firms' chances of winning approval in the U.S. At least until recently, FDA—quite probably reflecting the views in Congress—has been singularly unimpressed by the results of foreign drug testing; but in recent years, overseas studies conducted in accordance with modern testing standards have been increasingly acceptable to FDA.

Although the American companies have been appropriately and openly proud of some of their research accomplishments, they have often shown equal pride in what are commonly called "me-too" drugs. These are products that are essentially minor modifications of an important, innovative drug which is still under patent. The me-too versions by definition have no advantages in safety, efficacy, or economy. They can be sold only by means of massive promotional campaigns. The me-too products merely pollute the pharmaceutical atmosphere.

The matter of drug promotion is still sensitive in drug company circles.[18] Company spokesmen show no eagerness to discuss it, and promotion expenditures are rarely if ever revealed in reports to stockholders. In the past fifteen years, or especially since the forceful application of the Kefauver-Harris Amendments, FDA has prodded most American drug companies to improve the quality of their printed advertisements in medical journals. Advertisements so biased, incomplete, or actually inaccurate that they disgust many physicians, and even many company researchers, are now uncommon. Seldom is a company forced to make a public retraction of its claims.

Journal advertising, however, represents only a minor portion of drug promotion. Most promotion—perhaps two-thirds or more—is accomplished by drug detailers or sales representatives who call on physicians and pharmacists. Their presentations are mostly oral, and it is difficult to prove or disprove any accusation that they may occasionally stray from the truth. It is our impression, and that of many of our clinical colleagues, that the quality of detailing has improved. This may be due in part to attempts by some firms to set higher standards in hiring detailers, and to train and retrain them to stick to the facts. Some improvement may also be due to the growing skepticism of the medical profession—especially the younger members—and to the increasing willingness of many physicians to depend on specially trained clinical pharmacists to recommend which drug product should be prescribed.

What remains virtually unchanged is the staggering amount of all this promotion. It is our estimate that all forms of drug promotion represent roughly 20 percent *and possibly more* of sales at the manufacturers' level. This would come to about $1.8 billion in 1978 and an estimated $2.0 billion in 1979. Such expenditures are significantly larger than the industry's total investment in research. They are also larger than the total spent on all educational activities conducted by all the medical schools in the United States to train medical students.[19] This detailing and advertising avalanche is the most intense promotion that physicians will face during their entire professional lifetimes. Too often, drug promotion in its sheer volume is more confusing than educational. Too often, it leads a physician to prescribe a drug when no prescription is medically needed.

Some U.S. firms have insisted for many years that the FDA's regulation of promotion is needlessly harsh. "We recognize our social responsibilities now," one official said to us. "Whether the FDA was around or not, we would tell physicians the truth, the whole truth, and nothing but the truth."

A few years ago, it became possible for us to learn how American and other multinational pharmaceutical firms comport themselves when there *is* no FDA around. We compared what a company said about one of its products to physicians in the United States and to physicians in about a dozen countries in Latin America. In the United States, with the FDA watching, the company invariably told the truth: it gave a limited number of indications and disclosed in great detail the warnings, contraindications, and potential adverse reactions. In Latin America, most (although not all) companies grossly exaggerated their claims for efficacy and minimized, glossed over, or completely omitted any mention of hazards.[20] During the past few years, their activities in East African countries have been shown to be at least equally revolting.[21] Since these findings were made public, many American multinational firms (although not all of them) have dramatically improved their promotion in foreign countries. In general, they have found that they can tell the truth and still make a profit.

In Great Britain, officials of the National Health Service recently took steps to reduce somewhat the flood of drug promotion, at least in Britain. In its agreement with the Association of the British Pharmaceutical Industry, the government announced, the industry would reduce its promotion of products purchased by the National Health Service from 14 percent of sales to 12 percent in 1977 and 10 percent in 1979. "This will release 13 million pounds a year for patient care in 1979," stated David Ennals, the Secretary of State for Social Services. "Of course the industry can spend as much as it likes on promotion— but not at the expense of the NHS."[22]

As part of the British understanding, the industry agreed that each advertisement must contain not only essential information on efficacy, side effects, precautions, and contraindications, but also on cost. In addition, Ennals said, he would soon introduce regulations to prohibit misleading graphs and tables and "to stop misuse of words like 'safe.'"

In the United States, the drug industry consists of about 750 companies in interstate commerce (nobody seems to know the exact number) and an unknown number in intrastate commerce. Generally they are grouped into the PMA (for Pharmaceutical Manufacturers Association) companies and the non-PMA companies. As of the end of 1979, PMA had 143 members, all either U.S. firms or U.S. subsidiaries of foreign companies. They accounted for some 90 percent of all prescription drug sales, drug profits, and drug research, and close to 100 percent of all drug promotion. They controlled about 90 percent or more of all drug patents.

At one time, it was customary to describe the PMA members as brand-name companies, while the non-PMA firms supposedly sold mainly generic-name products. Such a grouping is no longer valid. Many PMA companies have gone into the generic-name business, and one—Eli Lilly—is reputedly the largest manufacturer of generics in the world. Furthermore, some generic firms market their products under new brand names.

For many years, strong bonds linked PMA with the American Medical Association. The reasons seemed obvious: PMA needed expert medical witnesses to testify on its behalf before the hearings chaired particularly by Senators Estes Kefauver and Gaylord Nelson, while the AMA needed the revenues from drug advertising in its journals to finance its disastrous attempt to block the Medicare program. Where other groups and agencies were concerned—industry critics, consumer groups, the American Pharmaceutical Association, the American Public Health Association, and FDA—there appeared to be within PMA a state of multiple industrial paranoia. As one industry witness put it after a congressional hearing, "It's them against us."

"Anything we propose is always wrong," a PMA official complained to us. "And anything we oppose is always right."

During the last several years, and for reasons which are not exactly clear, the situation has perceptibly changed. FDA officials, industry leaders, pharmacy leaders, and consumer advocates can gather amicably around the same table.

"In the old days," one of our associates recalls, "practically every meeting ended with table-pounding, profanity, denunciations, and everybody walking out of the room furious. Now we still have disagreements, but at the end of the meeting we all go out and have dinner together. And nobody accuses anybody else of selling out."

Another industry critic put it this way: "I'll be damned, but an industry vice-president turns out to be one of my best and most trusted friends!"

Perhaps our most cherished reaction came from a PMA official after we had commented—somewhat unfavorably—on certain drug company promotional activities. "How in hell can we argue with you," he wrote, "when you insist on being accurate and fair?"

Total peace in this arena has not yet broken out, but the new level of discussion has proved to be a pleasant relief to many of us. And also productive.

DRUG NAMES, DRUG APPROVAL, AND THE "DRUG LAG"

Practically never does a patient swallow a pure drug. What is actually used is a drug product: a mixture of the active ingredient (the actual drug) plus a combination of binders, buffers, flavors, colors, and perhaps other ingredients. Such an agent usually carries three names:

- The *chemical* name, generally long, complex, and decipherable only by chemists. It gives the molecular structure of the drug and may suggest its probable action on the body.
- The public, established, or *generic* name, usually simpler but often impossible for a prescribing physician to remember.
- The trademark or *brand* name, short, simple, and easy to write on a prescription pad. In most instances, the brand name is monopolized forever by one company.

One drug product, for example, has the chemical name of 10-(3-

dimethylaminopropyl)-2-chlorphenothiazine—the   "phenothiazine"
will suggest to a drug expert that the chemical will act as a tranquilizer
—the generic name of chlorpromazine, and the brand name in the
United States of Thorazine. It was, in fact, the first major tranquilizer
to be synthesized.

Under the patent system in the United States, the creator or
discoverer of a new patented product has the exclusive right to market
it for the life of the patent. That patent life is seventeen years in this
country. For many inventions—a new kind of light bulb, for example,
or a new spot remover—the manufacturer may be able to get his
product on the market in a year or less, and then have sixteen years of
full protection. With a new drug, however, the situation is far different. Before it can be marketed, it must be approved for relative safety
and efficacy by the Food and Drug Administration. This is not
so simple.

FDA's New Drug Application (NDA) process[23] usually requires
years of testing on animals and then on human subjects—first on
normal, healthy volunteers, then on several hundred patients being
treated by experts in special clinical facilities, and finally on several
thousand patients treated by specialists or other physicians. Along the
way, many proposed products drop out; their efficacy is not substantial, or the subjects may suffer unanticipated and undesirable side
effects. Before a new product wins FDA's stamp of approval, five to
ten years have elapsed, and the company may have invested as much
as fifty or sixty million dollars. A new study based on 1976 data from
fourteen companies puts the average figure at $54 million.[24] Mean-
while, the life of the patent has been steadily ticking away, and the
company has on the average only nine years or so remaining to recoup
its investment.[25]

This situation, which developed largely since passage of the Kefauver-Harris Amendments in 1962 and their implementation a few
years later, has been understandably galling to the drug industry.
Leaders of the industry charge that the NDA procedure is needlessly
complex and that FDA makes unrealistic demands to get what it feels
is essential evidence, while most other countries seemingly get along
comfortably with a more relaxed and far more speedy system. FDA's
defenders say that the American system undoubtedly saved this country from having a thalidomide disaster, a rash of cancer cases caused by
supposedly safe heart disease remedies, and an epidemic of deaths
caused by a superpotent anti-asthma drug. They also note that the

American drug industry has not been too badly damaged financially. "The average new drug commercialized by the pharmaceutical industry today," a drug security analyst said recently, "will generate approximately $50 million in sales worldwide in its fifth year on the market."[26]

Nevertheless, it is evident that the problem of delays is being partially alleviated. FDA is moving more rapidly. Top priority is being given to the review of breakthrough drugs urgently needed to control a hitherto uncontrollable disease, while unimportant me-too drugs are put on a slower track and given less prompt study.[27] As further improvements, it is being suggested now that the rules be changed so that the manufacturer is given a guaranteed ten years of patent protection after marketing begins, or that the patent protection should start only at the moment FDA approval is received.

In proposed legislation introduced in 1978,[28] Congressman Paul Rogers and Senator Edward Kennedy called for a change in the law so that FDA could approve a new drug after trials on a few hundred patients and officially recognize human trials in certain foreign countries. This kind of approval would presumably be restricted to urgently needed breakthrough drugs. It would not be applied in the case of one more antihistamine or another antibiotic no better than penicillin or tetracycline. Furthermore, it could and probably would be conditioned on the willingness of the company to maintain postmarketing surveillance and check on any unexpected adverse reactions that did not appear in the early trials. The proposed legislation was passed by the Senate but did not get out of committee in the House in 1978. It was reintroduced by Senator Kennedy and Representative Henry Waxman with significant modifications in 1979.[29] By late 1980, the bill had not yet been considered by the House.

On the other hand, some critics insist that FDA cannot solve the problem of delayed drug approval because FDA *is* the problem and should be abolished. Moreover, there are some critics who declare that FDA is moving too fast and approving drugs without adequate trials. One problem that has been recognized only recently is that some adverse reactions may not be detectable until patients have used a drug for twenty years or so, while other reactions may not be detected until they affect the next generation. For example, diethylstilbestrol (DES), a hormone-like product used many years ago in an attempt to prevent an impending miscarriage, was found to cause cancer of the vagina in the daughters of some of the treated women—and, in fact, to be worthless in the prevention of miscarriage.

Regardless of the propriety of FDA's operations, it is obvious that the introduction of new drugs each year in the United States has dropped markedly since passage of the Kefauver Amendments. For this reason, there have been increasing demands that the law be scrapped and that the companies themselves be allowed to decide on their own whether or not to put a new drug on the market.[30] Such a proposal is truly frightening; we believe some companies could be trusted to behave responsibly, but others—on their past record—could not. In the past, the latter have marketed drugs that were unsafe or ineffective and whose promotion was inaccurate, biased, or false.[31]

In any consideration of the drop in the number of new drugs introduced annually, three facts have often been ignored:

- The same or a similar drop has occurred at about the same time in other countries.
- In the United States, the drop began in 1959, three years before the Kefauver Amendments were passed and about five years before they were put into effect.
- The number of new drugs introduced annually—that is, new single drug entities and not merely new dosage forms or new combinations of old drugs—tells only part of the story. Many drug experts have indicated that only a very few of these products, perhaps half a dozen per year, represent *important* new therapeutic advances.[32] Most of the others provide little or no therapeutic gain; in short, they are only me-too drugs.

Related in some way to this delay in getting approval of new drugs in the United States, and perhaps to the fact that research in this field is becoming more difficult, is what has been termed the "drug lag." Regrettably, there is no agreement on how to define the drug lag or on how to measure it. There is, in fact, no agreement on whether it has been a good thing or a bad thing for the health of Americans. On the one hand, it has been likened to a disaster ranking with bubonic plague and used to bludgeon the FDA into speeding the approval of new drugs;[33] on the other, some concerned individuals have insisted that the drug lag is not big enough.[34]

In a general way, the drug lag refers to the fact that some newly discovered drugs—including a number discovered by American drug companies—are marketed in other countries months or years before they are approved for marketing in this country. Some may never reach the market in the United States. The existence of the American drug lag can scarcely be denied.[35]

It is vital to note, however, that the lag is not found only in the United States. There are some drugs, for example, that were available in West Germany before they were available in Switzerland, some that were available in Switzerland before they were available in Sweden, some that were available in Sweden before they were available in the United States, and some that were available in the United States before they were available in Norway.

What has been unclear is whether these various lags represent a threat mostly to the health of the people in the countries involved or mostly to the sales of the companies whose products are concerned. According to European experts, there are far fewer prescription drugs on the market in the Netherlands, Denmark, and Sweden than there are in such nations as France, Italy, West Germany, and Great Britain.[36] From such information, it might be concluded that the Dutch and the Scandinavians cannot be treated as well as the French, the Italians, the West Germans, and the British. It is our opinion, however, that the health care—including drug therapy—available in the Netherlands and Scandinavia ranks among the best in Europe.

Some European physicians—mostly those in general practice but also including some specialists—have expressed their dismay that products which they were accustomed to using in their own countries were not available in the United States or, for that matter, in Canada.

Many foreign physicians seem to be unaware that most drugs not approved—or not approved quickly—by FDA were blocked on the grounds that the manufacturer had failed to submit adequate data to prove objectively that the product was safe and effective. Many foreign physicians also seem unaware that some drugs they use customarily in Europe have been taken off the U.S. market as unsafe. It is likewise not appreciated by many physicians, American and foreign alike, that most FDA decisions are based on the advice of its advisory committees, which include some of the most knowledgeable drug experts in the nation.

The impact of the drug lag in the United States is difficult to assess. The three-year delay in gaining FDA approval of the Italian anti-tuberculosis drug rifampin was probably a disservice to some American patients. An even more glaring case involves the so-called beta-blockers, some of which have been widely accepted for the treatment of hypertension, cardiac arrhythmias, and angina. For roughly a decade, against the advice of leading nongovernmental drug authorities, and for reasons which we find difficult to comprehend, the FDA adamantly refused to approve any beta-blocker. Yet, it has turned out that FDA's actions were not all irrational: some members of this drug group—including the first one to be approved in Great Britain—were later found to be associated with the development of malignant or nonmalignant tumors in experimental animals, and one had to be taken off the market in Europe because of its probable relation to eye damage.[37]

FDA's decision not to approve thalidomide, later disclosed to be a cause of fetal deformities, was a blessing for Americans.[38] So were FDA's actions to remove from the market such headache remedies as aminopyrine and the dipyrones, still commonly used in many countries but now held responsible for serious or fatal blood diseases. Particular abuse was heaped on FDA for holding up a new anti-epilepsy drug, sodium valproate, indicated particularly for the treatment of a form of the disorder known as "absence seizures." Approved in France in 1967, the drug was not cleared by FDA until 1978. The 11-year delay, it was charged, had "cruelly" prevented patients from getting desperately needed help. This was a low blow, for it was, in fact, the company which had lagged in requesting approval, and which had even had to be urged by FDA to put in an application for approval. [39] Furthermore, it now appears that sodium valproate is not an unmixed blessing: its use has recently been associated with rare but serious and sometimes fatal liver destruction.[40]

Another curious aspect of the drug lag controversy has involved a drug known as clioquinol or Enterovioform, marketed for decades by Ciba or Ciba-Geigy and now also by other companies for the prevention and treatment of diarrhea and amoebic dysentery. Although it is still widely available—in some countries, without a prescription—it was removed from the market in the United States in 1961 and in Japan in 1970. After prolonged lawsuits, the Japanese courts ruled that the drug was responsible for an epidemic of drug-induced paralysis, visual defects or blindness, and even death in some 10,000 patients—a situation that was termed the worst drug disaster in history. Victims were reported not only in Japan but also in a number of other countries. Significantly, the disease virtually disappeared in Japan when clioquinol was banned.[41]

The drug lag in the United States has been blamed both on the policies of FDA and the provisions of the 1962 Kefauver Amendments. One of the most thorough studies in this hotly disputed field was that undertaken by the Department of Health, Education, and

Welfare's Review Panel on New Drugs, under the chairmanship of law professor Norman Dorsen of New York University. In May 1977, the panel concluded in its report to the Secretary of HEW that

> the available evidence does not justify a departure from the system of regulation instituted by the 1962 Amendments. While in the last decade there has been an increase in the cost of drug development and a decline in the average number of new chemical entities approved annually by FDA, the studies to date do not show persuasively that these trends are principally attributable to the 1962 Amendments. . . . Although drug approvals declined after 1962, data indicate the decline began earlier. Furthermore, the 1962 Amendments were implemented gradually, and their full impact was not felt until the 1970s.[42]

A revealing analysis in this field was carried out by Paul de Haen, generally regarded as the foremost authority on the subject of which drugs were introduced in which countries and in which year. For this study, he surveyed twenty-nine drugs in fourteen major therapeutic classes marketed between roughly 1967 and 1976 in England, France, West Germany, and Italy.[43] He found that (1) during that decade, only 24 percent of the drugs reached all four countries; and (2) the time to achieve marketing in all four, where this actually occurred, ranged from one to thirteen years.

There were no clinical or scientific explanations for these lags— for example, why one new anti-arthritic was marketed in England in 1962 but not in Italy until 1974; or, for that matter, why the widely used sedative flurazepam (Dalmane) was introduced in the United States in 1970 but had still to be marketed in France by 1979.

One explanation, de Haen said, may rest on industry management decisions. "In some instances, there may be commercial and competitive reasons why it is not practical to offer a drug in a given country."

He observed that the costly delays in winning approval of a new drug are not limited to the United States. "Progress in science and the requirement of extended pharmacologic and therapeutic evaluations have placed a heavy burden on innovating manufacturers in all countries, for which the patient has to pay eventually. However, he may be rewarded with greater therapeutic efficacy and reliability."

The drug lag is therefore not unique to the United States. What seems to be unique is the fuss that has been made about it in this country.

"In spite of the fact that there are many drugs that have only been introduced in a limited number of European countries, and that there has been a considerable delay in the transfer of others from one country to another," de Haen said, "no complaints about this subject have been expressed in the European literature."

More important than further fruitless and sometimes paranoid debate about the nature of the drug lag in the United States and who or what is responsible, it seems to us, is determining what should be done about it. What should be done to help the patients—usually few in number—who, in the clinical judgment of competent physicians and drug experts, may be helped by a drug not yet approved in this country but on the market elsewhere?

Erasing the 1962 Amendments or demolishing FDA do not seem to us to offer attractive solutions. One possible technique might be to enable FDA, under existing cr new law, to provide for such patients by setting up a simple "compassionate approval" procedure, allowing a company to furnish supplies to a limited number of physicians, possibly on the condition that each physician be required to make a complete report to FDA on the outcome of treatment, until such time as the drug is finally approved or rejected.

As will be seen in Chapter 10, a number of European countries have established mechanisms whereby a drug not available in one country can be specially imported from another, provided that the physician will simply say to his own government, "I need this drug for the best care of this particular patient." Once such a provision is on the law books, European drug officials say, it is practically never used. It has, however, convinced these officials and the physicians in those countries that the drug lag problem is no problem.

Such solutions as these may be strongly opposed by some drug companies and by some consumer groups. They may be viewed with suspicion by American physicians who, unlike their colleagues in foreign countries, are more likely to be sued for malpractice if something goes wrong, although this risk might be minimized by obtaining in advance the informed consent of the patient. On the other hand, these approaches might conceivably mark the end for too many years of noisy, wasteful rhetoric. And they could, in probably a limited number of cases, improve the quality of health care.

Thus, it may be concluded that the drug lag—which probably never was and certainly is not now a significant problem in most other nations—will continue to exist in the United States. It will probably do this at least as long as the attack on it is financially fueled by those drug companies which believe, at least in the short run, that they have most to gain from a quick and easy drug approval process in this country. Our own drug lag may have inconvenienced or, more infrequently, harmed some American patients, but it has probably safeguarded the health and even the lives of many more Americans.

As Mark Twain once said of the music of Richard Wagner, the drug lag may not be as bad as it sounds.

PRICES, PRICE ADVERTISING, AND PRICE CONTROLS

It seems to be an inescapable fact of economics and the free enterprise system—or of the orneriness of human beings—that buyers and sellers rarely see eye-to-eye on the fairness of prices. Most drug buyers seem convinced that the prices they have to pay are too high. Most drug sellers, notably manufacturers and pharmacists, are equally positive that the prices they get are reasonable, justifiable, or even too low. One explanation for this gap is obvious: there is no substantial agreement on the definition of a fair or reasonable price, and perhaps there never will be. If ten economists were to be asked for a definition, it has been charged, they would come up with fifteen different answers.

During the 1950s and 1960s, and especially during the economic pinches of the 1970s, patients and the governmental or private agencies that provide health care for them have placed increasing pressure on the pricing structure used by pharmacists and drug manufacturers, and on the prescribing patterns of physicians. As we have noted elsewhere, it may be confidently expected that these protests will continue.[44]

It has also been asserted, especially by economist Milton Friedman while he was still at the University of Chicago, that regulation by governmental agencies—the Food and Drug Administration in particular—adds unjustifiably to higher prices and for this and other reasons should be abolished. To this, FDA Commissioner Donald Kennedy retorted: "Although this is sometimes regarded as a law of economics, it is really only a law of Chicago economics."[45]

Regardless of whatever influence FDA might have on prices, the prospect of an unregulated drug industry or any other major industry involving the welfare of millions of people is chilling. It is barely conceivable that socially irresponsible drug companies would eventually lose out in a competitive marketplace, as some economists have said, but the price involved in that "eventually" in terms of false hopes, unjustifiable drug expenditures, and needless drug-related injury and death is fearful to contemplate. Moreover, in the past, when it was disclosed that certain firms had been producing dangerous or deadly drugs, or ones that were without value, these firms lost little of their reputation—or their dollars—in the marketplace.

As the patient sees it, it is beyond question that drug prices have increased sharply in recent years. The price of an average prescription in community pharmacies has risen from $3.72 in 1970 to $7.03 in 1979, amounting to a jump of about 89 percent in nine years. Most of this rise, however, has been the effect of inflation. In constant dollars, with the effect of inflation erased (1967 = 100), the increase from 1970 to 1979 was from $3.75 to $4.97 or 33 percent. In glaring contrast, expenses for physician services and especially for hospital care have skyrocketed.

Drug industry spokesmen have used such figures to support their arguments that the prices of their products have risen only modestly. Furthermore, company representatives declare, the prices of their products have remained relatively low because there is keen competition in the drug industry. On the other hand, industry critics have insisted that there is little or no competition in the drug business.

The key question, then, may be: *Is there or is there not real competition in the drug business?*

The answer is simple: *Yes and no.*

If competition is defined as the rivalry among chemically different drugs for the same market—for example, among various substances to treat high blood pressure—then competition in the industry is fierce. But if competition is defined as the rivalry between two or more different versions of the same active ingredient, then it has been only moderate at best. This lack of effective competition has been visible in the case of drugs which are available in the form of a relatively high-cost innovator's brand-name product no longer under patent and also in the form of several competitive generic-name products marketed at prices 10 percent, 20 percent, 30 percent, or even more below the price of the original version; in many such instances, the innovator's product maintains the dominant portion of the market, regardless of price. The explanation is usually that the brand-name product is heavily promoted and is familiar to physicians, while the generic-name versions are not. (This situation exists primarily in community pharmacies; in hospital pharmacies and similar institutions, where drugs are usually purchased on competitive bid, price competition is more evident.) Especially during the last five years, however, there have been increasing signs of significant price competition stemming at least in part from new state substitution laws and the Maximum Allowable Cost program for Medicaid beneficiaries.

In the Medicaid program, pharmacists are paid a fixed professional fee per prescription, based on rates that are set periodically in each state. Pharmacists have bitterly attacked the implementation of this arrangement, claiming that they are being ground between rigidly fixed—and paltry—fees, usually updated by the state only once a year or less often, and the rising costs of doing business. The protests from community pharmacists have been clouded by the fact that there is yet no agreement on how much it costs a pharmacist to dispense an average prescription. Furthermore, if pharmacists actually lose money in dispensing prescription drugs to Medicaid patients, they can legally recoup their losses by charging more to non-Medicaid beneficiaries. This practice is, in effect, a hidden extra Medicaid tax paid by taxpayers.

It has been frequently proposed that competition at the pharmacy level could be stimulated by price advertising, a technique that was long held to be "unprofessional" by pharmacy leaders. As the result of recent court decisions, however, pharmacy price advertising or price posting can no longer be punished as unprofessional conduct; and in various states, pharmacies are permitted or required to notify the public of their drug prices, usually the prices of those products most frequently dispensed. Where these price-posting programs have been instituted, their effects have so far been minimal or unclear. (In California, the price-posting law has been repealed.) This could have been predicted. In the case of a drug needed for a sudden or brief illness, most patients will probably select a pharmacy on the basis of convenience. Only when the drug is required in relatively large amounts for long-term chronic disease—for example, diabetes, arthritis, asthma, or high blood pressure—will people be expected to indulge in comparison shopping. Moreover, it does not seem likely that an individual would spend the time or the money for bus fare—or gasoline—to save perhaps sixty cents on a twelve-dollar prescription. What is more serious is that this emphasis on price alone ignores the professional services that a pharmacist can render. It makes him seem to be simply a pill counter. A patient who selects a surgeon on the basis of how much he charges per stitch is asking for trouble. One who chooses a pharmacist merely on the basis of price per capsule is similarly inviting disaster.

In any effort to control drug expenditures, the manufacturer's drug prices—linked as they are to the manufacturer's profits—are a particularly tempting target. It is beyond dispute that the drug industry's profits are high. Industry spokesmen have defended these profits as justified on the grounds that the drug business is peculiarly risky and that the profit rates are essential if the companies are to continue their vital research and to attract investment capital. Such arguments have lost much of their force since it has been noted that the profits are what is left *after* all expenses—including those for research—have been paid. On the other hand, the drug companies have been assailed for making outrageously and even obscenely high profits, and for fattening themselves on the sickness of Americans. (A similar charge could be made that some farmers, ranchers, and grocerymen are fattening themselves on the hunger of Americans.)

It is clear that drug prices—and drug profits along with them—could be limited by governmental action. Drug profits could be reduced to zero, and the industry transformed into a national public utility. Such a drastic step would, as one critic has gloated, "teach those bastards a lesson." It would also put American pharmaceutical research, now the most innovative and productive in the world, under the unpredictable whims of the Congress or some administrative agency. Also, it would not save much money for patients or taxpayers. Of an average $6.00 prescription, for example, roughly $3.00 now goes to the manufacturer; and of this, only about $0.30 or less represents net profits. Thus, if industry profits were to be abolished, the price of a $6.00 prescription would be reduced to $5.70. If the drug industry were obliged to cut its profit rate to what is typical of all manufacturing industries, the price of the $6.00 prescription would be reduced to about $5.85.

As another approach, it has frequently been proposed that the industry should throw out or at least reduce its enormous expenditures for drug detailing, advertising, and other forms of promotion.[46] Critics charge that these activities, especially at their present level, are wasteful, have nothing to do with the quality or value of the drug products themselves, contribute little to their effective use, and create more confusion than enlightenment. In a substantial national health insurance program, the United States government could—as the British government has done—induce the drug industry to reduce its promotional expenditures.

At least in theory, the government could provide incentives for price competition by allowing or requiring the selection of low-cost generic-name products instead of the more costly brand-name product actually prescribed. This approach, in fact, has been implemented in some states in their respective Medicaid programs. The results to date are not clear: for whatever reason, many pharmacists have been unwilling or reluctant to do the product selecting; and in some states, the whole matter has been tied up in the courts.

As we have shown elsewhere,[47] this maneuver cannot be expected to yield rich savings now for patients or taxpayers. It can be applied only to products no longer under patent, and for which economical substitutes are legally on the market. Today, about half of the most frequently prescribed drugs are still under patent protection. If a company is required to face real competition from low-cost products, it can recoup its losses by raising the prices on its brand-name products that still have patent protection. Society would get not a bit of benefit.

But this situation is likely to change. In the coming decade, most of the new drugs that flooded onto the market in the 1950s and 1960s will have lost their patent protection and will be exposed to competition from generics. Relatively few drugs were introduced in the 1970s, and so only those few will still have viable patents in the 1980s and 1990s. Thus, the impact of substitution will probably become more noticeable. For the first time, price competition on most important products may become a reality.

In addition, drug coverage under a national health insurance program may also become a reality. In such a case, the government, which now pays for about one-quarter of all drug expenditures, would be paying for perhaps 50 percent, or even 80 or 90 percent. Such a customer might be expected to have considerable influence.

One experienced official, Vincent Gardner, formerly of the Health Care Financing Administration, predicted the creation of "machinery making possible direct negotiation between the pharmaceutical industry and the Federal Government over the cost of prescribed drugs dispensed under national health insurance."[48] Such a prospect in the United States is scarcely reassuring to the industry. Frank Markoe, Jr., vice-chairman of the board of Warner-Lambert, commented: "It would seem most unlikely that the industry could survive many such negotiations."[49] On the other hand, other industry spokesmen note that American drug companies seem to have survived such negotiations in a number of foreign countries. (See Chapter 10.)

In this continuing controversy over drug prices, it is essential to emphasize the strategic role that is played by physicians—or that *could* be played by them. It is physicians who are in the best position to influence drug prices—or, more importantly, drug expenditures—by the way in which they write their prescriptions. They can put an abrupt but decisive end to the continuing hassle over brand-name versus generic-name products by prescribing a generic in the first place. This will place a slight burden on them, since it will require physicians to learn the generic names of the drugs they order. If no competitive version is available for a high-cost drug they intend to use, they can—if they know the relative prices—prescribe a different and less expensive product, brand-name or generic, which may be expected to have the same clinical effect. Such activities may in themselves induce drug companies to reduce their large expenditures for promotion, especially for drug detailing, since such promotion would no longer be worthwhile. And finally, physicians can decline to write a prescription when no prescription is clinically needed. This, too, could be a burden. Instead of using a few seconds to write the prescription, the physician would be obligated to give other advice such as modifying eating, drinking, smoking, and exercise habits—advice which the patient may or may not accept. This advice, if accepted, would not only save dollars. It might save lives.

ADVERSE DRUG REACTIONS AND POSTMARKETING SURVEILLANCE

It should be beyond argument that virtually any drug powerful enough to do good can also, under certain conditions, do harm. It can destroy cells, injure tissues, and even cause death.

What remain as subjects of controversy are, first, the definition of adverse drug reactions; second, how frequently and how seriously they occur among patients; and, third and perhaps most important, what can be done as part of a national drug program to minimize these unhappy or calamitous events.

For a definition of an adverse drug reaction, we have suggested the following characteristics:[50]

- It is adverse—that is, noxious, unfavorable, untoward, and pathological.
- It is unintended or unanticipated, and not sought as a goal of therapy.
- It results from the use of a legally available drug in normal dosages, administered for the diagnosis, prevention, or treatment of a disease, or to modify bodily functions.

- It is not mild or trivial in degree, but serious enough to cause significant illness or disability, or to call for hospital admission or additional hospitalization, or to require significant changes in the planned strategy of treatment.

The occurrence of such reactions is scarcely new. What *has* proved surprising are the scope of the problem and the apparent difficulties faced by many physicians and pharmacists in recognizing that the reactions were actually caused by drugs rather than being the symptoms of an underlying disease or marking the failure of the patient to cooperate.

Perhaps the most disquieting report was that published in 1971 by Kenneth Melmon, then of the University of California in San Francisco. Reviewing earlier studies by other workers in the 1950s and 1960s, he said: "Poor documentation of drug reactions has minimized the apparent frequency of drug toxicity in the United States. Reporting in the past has relied on the volition of the physician or hospital staff; the quality of data gathered is deplorable."

Too many physicians, he noted, have a low index of suspicion. "A physician is naturally reluctant to think that his treatment contributes to a patient's disability.... Too frequently, laboratory data or new symptoms that do not 'fit' into the anticipated course of the disease are ignored."[51]

Melmon estimated that the economic cost of these reactions in 1971, measured only in terms of hospital room-and-board charges—then about $60 a day—was roughly $3 billion a year. In 1974, with hospital charges up to $90 a day, we put the figure at more than $4.5 billion a year.[52] In 1980, with hospital charges amounting to about $200 a day, the annual cost would be more than $10 billion.

It was calculated from the few studies then reported in the medical literature that from 3 to 5 percent of all patients in the *medical* services of hospitals—not the surgical, obstetrical, or other services—were admitted because of a drug reaction, and from 10 to 30 percent of patients admitted to the medical services for any reason were likely to develop a drug reaction during their hospital stay.

Approximately 80 percent of these drug reactions—involving both prescription drugs and over-the-counter products—could have been predicted, Melmon said, and most of those could have been prevented. The obvious exceptions to this rule, it seemed, were last-ditch treatments given to patients with serious but undiagnosed bacterial infections or those with inoperable cancer.

The Reporting System

Much of the confusion surrounding this situation in the early 1970s—and much of the stormy controversy it created—was clearly attributable to the inadequacies of the reporting systems then in effect. In spite of efforts first by the American Medical Association beginning in 1952[53] and later by FDA, physicians in this country were singularly unwilling to report incidents of adverse drug reactions. With the mounting concern over malpractice suits, this unwillingness may be somewhat understandable.

During the past five or six years, however, the situation has been significantly clarified, and reporting of adverse reactions has improved. This has been due in large part to the cooperative efforts of such groups as FDA's Division of Drug Experience, the Boston Collaborative Drug Surveillance Program, the Center for the Study of Drug Development at the University of Rochester, Boston University's Drug Epidemiology Unit, and, most recently, the Joint Commission on Prescription Drug Use. Proposed originally by Senator Edward Kennedy and other congressional leaders, and financed largely by no-strings-attached support from the Pharmaceutical Manufacturers Association, the Joint Commission was chaired during its existence from 1976 to 1980 by Kenneth Melmon, now at Stanford University. Many individual investigators also contributed to the analysis of drug reactions.

Although the various groups and individuals did not use precisely identical methods, and although the results were not completely comparable, the findings were alarming. The Boston Collaborative group, for example, which began its systematic long-term project in 1966, reported that about 30 percent of the hospitalized patients they monitored suffered adverse drug reactions.[54] These patients were primarily those treated on the medical services in hospitals in the United States, Canada, New Zealand, and Israel. For most aspects of the study, patients on other services—surgery, pediatrics, obstetrics, and so on— were not included. In addition, from 1.0 to 3.5 percent of the patients on the medical wards had been admitted to the hospital because of an adverse drug reaction.[55]

Many of the hospital-acquired reactions were considered to be minor, the most common being nausea, drowsiness, diarrhea, vomiting, and rash.[56] But in 3 percent of the drug reaction patients, the reactions were categorized as life-threatening;[57] of these, the most frequent were cardiac arrhythmia, depression of the blood-forming bone marrow, emotional depression, excessive accumulation of fluid in the tissues, and hemorrhage. Of the patients with these life-threatening reactions, 10 percent died.

The nature and size of the problem in most other countries is poorly understood or completely unknown. In Great Britain, for example, the voluntary reporting program—the so-called "yellow card" system—failed for four years to connect the newly introduced beta-blocker practolol with the occurrence of serious eye damage and injury to the peritoneum, the lining of the abdominal cavity.[58] In Sweden, where adverse drug reaction reporting is mandatory for physicians, it has been claimed that only 31 percent of the actual cases are disclosed.[59]

The Pharmacological Culprits

Although practically any drug can produce an adverse effect, the offenders that have been mainly responsible for hospitalization include (not in any order of ranking): oral contraceptives, conjugated estrogens taken for problems of the menopause, diethylstilbestrol, antibiotics such as lincomycin and clindamycin, propoxyphene, amphetamines, sedatives, and tranquilizers (usually when they are used for prolonged periods). Some studies have implicated digitalis products, aspirin-containing compounds, a number of different steroid hormones, oral antidiabetic agents, antihypertensive drugs, anticoagulating products, and anticancer drugs.[60]

Among the drugs causing adverse reactions in hospitalized patients, the most important are reported to be antibiotics, digitalis, quinidine, sedatives, tranquilizers, antidepressants, insulin, antihypertensives, analgesics, and diuretics.[61]

Postmarketing Surveillance

For most of the drugs considered here, the untoward effects have been well known to physicians for years or decades, and in some cases—as with digitalis—for centuries. The occurrence of most of these events might well have been expected. In the same way, a patient known to have had an allergic reaction to penicillin might be expected to experience an allergic response again if penicillin is administered a second time.

What is more difficult or even impossible to predict is the occurrence of an allergic reaction to penicillin or any other drug if the patient has never before demonstrated any such allergy. Equally difficult is the prediction of an adverse drug reaction that has never before been noted or reported, or that has never before been linked to a particular drug. If, for example, a new drug causes an adverse reaction in one patient in 10,000, the risk will scarcely be noted or will be completely missed if the product is put on the market after FDA-required trials on, say, only 3,000 patients. If the drug turns out to be hazardous only after it is used over a 20-year period, its dangers will probably not be recognized after only five or ten years of use. And if the toxic effect shows up only in the next generation—as happened with diethystilbestrol—the problem will be particularly difficult to detect.

During the past several years, the United States has been largely spared from three drug disasters involving unexpected (or unreported) drug hazards: the epidemic of paralysis and blindness apparently caused by the antidiarrhea agent clioquinol or Enterovioform; the tragic birth of deformed infants to women who had used thalidomide as a sedative in the first three months of pregnancy; and the occurrence of damage to the eyes and other tissues that has been associated with the use of practolol to control cardiac arrhythmias or high blood pressure. It is not clear in all these cases, and perhaps others, if Americans were protected by alert regulatory officials, or whether, as the old saying goes, "God looks after drunks, children, and the United States of America."

Since the mid-1970s, there has been a growing feeling among drug experts that it is not prudent to place complete reliance for the protection of patients on any hit-or-miss reporting system or on the intervention of a merciful providence.[62] Instead, it has been proposed that a formal system be established for postmarketing surveillance on newly introduced drugs—and perhaps on others when there is at least a lurking suspicion that there is inadequate knowledge about the safety of the product.

This matter has been investigated by the Joint Commission on Prescription Drug Use and by the experts, governmental and nongovernmental, working with it. The commission has now issued its final report and recommended the establishment of a comprehensive, systematic surveillance program operated by a nongovernmental agency.[63]

At almost the same time that the commission issued its report, there was a dramatic demonstration of the need for surveillance and an example of how it could be carried out with considerable speed. In May 1979, Smith Kline & French won FDA approval to introduce a new antihypertension product, ticrynafen or Selacryn. By early January

1980, SKF and FDA had received reports of fifty-three cases of liver or kidney damage associated with the drug, along with ten deaths.[64] Nothing like this had happened in animal studies or earlier clinical trials. FDA, with the voluntary cooperation of the manufacturer, ordered that the drug be removed from the market. The company immediately halted sales and started recalling the drug. Physicians and pharmacists received almost instantaneous warnings. SKF likewise notified the press and, not content to await the receipt of reports from physicians, dispatched representatives to call on those who had been prescribing the drug, so that the company could determine if other patients had been injured. By early March, SKF had received reports of 363 cases of damage, with twenty-four deaths.[65] An FDA official emphasized, however, that "the public should know that a good reporting system, properly utilized by physicians, manufacturers, and FDA has worked the way it was designed to—promptly and effectively to protect the public health."[66]

The Drug Regulatory Reform Acts of 1978 and 1979 have also proposed the institution of a formal surveillance system, presumably not for all drugs but only for those representing therapeutic advances but whose safety, especially with long-term use, is inadequately known. Such proposals have been viewed with considerable favor by both FDA officials and some drug industry leaders. These proposals could make it possible for some new drugs—important or breakthrough drugs— to be released more promptly for short-term use while the products are monitored for safety in long-term use among small, carefully controlled groups of patients. Only when the drugs are found in such scientific studies to be relatively safe for long-term therapy would they be released by FDA for such general use.

This approach would make it possible to spot unexpected adverse reactions that did not appear in previous animal studies or in the early clinical trials on human patients. In addition, this kind of surveillance may well disclose possible valuable *new* applications of the drugs that had not been discovered in the previous trials.

Adverse Reactions and Drug Insurance

In almost any approach to the coverage of drugs under national health insurance, the matter of adverse drug reactions must receive careful consideration. Designers of program formularies, both of the formal and informal types, must decide whether or not to include a drug that carries a high risk of serious adverse reactions when a safer and equally effective alternative is available. They must likewise consider whether or how to reimburse persons for the long-term use of a drug that has been approved for only short-term use and is undergoing postmarketing surveillance.

Most important and probably most effective in the long run, we believe, is the establishment of drug utilization review programs, notably in hospitals where patients receive the most intensive drug therapy, to correct physician prescribing patterns that may be invitations to pharmacological disaster. The primary objective of such reviews, as we will note in a later chapter, is not to punish the irrational prescribers but to educate them.

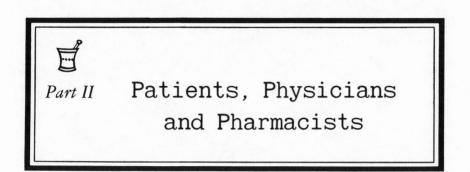

Part II Patients, Physicians
and Pharmacists

Patients

Rational drug use: the right drug for the right person, in the right amount at the right time, with due consideration of cost.

—HEW Task Force on Prescription Drugs

The health of Americans is better than ever, but it is far from what it might be. The infant mortality rate has fallen by 50 percent in the past fifteen years, and deaths from cardiovascular disease, the nation's number one killer, are continuing to be reduced. But the burden of chronic illness becomes ever heavier, and some problems—lung cancer and emphysema, for example—seem to resist the advances of modern medicine. Other conditions such as diabetes and high blood pressure can generally be controlled, but they may require a lifetime of treatment.

The problem of illness is reflected in many different statistics:[1]

- The people in this country average about two episodes each year of acute illness or injury sufficiently severe to require restriction of activity or lead to a physician visit.
- For the population above the age of 15, women account for 60 percent of all physician visits. For the group in the 15-44 age bracket, the rate of physician visits by women is almost double that by men.
- More than half of the population suffers from at least one chronic condition.

For middle-income individuals, increased use of health care has paralleled the growth of health insurance. For the elderly and the poor, the rapid rise in the use of medical care came after the implementation of the Medicare and Medicaid programs in 1966, which reduced many of the past inequities in access to care. At the same time, there has been mounting interest in the quality of health care—and a demand that the quality be improved.

A key dimension to the quality of medical care involves both the patient and the physician: the use of prescription drugs. Yet, despite the many medical advances during the past decade or two, there continues to be widespread evidence that the process of drug-taking is no more rational than the process of drug-prescribing. The problem, regardless of where the fault lies, may often be summed up in two words: patient noncompliance.

Although the availability of physicians has numerically outpaced population growth, and thus, except in a few circumstances, the demand for physician services is now more readily met, the average patient-physician encounter may be exceedingly short. It has been estimated that the typical office-based physician is asked to listen to each patient's trouble, conduct an examination, reach at least a tentative diagnosis, lay out a strategy of treatment (or perhaps nontreatment), usually write a prescription and explain how the medication is to be used—and do all this in an average of approximately fifteen minutes.[2]

During this exceedingly brief encounter, the conscientious physician is expected not only to order the appropriate drug but also to explain—in language that each patient can comprehend—what the drug is, what it is expected to accomplish, precisely when and how to take it and for what length of time, what side effects may occur, and what to do if they do occur.

Some physicians may decline to give out all this information. Some may not wish to mention such delicate matters as potential hazards, perhaps in the belief that these will needlessly alarm patients and induce them not to take the medication. Other physicians are poorly or at least inadequately informed about the drugs they prescribe. And some physicians refuse to discuss any such subjects on the grounds that "father knows best" and the patients should simply do what they are told to do. We disagree strenuously with the beliefs of this last group. Especially where drugs are concerned, patients have a *right* to know.

Furthermore, in most instances, patients have a *need* to know. They can scarcely be expected to use their drugs appropriately unless they clearly comprehend the details of appropriate use. Says FDA Commissioner Jere Goyan, "Americans deserve as much information as we can give them."[3]

Finally, many patients have a *desire* to know. How well do Americans use prescription drugs? The evidence suggests that the process of drug-taking may be far less rational than the process of drug-prescribing:

- Many patients are advised to take a particular drug before meals, but they take it after meals.
- Many patients are warned not to use alcohol while they are using some medications, so they give up whiskey and gin but continue to use beer and wine.
- Some patients are told to take an antibiotic faithfully for ten days, but they stop in three days because the fever is apparently gone.
- Some patients double the recommended daily dosage, perhaps in the belief that if three pills a day are good, six will be better.
- Some patients forget to take the medication for three days and then, to recoup, take quadruple the dosage on the fourth day.
- Many patients neglect to report an early adverse reaction to their physician or pharmacist, and delay until the time comes when costly hospitalization is needed.

It is not clear in each instance whether these and other unhappy events are the fault of the patient, the physician, or both—or whether a clinically oriented pharmacist should have intervened. Patients complain that the instructions they received from their physicians were confusing or inadequate, or that they received no instructions in the first place. Physicians complain that they were misunderstood, or that the patients forgot or were "uncooperative." (As will be noted later in this chapter, some of these same physicians may argue against handing out printed instruction leaflets for the reason that this might disrupt "patient-physician relations.")

THE COMPLIANCE PROBLEM

The failure of patients to comply with directions for the drugs prescribed for them represents a problem of almost staggering proportions. After reviewing almost two hundred studies, David Sackett, Brian Haynes, and their colleagues found that average rates of compliance ranged from a high of 89 percent to a shocking low of 18 percent among various groups of patients being treated for short-term illnesses. Among patients being treated for long-term illnesses, the average rate of compliance was only 54 percent.[4] One-third of the patients took all of their drugs as prescribed, one-third took none of them, and the remainder followed instructions only in part or only some of the time. Others who have studied the problem have found that between 25 and 59 percent of all patients fail to comply with instructions on drug use.[5] For many patients—up to a third—the non-compliance represents a serious threat to health or even life.

Noncompliance, it may be concluded, is widespread, it is danger-ous, and it is expensive to the patients themselves, to third-party pro-grams, and to taxpayers.

It is difficult to characterize the noncomplying patients. Non-compliance, it appears, has little or nothing to do with sex, age, race, income, education, occupation, marital status, ethnic background, reli-gion, or urban versus rural residence. Similarly, unlike what might be expected, noncompliance does not seem to be related to the type of illness, its severity, or its duration.[6] There are, however, some factors that *are* apparently related to noncompliance:

- In short-term illness, there is a tendency for patients to stop medication when there is the first relief of symptoms.
- In long-term, chronic illness, some patients tend to be-come confused, forgetful, or bored.
- When a patient is put on treatment with two, three, or more drugs at the same time, there is a risk of confusion or of unpleasant side effects resulting from the interaction between the drugs, which leads some patients to stop taking some or all of the prescribed medications.

Part of the blame for noncompliance clearly belongs to the pa-tient, and part obviously must be charged to the physician, but some seems to be the result of a breakdown in patient-physician communi-cations:[7]

- There is, first of all, the time constraint. In the fifteen minutes of an average office visit, the physician usually does not have an adequate opportunity to teach patients how to use the drugs prescribed for them.
- The physician may fail to communicate in terms that the patient can comprehend.
- Even if the physician does present the instructions clearly and simply, the patient may be so worried and anxious that the instructions are simply not received. The patient may be temporarily incapable of understanding the advice and prone to forget it.

- The physician may fail to recognize the patient's lack of understanding or lack of motivation.
- Too often, physicians do not monitor their patients' drug use, even in follow-up visits.
- Critical for effective physician-patient—or patient-physician—communications are flexibility in the physician's communications style, adaptability, and a willingness to listen to the patient's point of view. At least until now, such matters are not taught—or not taught effectively enough—in medical schools.

PPIs AND PATIENT INFORMATION

For decades, many European patients were accustomed to receive with each package of drugs a brief description of how the product should be used. These statements were written in simple language supposedly understandable by anyone. Rarely was there mention of possible side effects; the statements were designed to instruct patients on usage but not to give them information on benefits or risks.

In the United States, such informational material for patients—except for over-the-counter products—was essentially unknown until the 1960s, when a rash of sudden deaths—3,500 in Great Britain alone—struck asthma patients using isoproterenol in a high-potency aerosol nebulizer.[8] This country was spared because FDA had not approved the high-potency product. In 1968, however, FDA ordered manufacturers to include with each nebulizer a package insert written specially for patients. During the next few years, similar patient package inserts (PPIs) were required for oral contraceptives, the so-called morning-after pill or diethylstilbestrol, estrogens for use in treating menopause or postmenopause problems, and intrauterine devices (IUDs).

In every instance, FDA was bitterly denounced by manufacturers, the American Medical Association, and other groups of physicians. The PPIs, it was held, were not needed, they would rupture delicate physician-patient relationships, and FDA probably had no legal authority to require them in the first place.

FDA disagreed on all points. Survey after survey revealed that the overwhelming proportion of patients found the PPIs helpful and informative. Joubert and Lasagna, for example, found that 93 percent wanted to know the reasons for taking the prescribed drug, 89 percent wanted to learn the common risks that might be involved, 86 percent wanted to know the risk of overdosage, 80 percent wanted to know the risk in taking too little, and 79 percent wanted to know the risk in not taking the drug at all.[9]

In general, the studies showed, patients want to have more information, and more detailed information, than they seem to obtain from their physicians and pharmacists. They want to know the indications, contraindications, warnings, precautions, proper methods of use, and the possible risks and benefits. To FDA leaders, providing such information would recognize the patient's right to know and his need to know—and it might help to alleviate the problem of noncompliance.

The consumer health movement was a strong force in creating the momentum for a far wider dissemination of PPIs. In 1975, a petition was filed with FDA on behalf of a number of consumer organizations that called for PPIs on many if not most prescription drugs.[10] The petition demanded the provision of sufficiently detailed information on risks and benefits so that patients could give (or withhold) really informed consent—so that they could have a voice in deciding whether or not they should start or continue treatment recommended by a physician. Consumer activists declared that PPIs would thus give patients an appropriate involvement in decisions that would affect their own health. Organized medicine and the drug industry said it would bring absolute chaos.

To date, the PPIs now in use—some developed by FDA and some developed and distributed by pharmacy groups—have brought neither chaos nor the eradication of noncompliance. They have undoubtedly been a useful tool to help educate patients. In short-term treatments, such as with an antibiotic for an acute infection, they seem to improve compliance.[11] For drugs used by patients with chronic ailments, such as hypertension and asthma, the PPIs by themselves do not seem to have lasting benefits.[12] Unfortunately, setting up adequately controlled studies in this immensely complex area is difficult, and the evaluation results are not altogether clear.

At this stage in the development of PPIs, there are various questions that have not yet been satisfactorily answered:

- What information should PPIs contain?
- Who should write them? FDA? The drug companies? Nongovernmental groups?
- Who should hand them out, the physician or the pharmacist?
- Should they be required for all prescription drugs? For those most frequently involved in noncompliance? For most drugs? For only those used in short-term treatment? For drugs administered to hospitalized patients?

- Should a physician be authorized to direct that a PPI should not be distributed to a particular patient? To all his patients? Should FDA be authorized to veto such an order?
- Should studies be conducted on the value of PPIs in relation to their financial cost?

At the request of FDA, the Institute of Medicine has already conducted a preliminary survey and proposed a research strategy that would examine the ways in which PPIs would be distributed and used, their acceptance by patients, their effect on patient-physician or patient-pharmacist communications, their effect on patient compliance, and the long-term consequences of PPI use.[13]

Although there had been some enthusiastic support for early and widespread use of PPIs, there is evidence that FDA is determined to move cautiously. Originally, the agency had planned to issue and then evaluate PPIs for fifty to seventy-five drugs selected from the 375 most frequently prescribed products; FDA Commissioner Goyan has recently stated that the study will be restricted at the outset to ten drugs.[14] Consideration will be given to such approaches as having the inserts given routinely to patients, providing a supply of the PPIs to which the patients can help themselves, or maintaining in each pharmacy a volume of the information which could be consulted by any patient who was interested.

One reason for this more cautious approach is that there is no accepted estimate of the cost of the program to the drug industry, to pharmacists, to government, and to patients. Similarly, there is no agreement on what effect—if any—there will be on the liability of drug companies, pharmacists, or physicians in case of malpractice suits.

The eventual outcome of the PPI problem is difficult to foresee. For the immediate future, the expanded use of PPIs may be doomed by the war against inflation and the war against regulation. Eventually, however, we believe that they will win at least moderate acceptance.

Numerous studies have demonstrated that patients educated about drugs do not necessarily remain educated. They need constant reminders from physicians and every other possible source, including the public media. The complying patient, the one most likely to benefit from drug treatment, is the one who recognizes that every drug must be handled with care.

Physicians

The use of drugs is probably the most widely applied form of medical therapy. If it is applied wisely as well as widely, it is perhaps the most cost-effective.

Presumably, however, since the beginnings of drug treatment, drug products have not always been prescribed, dispensed, and used properly or even intelligently. But in recent years, the situation has been bedeviled by such factors as the abundant and effective promotion by the drug industry, the insistent belief that there is or must be "a pill for every ill," the pressure put upon physicians by prescription-demanding patients, the acceptance into everyday medical practice of what were once viewed as nonmedical problems, and the spread of third-party health insurance programs that make it easier—and less expensive—to gain access to physicians and hospitals and to pay for some drugs.

Over the years, there have been occasional reports in the medical literature that all was not well in drug-prescribing, that some drug therapy was irrational. In the late 1960s, the HEW Task Force on Prescription Drugs surveyed these earlier reports, conducted surveys of its own, and then published its findings.[1] A few physicians were irate, not so much because of the scope and nature of the problem, but because the findings were made public. Since then, there has been mounting concern about the whole area of irrational prescribing.

As noted earlier, rational prescribing was defined by the Task

Force as "the right drug for the right patient, at the right time, and in the right amount, with due consideration of cost."[2] From the outset, it was emphasized that costs were important, but not as important as the health of the patient.

Inappropriate or irrational prescribing may take many forms, but they all tend to fall into one or another of two general types. One is undermedication—for example, failing to treat moderate or severe hypertension, or providing only a two-day supply of an antibiotic to treat a case of pneumonia or "strep throat." The other, which is more common, is overmedication.

"We shall have to realize that overmedication is not simply overconsumption of drugs," said Mark Novitch of FDA. "When the more toxic of two equally effective drugs is used, that is overmedication. When a fixed combination drug is used and only one of the components is indicated, that is overmedication. And when a costly drug is prescribed where a less costly one of equal effectiveness is available, that, too, in a sense, is overmedication."[3]

There is overmedication if a drug is prescribed when no drug is clinically needed—for instance, the prescription of an antibiotic to treat the common cold, "flu," or other viral infections in which no antibiotic has value, or the administration of vitamin B-12 for any disease *except* pernicious anemia.

There is overmedication when a physician tells a patient: "You'll need to take this medicine for ten days, but I might as well order enough for twenty days."

Responsible for much modern prescribing, rational and irrational, is the nature of the complaints that bring patients to a physician's office. The ten conditions most commonly diagnosed by physicians during office visits are these:[4]

1. Acute respiratory infection
2. Neurosis
3. Coronary disease
4. Middle ear infection
5. Diabetes
6. Eczema and dermatitis
7. Acute pharyngitis (throat infection)
8. Refractive error (change in eye structure)
9. Hay fever
10. Obesity

It is important to note that in practically all of these conditions there are now prescription drugs that can either control the disease or, more frequently, at least control most of the symptoms. Accordingly, one or more drugs will be prescribed for about 82 percent of patients with upper-respiratory infections (excluding the "flu"), 40 percent of those with a neurosis, 55 percent of those with coronary disease, 78 percent of those with a middle ear infection, 48 percent of those with diabetes, 32 percent of those with hay fever, and a remarkably high 61 percent of those complaining of obesity.

HOW DO YOU DEFINE AN "ILLNESS"?

Two of the most frequent diagnoses of illness are relative new-comers to the list. Only a few decades ago, neurotics and overweight individuals rarely went to a physician for help, and, if they did, most internists and family physicians were able to offer them little more than sympathy and reassurance ("Go home and don't worry"), with perhaps a prescription for a mild sedative, or a reducing diet list. In those years, the true "illnesses" were considered to be only those that produced physical or biological derangement: infections, cancer, heart disease, diabetes, severe hypertension, parkinsonism, and the like. Neuroses and even some psychotic disorders were judged to be a different matter, and the victims were referred to a psychiatrist, a psychoanalyst, a counselor, or a clergyman.

What has significantly changed this situation—with a dramatic effect on the drug industry and on the prescribing, dispensing, and use of drugs—has been the redefinition of tension, anxiety, insomnia, depression, and an array of psychological problems as "diseases."

When a person is apprehensive before a school examination or a visit to a dentist, distressed because of a snub at the country club, or upset by strained employee-employer relations at the office or by marital stress, this is becoming redefined as an "illness." Abuse of alcohol, drug dependency, excessive cigarette smoking, and other self-destructive behavior today call more and more for medical intervention. Obesity is now considered to be one of the nation's major health problems. Many of these syndromes are being created by what Henry Lennard and Leon Epstein have called "mystification"—a process, they say, that has been stimulated at least in part by drug industry promotion.[5] Certainly, the process has had a remarkable impact on the use of drugs that influence the mind.

The prescription of a mind-altering drug—a sedative, a stimulant, or a tranquilizer—has a twofold effect. For the patient, it legitimizes the complaint: the symptoms are not imaginary. And for the physician, it strengthens his self-image as a healer.

Whether, in the long run, such drug use does more harm than good for patients—or, for that matter, for the ability of physicians to assess their own prescribing patterns—remains unclear.

PHYSICIAN PRESCRIBING PATTERNS

Certain of these prescribing patterns deserve particular attention, not because they are necessarily the most serious but because they have been examined by especially concerned groups and individuals.

The Minor Tranquilizers

The introduction of the first major tranquilizers—the Rauwolfia alkaloids and reserpine (Serpasil) in 1953, and chlorpromazine (Largactil or Thorazine) in 1954—and then the first minor tranquilizers—meprobamate (Miltown, or Equanil) in 1956, chlordiazepoxide (Librium) in 1960, and diazepam (Valium) in 1963—brought, for the first time, a whole range of psychoneurotic problems into the realm of drug treatment not only by psychiatrists but also by internists, physicians in general practice, and even pediatricians.

In the case of the potent major tranquilizers, use has generally been limited to the treatment of such serious psychotic disorders as schizophrenia. Members of this drug class are now known to have a significant potential for damage. Excessive dosage for prolonged periods is likely to produce temporary or permanent brain damage.[6] In some instances, the symptoms of schizophrenia may be controlled but replaced by a depression so deep that the result may be attempted suicide.

With the far more widely prescribed minor tranquilizers, psychosocial problems and psychosomatic complaints became legitimized as treatable illnesses simply because there now were drugs to treat them.

"By the very acceptance of a specific behavior as an 'illness' and the definition of illness as an undesirable state," Irving Zola has pointed out, "the issue becomes not *whether* to deal with a specific problem but *how* and *when*."[7]

For whatever reasons, the use of minor tranquilizers skyrocketed not only for tension, anxiety, and insomnia, but also for relief of musculoskeletal problems, hypertension, gastrointestinal complaints, asthma, menopausal symptoms, and postoperative care.[8] By 1973, 100 million prescriptions were dispensed annually for these agents, accounting for the sale of approximately 5 billion tablets. The rise in the number of such prescriptions dispensed by community pharmacists alone rose to 61.3 million in 1975. In 1976, however, the number of these prescriptions dropped abruptly, when serious questions about the safety of such products as diazepam began to be raised.[9] The rarity of side effects was no longer so evident. Yet, despite its declining popularity, diazepam remains the drug most frequently prescribed in the United States—and the number one drug named in drug abuse reports from the nation's emergency rooms.[10] In 1978, FDA alerted physicians that there was no evidence to show that diazepam and other minor tranquilizers have substantial effectiveness in the control of emotional problems in long-term use—that is, after about four months.[11]

The Psychostimulants

Perhaps the most blatant misuse of prescribed psychoactive drugs has concerned the psychostimulants, notably the amphetamines. The first of these was introduced in the 1930s by Gordon Alles and his associates, working mainly at the University of California in San Francisco and seeking to find an abundant substitute for Chinese ephedrine, then in short supply, for the treatment of asthma. Later, it was found that the amphetamines could (1) help truck drivers and students studying for examinations to stay awake at night, (2) give thrill-seekers an artificial "high," and (3) quench appetite.

There are now twelve different products still approved by FDA for the treatment of obesity. All (except mazindol) are chemically related, all are stimulants of the central nervous system, and all are now affected by the Controlled Substance Act of 1970, which limits the number and size of refills that can be obtained. Between 1971 and 1976, FDA took a number of steps that have resulted in a reduction of amphetamine prescriptions from more than 20 million in 1970 to about 5.5 million in 1973. The annual number of prescriptions has since remained at roughly that level. The Canadian government, however, no longer allows the labeling of psychoactive stimulants to indicate any value in the treatment of obesity. In Canada, as in the United States, the amphetamines are still approved for use in the treatment of narcolepsy and minimal brain dysfunction.

Sedatives and Hypnotics

These agents, commonly called sleeping pills and including notably the barbiturates, have been among the most carelessly prescribed

and dangerously misused of all prescription drugs.[12] As a result of
FDA controls and FDA education aimed at both physicians and the
public, their use has dropped dramatically, from about 42.1 million
prescriptions in 1971 to 27.3 million in 1976. For barbiturates alone,
the annual number of prescriptions dropped in that period from 20.4
million to 5.5 million.[13] Nevertheless, there are still about 5,000 deaths
a year associated with sleeping pills, and barbiturate users make
roughly 25,000 trips each year to hospital rooms because of drug-
related problems.[14]

Although some authorities deny that American physicians over-
prescribe psychoactive drugs,[15] it is our view and that of others[16] that
Americans are overmedicated with these potent products. It must be
recognized, however, that at least a part of the problem—if problem
there is—depends not on clinical but on strategic factors.

When a busy physician knows that his waiting room is crowded
with other patients, and he recognizes that it might require an hour of
his time to provide emotional support and reassurance to the patient
in his office but only a minute or two to write a prescription, what
should he do?

Most drug experts would agree that patients would be well served
if physicians followed one recommendation:

> Every time a physician reaches for his prescription pad, he [should] ask
> himself if he is prescribing a sedative or tranquilizer because he has a
> roomful of patients waiting and is in a hurry to get on to the next patient,
> whose illness he considers more serious, or whether he has carefully
> considered all the evidence, has found that sympathy, understanding,
> suggestion and reassurance are not sufficient, and has decided to pre-
> scribe a sedative or a tranquilizer for positive reasons rather than as an
> easy way out.[17]

Anti-infective Agents

Drugs to fight infections, particularly antibiotics, have been for
many years the most frequently prescribed of all classes of prescription products. Year in and year out, antibiotics continue to represent
from 15 to 20 percent of all prescriptions filled by community pharmacists, and from 25 to 28 percent of all drugs prescribed in hospitals.
Evidence of the unjustified and inappropriate use of antibiotics also
continues to be found year in and year out.

Among the commonplace errors in antibiotic therapy are these:
    • Prescribing an antibiotic without ordering a laboratory

test to obtain a firm identification of the organism causing the illness, especially in upper-respiratory infections.

- Prescribing an antibiotic by telephone without examining the patient.
- Prescribing an antibiotic for a virus infection (since it has been repeatedly demonstrated that antibiotics do not control or shorten most virus infections or prevent complications).
- Prescribing chloramphenicol to treat infections that could be controlled by safer and equally effective drugs.
- Prescribing an antibiotic, especially for prolonged periods, to prevent complications (except under special circumstances that will be noted below).

We have described elsewhere the more than twenty years of excessive prescribing of chloramphenicol and the development of more prudent use of this potent but hazardous agent by most physicians.[18] Sad to say, the practice of excessive prescribing of chloramphenicol still persists among a small percentage of physicians. The once widespread use of most fixed-ratio combination anti-infectives—two or more antibiotics, or an antibiotic plus a sulfa drug, or an antibiotic plus an antihistamine—has been largely terminated in this country, although a few of these combinations have been approved. When studies by the National Academy of Sciences/National Research Council found that these "piggyback" products were "ineffective as a fixed combination," FDA ordered nearly all of them off the market.[19] But problems remain.

Investigations spanning more than a decade continue to reveal overuse and misuse of antibiotics in hospitals, whether these be private, government, university, or community institutions.[20] With wide differences in the extent of use, depending on the nature of the hospital and on the service concerned—medical, surgical, obstetrical, and so on—antibiotics have been administered to roughly 21 percent of inpatients in some hospitals and to more than 61 percent of inpatients in others. In a number of studies, it has been found that the administered anti-infective therapy was either not needed in the first place or that an inappropriate drug or dosage had been employed in from 30 to 60 percent of all patients treated.

The problem of using antibiotics on patients about to undergo surgery, not in order to treat an infection but to prevent one, remains tricky. Some surgeons apparently continue to believe that antibiotics *must* be administered preventively to virtually all of their patients undergoing any procedure from simple hernia repair to delicate brain surgery. Studies show that about 30 percent of all hospital antibiotics were ordered for the prevention of possible complications, and often the preventive treatment was continued for five days or more.

The value of such wholesale use of antibiotics has been seriously questioned, especially when the drugs are applied systemically to the entire body rather than to the actual area of the incision. Except for certain procedures—for example, genitourinary and cardiovascular procedures, hysterectomies, cesarians, total replacement of the hip, and microsurgical procedures in the brain—some investigators have concluded that "current practices of antibiotic prophylaxis in surgery too often result from custom, unsupported belief, or dependence on poorly designed clinical trials."[21]

Similarly, it has been charged, the prophylactic use of antibiotics for more than two or three days is, in most cases, unneeded, needlessly expensive, and poses an unnecessary risk to patients.[22] (Of course, if an infection actually develops, the situation calls for different rules.) The risk, involving the emergence of antibiotic-resistant strains of organisms, has been described by one eminent expert on infectious disease in these terms:

> As a result of indiscriminate prescribing of antibiotics, more and more hospital patients are contracting infections more severe than the diseases for which they were admitted. Some of the infections are due to organisms once considered harmless. New strains of bacteria that cause diseases like gonorrhea, pneumonia, and meningitis (which once responded quickly to antibiotics) have developed and do not succumb to traditional antibiotics. And people suffer and even die from the side effects of antibiotic therapy. These concerns overshadow the fact that antibiotic therapy remains one of the most miraculous tools ever used by physicians.[23]

Regrettably, the irrational use of antibiotics and other anti-infective drugs is not restricted to hospitalized patients. In ambulatory patients, especially in the case of acute respiratory diseases—the common cold, "flu," rhinitis, pharyngitis, bronchitis, and the like—the prescribing of antibiotics is woefully excessive. These complaints, according to one classical study, account for nearly 63 percent of all ailments that bring patients to physicians' offices, hospital outpatient clinics, and neighborhood health centers.[24] Yet, barely 3 percent of these respiratory ills are caused by infectious agents such as streptococci that are susceptible to antibiotics or sulfa drugs, while the rest are caused by viruses that cannot be controlled by any drugs. Yet, in more than 80 percent of these visits, drugs—most often antibiotics—are prescribed by physicians.[25]

Finally, there is one other sin which deserves attention: ordering an expensive antibiotic when a less costly but equally effective drug is available. Here, the case of the new cephalosporins is of particular interest. These antibiotics are unquestionably effective, but they are also unquestionably expensive. For hospitalized surgical patients, in whom the cephalosporins have been frequently used to prevent complicating infections, cephalosporins may cost about $2.50 per day, as opposed to about $.50 per day for such equally useful antibiotics as penicillin, tetracycline, or erythromycin.

The cephalosporins, according to the AMA's *Drug Evaluations*, have been very actively promoted, popular antibiotics. But "published reports of surveys indicate that their broad usage, particularly by surgeons, may prove to be out of proportion to their ultimate importance in the field of anti-infective therapy. Despite the fact that cephalosporins have been effective in many different infectious diseases, they generally should not be regarded as a first-choice group of antibiotics."[26]

In some hospitals in which cephalosporins could be prescribed only with the blessings of an infectious disease expert, or in which an effective antibiotic utilization review procedure has been instituted, prescriptions for these agents have dropped dramatically by as much as 50 percent.[27] In some out-of-hospital programs, as in the New Mexico Medicaid program, physician education has resulted in decreasing some irrational uses of antibiotics by as much as 60 percent.[28]

In many third-party drug programs, the ultimate defensive maneuver is available: Physicians may prescribe any antibiotic they desire for any patient, but if the prescription is judged by experts to be irrational, the program will not pay for it.

Analgesics

Propoxyphene, marketed in various forms (Darvon, Darvon Compound-65, Darvocet-N, and others), is one of the most commonly prescribed drugs in America. Supposedly bridging the gap as a painkiller between aspirin and the narcotic drugs like meperidine (Demerol) and morphine, by itself it is no more effective in the relief of pain than aspirin or aspirin with codeine, if it is even as effective.[29] Yet, largely because of the adept promotion by manufacturers, propoxyphene products have represented a pharmaceutical gold mine. In 1976, even after reports questioning the efficacy and safety of these drugs had been accumulating for years, their prescriptions exceeded 30 million.[30]

In the mid-1970s, propoxyphene-related deaths reportedly reached a frequency of 6 per million population in the United States. About 46 percent of these deaths were listed as apparent suicide, 26 percent as accidents, and the remainder as undetermined. Most of the victims were middle-class, white, urban dwellers who were *not* members of the illegal drug abuse population.[31]

Estrogens

A major part of the problem with the prescription of estrogens, or female sex hormones, to control many symptoms in menopausal or postmenopausal women is that these drugs are so clearly effective in some women in relieving symptoms. In many patients, they can alleviate hot flashes, anxiety, depression, fatigue, headache, osteoporosis (bone-softening), and atrophic vaginitis (a shrinking or irritation of the lining of the vagina).

Unfortunately, this coin has another side. Use of the estrogens in postmenopausal women has been associated with a four- to eightfold increased risk of developing cancer of the endometrium (the lining of the womb),[32] a two- to threefold increase in the risk of ovarian cancer,[33] along with an increased risk of developing hypertension,[34] glucose intolerance,[35] and venous blood clots and gallbladder disease.[36]

Although evidence of these dangers has been steadily accumulating, the use of estrogens has likewise increased. In 1977, FDA estimated that three million women—about twice as many as two years before—were given estrogen prescriptions for menopausal or postmenopausal symptoms.[37]

Primarily because of the risk of endometrial cancer, in 1977 FDA began requiring pharmacists and physicians who dispense estrogens to provide patients with a special brochure that emphasizes the risks of long-term use. The decision was greeted with consternation or outright fury by many gynecologists and other physicians, largely on the grounds that the decision to prescribe or not to prescribe should be made by the physician. Some physicians insisted—and some still claim —that many of their patients do not wish to be given "frightening" information about risks, and it is these women who place pressure on the physician to prescribe.

It is our strong belief in this and similar situations that, with few exceptions, such a prescribing decision must be made jointly by the physician *and* the reasonably informed patient.

OBSTACLES TO RATIONAL PRESCRIBING

More than ten years ago, the HEW Task Force on Prescription Drugs found ample evidence to support the view that rational prescribing was far from a universal practice.[38] A number of problems were identified:

- The inadequate training of physicians during their medical school years on the day-to-day application of drug knowledge.
- The inadequate sources of objective information available to practicing physicians about drug properties and indications.
- The widespread custom of physicians to continue their drug education by relying mainly on the promotional activities of the drug companies.
- The exceedingly rapid turnover in the popularity of prescription drugs.
- The limited time available to practicing physicians to study and evaluate the therapeutic claims for newly marketed drugs.

When we reexamined these problems in 1974, we found that little had changed in this aspect of medical education.[39] There was still no source of information readily available to physicians on the properties, indications, and hazards of all drugs on the market. Such information was included in the so-called package inserts, but these were infrequently seen by physicians and usually ended up in the pharmacist's wastebasket. This kind of information was included in the *Physicians' Desk Reference (PDR)*, but only if the manufacturer elected to advertise his products in that publication. Physicians continued to be influenced by drug industry promotion.

TOWARD MORE RATIONAL PRESCRIBING

A number of strategies can significantly improve drug-prescribing. Some of these focus on improving physician education and access to information. Others involve the use of computerized drug utilization review systems, both hospital-based and areawide. Still others concern the development of close cooperation between physicians and clinical pharmacists. And, if need be, regulatory steps may be taken.

Physician Education

Medical students, interns, and residents must have better training in *clinical* pharmacology and therapeutics: the application of fundamental knowledge to actual practice. Not only should classroom instruction be improved, but clinical instruction in hospitals and outpatient clinics should devote more time to proper drug use.

Young physicians may be adequately trained in the use of those drugs which were in vogue at the time of their formal education, but apparently many have not been trained to evaluate the new products which will appear during their years in practice.

Physician Information

Physicians cannot continue to rely so heavily—or, in some cases, exclusively—on the drug industry for information, provided in large part by industry detailers or sales representatives, that is too often designed not to inform but to promote. Medical journals and, to a lesser extent (because they may be quickly outdated), textbooks and monographs are more often reliable sources of drug information for physicians. But more sources are required.

The continuing development of new drugs, the unearthing of new information on old drugs, and the time constraints on physicians have made an old proposal take on new urgency. More than a decade ago, the HEW Task Force on Prescription Drugs recommended the publication of an HEW drug compendium, updated at reasonable intervals, giving both clinical and price information for all prescription drugs on the market. The introduction of the Health Care Financing Administration's new *Guide to Prescription Drug Costs*[40] is aimed at filling part of the need. The publication of *AMA Drug Evaluations*,[41] with its periodic revisions, has marked an important advance, as has that of the *FDA Drug Bulletin. The Medical Letter*, a review of up-to-date prescribing information, continues to be a valuable source. Yet, the need for a complete compendium remains. Physicians and pharmacists must have this information readily available to them.

Hospitals

Hospitals and their medical staffs must accept more institutional responsibility for not only the medical care they provide but also the training they conduct. In the United States and other developed countries, hospitals provide the opportunity for greater emphasis on clinical pharmacology in their intern and residency programs and in their programs of continuing education of physicians.

In many hospitals, there is a pharmacy and therapeutics committee, usually including pharmacists and physicians, which seeks to rationalize drug use. In some instances, the committee offers only informal advice. In others, it has the authority to determine which products will be approved for use in the hospital (except in special circumstances) and which will be stocked in the hospital pharmacy. (See Chapter 6 on formularies.) Often, costly brand-name products which duplicate less expensive generic forms are banned.

Utilization Review

A dramatically effective measure to modify irrational prescribing habits is the creation of a computerized drug utilization review system. (See Chapter 8.) Such a system may be used retrospectively, after—and generally long after—the prescription has been dispensed, to analyze physician prescribing and patient drug use patterns. Even more dramatic, however, has been the use of a prospective system in which the prescription is reviewed and checked against patient records and established guidelines *before* it is filled.

The Regulatory Approach

The advent of Professional Standards Review Organizations (PSROs) to review health care provided at federal expense has provided a new version of utilization review. Under already existing authority, PSROs can review physician services, hospitalization, and drug use. In addition, they can combine utilization review techniques with the laying on of economic sanctions.[42]

In the following chapter, we will examine the effective relations that may be created between physicians and pharmacists, and the role of the clinical pharmacist. One noteworthy example of this cooperation, however, may be mentioned here.

Several years ago, in Jacksonville, Florida, leaders of the county medical society became convinced that there was gross overprescribing of amphetamines. More than a million such prescriptions were recorded in a four-month period in 1977. Furthermore, pharmacies were being robbed alarmingly often, and street traffic in the drugs was believed to be enormous.

In an effort to alleviate the situation, the medical society sponsored a verbal campaign to inform physicians in the area of the seriousness of the problem and urged them to use the greatest prudence in their prescription writing. At the same time, pharmacists volunteered to remove all stocks of amphetamines from their shelves and to institute a two-day delay in filling orders for these drugs—a period that enabled them to track down false prescriptions.

Later, the president of the medical society reported that physicians almost unanimously welcomed the program and expressed their interest in applying the program to other dangerous drugs.

Of particular interest, there was an 81 percent decrease in amphetamine prescriptions and a significant drop in the number of pharmacy robberies.[43]

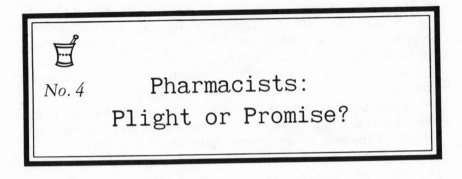

No. 4   **Pharmacists:
Plight or Promise?**

Except for the nationalization of pharmacies, which has occurred in Sweden but which most American pharmacists would probably view as an unmitigated disaster (and which probably will not happen here), it seems most likely that prescriptions written under any kind of national health insurance program would be dispensed under something like the existing system.[1] But, it may be hoped, not exactly like that system.

Most prescriptions for nonhospitalized patients are now filled in what are termed community pharmacies, either independent or chain stores. In this connection, a chain is generally defined as four or more units under the same ownership. Other prescriptions are dispensed by mail-order pharmacies, pharmacies in clinics, Health Maintenance Organizations, and discount stores, and to a growing degree by hospital outpatient pharmacies. Some prescriptions are filled by physicians who dispense for their own patients.

Except in special circumstances, as in remote regions where there is no pharmacy, physician dispensing no longer seems to be justified. This is particularly true when the taxpayers are paying the bill. Some dispensing physicians assert that they are better qualified than pharmacists to order high-quality products and to save money for their patients. We are inclined to doubt both claims. In most cases, it appears, physicians dispense their own drug products simply because it gives them additional income.

It is beyond question that patients can save substantial sums by ordering some drug products through a mail-order pharmacy. This method, however, has serious drawbacks. It may be advantageous when the product is needed for a long-term, chronic condition and can be ordered in a supply that will last for several months. It is useless when, for example, an antibiotic is needed promptly for an acute infection.

Patients may save money by comparison shopping in a number of independent and chain stores. Some chains and hospital outpatient pharmacies can purchase drugs in large quantities and become entitled to large discounts, and thus may be able to sell *some* of their products at relatively low prices. Other chain stores and hospital pharmacies, even though they can purchase at these low costs, sell at the same prices as those charged by their independent competitors and simply pocket a larger profit. Whether or not a hospital can use its discounts to benefit persons other than inpatients is an issue now being tried in the courts.

Most patients will presumably select a pharmacy primarily for convenience when a drug is needed urgently. When maintenance drugs for long-term therapy are required, money-conscious patients will undertake comparison shopping. But the most prudent patient will consider all factors—including convenience, prices, professional services, and particularly the pharmacist's personal interest—and select a family pharmacist with as much care as he or she uses in choosing a family physician.[2] Once a family pharmacist is chosen, it is important that the patient obtain all drugs, prescription or over-the-counter, from that pharmacist. This is especially important for elderly patients suffering from chronic disease and for patients obtaining prescriptions from several different physicians, dentists, or podiatrists.

There is still no uniform system of setting pharmacy prices. For a patient who is covered by insurance or some other third-party program, many pharmacists would like to charge what is known as the "usual and customary" price. That is, the charge for the beneficiary's prescription will be the same as that for the same prescription filled for a nonbeneficiary. Many third-party programs take a dim view of this approach, because the various amounts of reimbursement make program management difficult, the system is subject to abuse, and it provides no incentive to hold down program costs.

For government programs, drug reimbursement is based on two elements: the *acquisition cost*, or what the pharmacist had to pay to the wholesaler or manufacturer to acquire the product; and the mark-up or *professional fee*, which is to cover professional services, rent, salaries, heat, light, taxes, and the other costs of doing business, plus whatever profit the pharmacist deserves—or the program adminis-trator thinks he deserves. There may be a distinct difference between the latter two amounts, especially when negotiations with a govern-mental agency are under way. The fee is set as a fixed dollar amount, such as $1.00, $2.00, or $3.00 per prescription. This method is most commonly applied in other third-party programs.

There is comparable confusion over the matter of reported ac-quisition costs. The acquisition cost for the same quantity of the iden-tical product obtained from the identical manufacturer was given in one survey as $10.00 by one pharmacy and $52.20 by another. As one observer has asked: "Can any third-party program be expected to believe that the two pharmacies at the extremes of this range, as well as those whose invoice price fell in between these limits, are entitled to such variable amounts?"[3]

The profits on sales reported by pharmacies would appear to be modest, now averaging about 3.3 percent *before* taxes.[4] (This com-pares unfavorably with the roughly 10 percent net profits *after* taxes reported by most major drug companies.) But the low profit figure for pharmacies covers all storewide operations, including sales not only of drugs but also cosmetics, film, stationery, gardening equipment, liquor, and whatever else may be merchandised.

One reason for the continuing controversy between pharmacy groups and governmental agencies is the unhappy fact that most pharmacists cannot seem to agree on what it actually costs them to fill the average prescription. Each pharmacy has its own accounting sys-tem, but there are astounding differences among the various systems used throughout the country. The same system may be used by all the units of a particular chain, but this is not necessarily similar to the method applied by a different chain.

"It's not simply that one pharmacist's way of calculating his dis-pensing costs is different from that of another pharmacist," says one experienced economist. "Too often, the pharmacist doesn't even *know* what it costs him. And when he tries to negotiate with the govern-ment representatives and get a reasonable professional fee, they can make hash out of him."[5]

There is, accordingly, a pressing need for the development, test-ing, and nationwide acceptance of a uniform cost-accounting system—

one that would be fair to pharmacists, patients, and third-party programs.[6] Such a system has recently been designed, tested, and marketed by the American Pharmaceutical Association (APhA).[7] There is also a need for a reimbursement system that would recognize the value of such features as 24-hour-a-day or weekend operations, delivery service, differences in cost-of-living levels in different parts of the country, differences between urban and rural operations, and differences in volume of business.

"You've got to realize," the economist emphasizes, "that a small-town pharmacy that fills perhaps thirty prescriptions a day cannot possibly survive on a fee schedule that means juicy profits for a big city pharmacy that fills thirty prescriptions an hour."

A similarly irritating problem has been involved in determining how much it costs a pharmacy to handle all the administrative details of processing a prescription for a beneficiary of a third-party program. What are the pharmacy's expenses for verifying the eligibility of the patient, referring to details of the specific third-party coverage, selecting the correct price, completing the appropriate claim form, getting prior authorizations where these are necessary, investigating rejected claims, keeping the proper accounting records, and all the other duties that may be required?

Without such information, it has been largely impossible for pharmacists and third-party program representatives to agree on how much additional reimbursement should be paid to each pharmacist for his added expenses, to determine if a standard fee should be set for all pharmacies. It has been totally impossible to reach such agreement for all pharmacies in the United States, or even for all pharmacies in a single state or city. It is sometimes impossible to reach agreement with an individual pharmacist. Accordingly, it has been difficult to determine who—the pharmacist or the third-party program—has been taking advantage of whom.

In July 1979, the first major step to solve this frustrating situation was announced by the American Pharmaceutical Association and the National Association of Chain Drug Stores (NACDS), which had jointly financed a preliminary time-and-motion study conducted by Health Information Designs, of Washington, D.C. Involving nearly one hundred community pharmacies, both independent and chain, the investigation showed that these added administrative expenses amounted to a low of $.19 to a high of $1.86 per third-party prescription, with a mean average of about $.67.[8]

A few pharmacy trade journals promptly picked up these findings and used them to prove that current reimbursement levels were too high or too low. The findings proved nothing of the kind. As the investigators themselves emphasized from the outset, the study covered only about one hundred pharmacies, all located in metropolitan areas with a population of a million or more, and all of them having agreed to participate in the study.

What was far more important, as APhA and NACDS officers—as well as HEW officials—recognized, was that a long-needed method had been developed. If verified, it could be applied to any or all pharmacies to create future guidelines that would be based on accounting rather than on argument.

As irksome as these economic problems may be to modern pharmacists, they are not as emotionally painful as is a professional problem that is now increasingly acute—namely, that most pharmacists have been overeducated for the services they are allowed to perform. They know it. They don't like it. And the public shouldn't like it, either.

WILL THE REAL DRUG EXPERT STAND UP?

It has long been our firm belief, and is now the opinion of many of our medical colleagues, that many pharmacists are far more knowledgeable about drugs and drug products than are most physicians. Modern pharmacists—especially those who graduated during the past decade or so—*should* be more knowledgeable in this area than the average physician. They have received five or six years of intensive training on the nature of drugs, their probable effects on patients, their potential hazards, when they should be used and when they should not, their possible interactions with other drugs and with foods, their interference with certain laboratory tests, their appropriate storage, and the dosage schedules to give the best possible results. Usually pharmacists are vastly better informed than physicians on relative drug prices; they know when a patient can save significantly by using a generic rather than a brand-name product and when such savings would be trivial.

Few physicians in their crowded medical school days had a chance to learn much about such matters. Less than half of the nation's medical schools have departments of clinical pharmacology designed to teach such subjects. Few physicians in practice have the time—or sometimes even the interest—to keep up-to-date in this complex field.

There are, of course, some physicians—most of them specialists in clinical pharmacology—who are outstanding experts on drugs. There are some physician specialists, as in cancer chemotherapy, who are the most knowledgeable in their particular field. And it must be pointed out, at the same time, that there are some pharmacists who do not keep up-to-date, or who never learned the facts adequately in the first place, or who do not feel comfortable in discussing these matters with patients; they are content to limit their professional activities to counting, pouring, and typing labels.[9]

Most pharmacists, however, except for those in progressive hospitals and perhaps some community pharmacies and clinics, are highly frustrated to find that they have little or no chance to put their vital professional knowledge to work. As a consequence, millions of patients who could have received helpful and perhaps lifesaving advice about drugs have not obtained it.

It is much as if a service station attendant were sent to school, trained to become a skilled automobile mechanic, awarded a certificate of proficiency, and then returned to his former employer, only to be told: "Son, keep your hands off people's carburetors and ignition systems and transmissions. You just pump gasoline and check the oil and water. And don't talk to the customers."

There are two major reasons for this unhappy situation in pharmacy. One is rooted in professional pride and marked by interprofessional squabbling: many physicians (although the number seems to be decreasing) have not been happy at the thought that a pharmacist might consult with patients about the prescription drugs that are ordered for them. Such physicians fear that a pharmacist might give advice that could conflict with their own. They even challenge the right of a pharmacist to ask the physician directly and discreetly about what seems to be an inappropriate or irrational prescription. Typical of this last group was a Los Angeles hospital physician who told a questioning pharmacist: "Don't tell me how to prescribe. I write the prescriptions. You fill 'em."[10] That physician's hospital appointment was soon terminated.

The second reason for the pharmacist's unhappy situation is an inescapable fact of economic life: when a pharmacist consults with a patient, especially one who is a beneficiary of some government program, the consultation takes time, and, under most such programs, there are no provisions to reimburse the pharmacist for investing this extra time. (A notable exception is the Blue Cross Plan of Central

Ohio, which obviously has felt that a pharmacist's time, knowledge, and advice are important for patients and thus are worth money to the program.)[11]

"I'd like to devote a few extra minutes with each patient, telling him or her how to use the prescription drug to get the best possible results," says a community pharmacist. "But those few minutes I'd spend with one patient—maybe two, or five, or ten, giving suggestions and answering questions—are minutes I couldn't spend to fill another patient's prescription. I'd have to charge a little more for the prescription itself. But that would put me at a disadvantage against my competitor in the next block, who just counts the pills and types the label."

How much more would this extra charge need to be for such consultation? Perhaps a dollar or two for each prescription. Would the public be willing to pay?

It must be emphasized again that most of today's pharmacists do not need extra training in order to provide this kind of consultation. They have already been trained.

"Paradoxically," says Michael Riddiough, of the U.S. Congress's Office of Technology Assessment, "the federal government requires pharmacy schools to provide clinical instruction, in order to receive federal capitation funds, but it does not pay pharmacy graduates to use this clinical training in their practice."[12] On the other hand, Dr. Riddiough warned his fellow pharmacists that they are going too far if they publicly proclaim that all pharmacists are willing and able to furnish helpful consultation to patients. "Pharmacists must admit to themselves what is painfully obvious," he wrote in a sharp letter to the editor of a leading pharmacy journal. "Their profession provides diversified services which vary dramatically from hospital to hospital, drug store to drug store, and pharmacy school to pharmacy school. . . . Somehow, miraculously, we all are supposed to provide all services for all people in all types of health care settings." But, he added, "a Senator or a Congressman who patronizes a chain drug store has difficulty in believing that all pharmacists should be paid for providing clinical services." It is time to tell the world that, "unlike a rose, a pharmacist is not a pharmacist is not a pharmacist."[13]

In theory, the need for any pharmacy consultation could be obviated by the prescribing physicians. Presumably physicians tell each patient what the prescribed drug is, what it is supposed to do, and how to use it properly. We would like to believe that most physicians so advise all of their patients. But some do not, and some fail to give the instructions clearly and understandably. Some patients, on the other hand, do not understand, or they forget, or they simply do not listen. There is, for instance, the case of the frightened patient who had been told in detail by her physician about the drug he was prescribing. The instructions were forgotten instantly—if they were ever heard. When the woman saw her husband in the waiting room, all she could remember was, "Thank God, he says it isn't cancer!"

Another irritating and even senseless aspect of the underutilization of pharmacists has been described by Robert Johnson of the California Pharmacists Association:

> One thing is obvious: the existing medical community (i.e., physicians) has neither the time nor the inclination to monitor adequately patients' drug therapy. Today's practicing physician is clearly the most over-utilized person in the health care system. He is called upon to do routine physical examinations, remove splinters, deliver babies, take blood pressures of mild hypertensives on a regular basis, and perform a myriad of other tasks commonly referred to as "medical problems" that detract from the time that could and should be spent on acute care conditions.

In glaring contrast, said Johnson:

> Pharmacists represent an immediately available, easily accessible, well-identified but under-utilized professional health manpower pool able to make a significantly larger contribution in the delivery of health care service. As a highly trained member of the health care team located primarily in the community, the pharmacist in his "store-front" clinical setting is in a unique position to provide personalized care at a reasonable cost.[14]

In special situations, as in some Public Health Service programs, pharmacists have been measuring blood pressures, taking throat cultures, ordering laboratory tests, and—under the general supervision of physicians—providing long-term care for patients with such chronic ailments as high blood pressure, diabetes, and pernicious anemia.[15]

It is becoming clear that the pharmacist can be particularly helpful by practicing what has come to be known as clinical pharmacy.

CLINICAL PHARMACY

There is no agreement on a precise definition of clinical pharmacy, which in general is thought of as the provision of full pharmaceutical services. It has been said to mean anything from diagnosing hypertension in a particular patient to pointing out the Surgeon General's warning on a pack of cigarettes.[16] Perhaps the most useful definition rests on the concept that the nonclinical, or garden-variety, pharmacist is product-oriented, while the clinical pharmacist is patient-oriented. Thus, a clinical pharmacist may be practicing his special profession when he advises someone not to buy a particular over-the-counter product or when he refuses to fill a seemingly irrational prescription until he has double-checked with the prescriber.

In recent years, there has been growing evidence that clinical pharmacy can be readily accepted and highly effective in some hospitals.[17] Clinical pharmacists have contributed substantially by serving on hospital pharmacy and therapeutics committees and drug utilization review committees, by helping to develop and update hospital formularies, and particularly by working on the wards and outpatient clinics with physicians, nurses, and patients. With hospitalized patients, pharmacists have immediate access to the clinical records. They know the diagnosis. They participate regularly in ward rounds. They consult easily with physicians—often at the request of the physicians—on the best drug to be prescribed, the preferred dosage form, and the best dosage schedule, and often they can advise on needed changes in the treatment strategy. They can check for potential interactions between two drugs prescribed for the same patient, perhaps by two different physicians. Sometimes the pharmacist will detect an adverse drug reaction even before it is noticed by either a physician or a nurse. In outpatient clinics, the pharmacist can obtain detailed drug histories, including information regarding over-the-counter products that the patients often fail to mention to their physicians, or that the physicians neglect to ask about. And, in many instances, the pharmacist can work with patients to instruct them how to continue their medication—what to do and what not to do—after they are discharged from the hospital.

Even outside the hospital, many of these functions can be handled successfully by clinical pharmacists.[18]

Patient Profiles

One of the most valuable functions included in clinical pharmacy is the maintenance of patient profiles or patient medication records. Records should be kept of all prescription drugs dispensed to a patient, as well as of those filled for other members of the family. The records should also contain similar records of over-the-counter purchases. The goal should be to have a list of all the drug products that may be lurking in the family medicine cabinets. The record should likewise indicate all of the patient's known drug allergies and idiosyncrasies, and whatever the pharmacist may learn about the patient's clinical status.

With such information in his files, a clinical pharmacist can—and should—query a physician by asking such questions as: "Doctor, about this prescription you wrote for Mrs. Smith, did she tell you that she's receiving another prescription for the same drug from another physician?"

Or: "When you prescribed penicillin G, were you aware that your patient is allergic to penicillin V and will probably react badly to any penicillin?"

Or: "Doctor, when you prescribed this anti-blood-clotting drug for Mr. Smith, did he tell you that he's also on heavy doses of aspirin prescribed by another physician for his arthritis? The combination, you know, may cause hemorrhage."

Or: "I've noticed that you're ordering an adult dose for the Brown baby. Are you sure that this is what you want?"

It is to be hoped that the pharmacist will intercept such seemingly irrational prescriptions and consult with the physician rather than with the patient. Few if any pharmacists, it is to be hoped, would say to the patient, "Anybody who wrote such a prescription for you must be out of his mind." Unfortunately, some physicians have been known to utter such an unfelicitous comment about their medical brethren.

Patient records in the pharmacy can also serve an important role in consultations between pharmacists and physicians. Where good communications exist, a pharmacist can alert a physician to the fact that a particular patient with some chronic disease has apparently forgotten to obtain a refill, or that the patient is obtaining refills too frequently, or that the prescribed drug might be economically replaced by a low-cost generic or by a different but equally effective drug available at a substantially lower price, or that the patient is continuing to use alcoholic beverages while taking the drug, even though the physician had warned against such a practice. Pharmacists may be the first to know that a patient has suffered what may be an adverse drug reaction. Often, they can alert a physician that his patient is getting prescriptions that might interact seriously with other prescription drugs or with over-the-counter products which the patient neglected to mention he is using.

Some pharmacists have expressed concern that maintaining detailed patient profiles or patient medication records (PMRs) might expose them to legal problems. One expert claims that the opposite is true. Harold Hirsh of Washington, D.C., who is both a physician and an attorney, says: "The question is, 'What liability accrues here?' In my judgment, those who fail to keep patient medication records are leaving themselves open to lawsuits, even in areas where the PMR is not mandated. Conversely, if pharmacists properly maintain PMRs, their liability is minimized."[19]

Support of Prescriber Instructions

Once a patient is in a pharmacy to get a prescription filled, and is more relaxed and no longer so concerned about a possible diagnosis of a dread disease, the pharmacist can reemphasize and perhaps clarify the instructions that were given by the physician.

"I'm sure," the pharmacist can say, "that your doctor said that you shouldn't drink while you're taking this medication. That means not only no hard liquor, but also no beer or wine."

Or: "With this antibiotic, you'll probably start feeling better in two or three days. Do *not* stop taking the medicine. Keep on with the drug for the full ten days that your doctor has ordered."

Or: "I'm sure that your doctor told you to take no other drugs while you're on the medication that he ordered. 'No other drugs' means things like aspirin, even though you can buy them at a supermarket."

Or: "I know your mother-in-law has many of the same symptoms that you do, but it may not be the same disease. Don't share your prescription with her."

Or: "I honestly don't care where you buy your Maalox, or where you get your prescription filled for Tagamet, or Librium, or whatever. But please let me know what drugs you do get, so we can keep your medication record complete and up-to-date."

Although the details may differ from place to place, this kind of pharmacist-patient consultation is now required by law in such states as Kansas, Maine, New Jersey, North Dakota, Oregon, Utah, Washington, and Wisconsin.[20] In many instances, however, the job is made difficult for pharmacists unless they are aware of the diagnosis made by the physician. Sometimes the diagnosis is instantly apparent: a prescription calling for an oral antidiabetic agent such as tolbutamide clearly signals a diagnosis of diabetes; a prescription for nitroglycerine may indicate angina; and one for colchicine is a giveaway of gout. But these clear-cut diagnosis-indicating prescriptions are uncommon. Less informative are, for example, orders for an occasionally toxic antibiotic such as chloramphenicol, which may be prescribed for anything from typhoid fever to gonorrhea, the "flu," a sore throat, or the common cold, or for a hormone such as prednisone, which is used for arthritis, allergies, asthma, and a host of other conditions.

In some cases, the patients themselves are aware of the exact diagnosis and may be able to inform the pharmacist, but this can be a risky business, subject to misunderstanding of what the physician said or to the patient's incomplete recall of the precise diagnosis.

For a number of reasons, it has been proposed that all prescriptions should carry the diagnosis of the condition for which the drug is being prescribed, either written out in full or shown in code. The idea has not yet won much favor among physicians, who feel that this may be a threat to privacy, or a threat to professional dignity, or none of the pharmacist's business in the first place. Some physicians actually fear that a pharmacist may give advice that will be contrary to their own wishes.

In the state of Utah, where a law requiring pharmacy counseling was put into effect recently, an effort was made to determine what really happens. "Immediately after the law was passed," said Alan Nelson of Salt Lake City, then an official of the state medical society, "I met with the president of the Utah Pharmaceutical Society. We decided to find out how often situations were occurring in which such 'counseling' caused problems, either by being inconsistent with what the physician had informed the patient, causing some confusion on the part of the patient, or some misinformation being given by the pharmacist. In the nine months of operation since the bill was passed, I have not heard of one instance in which this created a problem. What this tells me is that, in a community where the physicians and pharmacists talk to each other, where they act as a team and have the patient's welfare as their final goal, this kind of situation can work quite well."[21]

PHARMACISTS AS PRESCRIBERS:
THE CALIFORNIA EXPERIMENT

During the 1970s, California—like most other states—was attempting to cope with soaring health care costs and a host of other problems related to an apparent shortage or maldistribution of physicians. In many circles, it was claimed that nonphysicians such as nurses, physician-assistants, and pharmacists could help to relieve the situation by taking on new or expanded roles. Unfortunately, most of these new roles were banned under existing state law. In an effort to find a solution, the California legislature passed a law permitting a number of experimental pilot projects: to provide special training when this was needed, to permit the trainees to use their knowledge and skill under the watchful eye of physicians, and finally to evaluate the results. If a project worked out satisfactorily, the legislature could then be asked to change the law and make the new role legal and permanent.

In 1977, the law was amended specifically to permit the organization of special projects in which clinically trained pharmacists— along with nurse-practitioners and physician-assistants—could prescribe for patients and monitor their progress.[22] The amendment was passed and signed into law by the governor, originally over the vehement objections of the California Medical Association. Later, but with no visible enthusiasm, the CMA agreed to cooperate.

For the pilot projects that involve prescribing by pharmacists, two programs have gone into effect, one centered in the School of Pharmacy of the University of California at San Francisco, and the other in the School of Pharmacy of the University of Southern California in Los Angeles. In total, about sixty pharmacists, all with Doctor of Pharmacy degrees, are participating.

"When they do their actual prescribing," an official of the program explains, "they will not prescribe just any drug for just any patient. Certainly at the start, they'll be working in a carefully controlled environment."

In most cases, the patients have already been examined and diagnosed by a physician. Some of the pharmacists have been assigned to work in such special units as a thyroid clinic, a hypertension clinic, an extended care facility, and even an inpatient cancer unit. Most of the patients are afflicted with a chronic disease. Eventually, the trainees may work in community pharmacies. In all cases, they are supervised every few days—and perhaps every day—by physicians.

According to Dr. Glen Stimmel, head of the program at USC, the project is aimed at determining (1) if specially trained pharmacists can prescribe safely, competently, and cost-effectively—and presumably minimize physician visits; (2) if patients will accept pharmacists as prescribers; and (3) what additional training is needed to qualify pharmacists for this function.[23] "We have until 1982 to draw our conclusions," says Dr. Stimmel. "If our findings are positive, changes in pharmacy practice legislation are very possible."

For clinical pharmacists who have insisted for years that they are knowledgeable about prescription drugs, and for the physicians who have supported them, the California experiment is—to use a hackneyed but accurate phrase—fraught with significance. If the experiment succeeds, it may have lasting effects on holding down some health care costs, on providing patients with easier and quicker access to the health care system, and possibly on improving the quality of drug therapy. It may inflate the pride of pharmacists in their profession, and also deflate the pride of some physicians. It will have to be considered in the design of any national drug insurance program.

"Of course, if it fails," says Jere Goyan, former dean of the pharmacy school at UCSF and later FDA commissioner, "there'll be egg on everybody's face. But it won't fail. We know these young pharmacists. They're good."

Part III. Cost-Containment:
Low Cost or High Quality — or Both?

No effort is made here to examine the possible cost of any particular drug insurance program. This was done in 1969 by the HEW Task Force on Prescription Drugs, which considered coverage of out-of-hospital prescription drugs under Medicare.[1] In 1979, a broader study was conducted for Roche Laboratories by Gordon Trapnell, who considered prototype programs for Medicare beneficiaries as well as for the entire population, along with the probable effects of different types of drug coverage and different varieties of cost-sharing.[2]

Trapnell's conclusion: the least costly program would be the provision of all prescription drugs (plus insulin) to Medicare beneficiaries, with an income-related deductible.

Instead, in the following chapters, we will focus on the clinical, economic, and tactical advantages and disadvantages of the most important approaches toward cost-containment.

The Great
Generic Controversy

Throughout the past decade, there has been a mounting outcry against the soaring costs of health care in the United States. Patients, notably those without adequate health insurance, have expressed their anger, especially at the rise in hospital charges and physician bills. Administrators of government and union health programs have been under increasing pressure to cut expenditures, or at least to slow their rise. In most cases, their efforts to contain costs have not been noticeably effective.

Although most of the recent attempts to hold down costs have been leveled at physicians and hospitals, the matter of pharmacy charges has not escaped comment—and, occasionally, bitter comment. Although drug company and pharmacy spokesmen have repeatedly noted that drug prices have risen only modestly, those prices *have* risen. Patients trying to cope on the basis of their limited incomes— the elderly in particular—are only too well aware of the situation.

Many approaches to cut health care costs have been proposed. Almost without exception, they have been strenuously opposed by medical and hospital leaders. Efforts to minimize what may seem to be needless hospitalization, needless surgical operations, needless laboratory tests, needless or needlessly expensive prescriptions, and expensive therapeutic procedures have all been denounced as unwarranted, clinically irresponsible, and probably unconstitutional.

The general reaction from organized medicine has been something like this: "To save a miserably few dollars, you'll force us to practice second-class medicine."

With each passing year, the "second-class medicine" argument has received a cooler and cooler reception from federal and state legislators, program administrators, insurance companies, many outstanding physicians, and even patients themselves. And, at the same time, more and more medical and pharmacy experts are stating openly that the second-class medicine defense is simply not true; costs, they say, can be cut without demolishing the quality of care.[1]

As the advent of national health insurance nears, especially if drug benefits are included, it may be confidently expected that the continuing controversy over drug costs and expenditures will continue. Among the approaches that will call for consideration are these:

- The selection of low-cost products, whether generic or brand-name, in place of high-cost brand-name products.
- The use of formularies, both in-hospital and out-of-hospital, to include drugs selected on the basis not only of relative safety and efficacy but also relative price.
- Government purchase on competitive bid of drugs for beneficiaries of government health programs.
- Patient cost-sharing through co-payment or some other means.
- Drug utilization review, designed to reinforce rational prescribing and dispensing patterns, and to detect errant ones.

It appears unlikely that all or any of these approaches will win unanimous endorsement from physicians, pharmacists, or drug manufacturers. They may, however, be tempting to patients and taxpayers.

STATE OF THE CONTROVERSY

Starting in the 1950s, American drug companies were distressed to learn that they were facing a new kind of competition: black-market products made illicitly in this country or abroad. In most instances, the legal products were still under patent. The counterfeits were usually shaped, labeled, flavored, and colored to mimic the originals.[2]

Whether this black-market competition was monumental or minimal has never been determined. Nevertheless, it resulted in the passage of what came to be known as antisubstitution laws by nearly all state legislatures.[3] Under such laws, a pharmacist could not legally substitute any other product for the one prescribed by the physician.

The laws apparently put an end to most of the black-market operations, although it became apparent in the 1970s that some enterprising operators were still in business. In October 1975, the Food and Drug Administration asked the U.S. Attorney in St. Louis to seize all of the prescription drugs made or held by Jamieson-McKames Pharmaceuticals, Inc. According to FDA, the St. Louis firm was marketing low-potency imitations of Roche's Librium, Librax, Valium, and Dalmane products, Pfizer's Urobiotic, and Burroughs Wellcome's Zyloprim, Septra, and Sudafed. All of these products were then under patent. In the case of Upjohn's Motrin, of which the active ingredient was ibuprofen, the counterfeit product contained an entirely different chemical, magnesium salicylate.[4] Later it was charged that bottles of penicillin were relabeled to show an expiration date about two years later than the true one. Bottles labeled as Upjohn's clindamycin were found to contain merely tetracycline. Bottles of penicillin were relabeled as ampicillin.

At the trial, the defendants' attorneys claimed that their clients were merely trying to save money for patients. However, the judge found that, "contrary to defendants' assertions, these actions were not taken in a sincere desire to save money for patients, but instead were the result of defendants' desire to reap profits. There can be no claim that defendants had a patient's interests in mind when said defendants sold drugs past their expiration date or substituted one drug for another."

In March 1979, the defendants were found guilty on all substantive accounts.[5] Four defendant companies were fined a total of $88,000, and James C. Jamieson, Sr., and James C. Jamieson, Jr., were each fined $50,000 and sentenced to eight years in federal prison plus five years on probation.

Regardless of their effect in stamping out this kind of pharmaceutical skullduggery, the antisubstitution laws had a far greater impact in another area, bringing on what has been termed the great generic controversy.[6] Under those laws, even if the original drug were no longer under patent, a pharmacist could not substitute a low-cost version without the physician's blessing. Thus, in the case of the widely used sedative chloral hydrate, if the physician prescribed "Noctec," the pharmacist was obliged to dispense the brand of chloral hydrate marketed by Squibb. The same was true if the prescription read "chloral hydrate Squibb." Only if the physician called merely for "chloral hydrate" could the pharmacist dispense a low-cost product— and presumably save the patient some money.

There has never been any question about the lower cost of nearly all generic products. A 1975 study by the Council on Economic Priorities revealed that the prices for one hundred 400,000-unit tablets of potassium penicillin G ranged from $1.50 or less for several generic products to $8.36 for Squibb's brand-name version marketed as Pentids.[7] For one hundred 100-mg tablets of nitrofurantoin, several generic versions were available for $3.65 or less, while Lederle's Cyantin was priced at $14.40, and Eaton's Furadantin (the original brand-name product) at $20.52. A 1979 survey showed that the price to pharmacists for five hundred 10-mg capsules of chlordiazepoxide was approximately $40.85 for Roche's Librium and $6.33 for Generix's generic version. The price for one hundred 2.5-mg tablets of Searle's Lomotil was $11.84, while that for Smith Kline & French's version was $4.91.[8]

Such massive price differences, it must be emphasized, are somewhat unusual. In most cases, industry experts estimate that the average saving will be about 20 percent.[9] In a few cases, it has been found that the brand-name and the generic versions are priced at essentially the same level; and in one instance, it was noted that a generic product was priced slightly higher than the brand-name version.[10]

The most recent source of drug price information is the Health Care Financing Administration's (HCFA's) newly published *Guide to Prescription Drug Costs*, which lists by therapeutic class the cost for each product to the pharmacist, the average daily dose, and the daily cost of treatment. The Pharmaceutical Manufacturers Association sought to prohibit publication of the *Guide* and filed for an injunction in the federal courts. In May 1979, the U.S. District Court for the District of Maryland ruled against PMA. "Release of this information," the court held, "is undoubtedly a public service in the public interest."[11]

HCFA officials have started distributing 500,000 copies of the *Guide* to physicians, pharmacists, and others, largely to help physicians in making prescription choices and to aid pharmacists in product selection. Updating is planned for twice a year.

It is evident that the pricing aspect of brand-name versus generic drug products is not and never has been a matter of controversy. When multiple-source products are available—that is, when there are two or more manufacturers or marketers of a drug—the potential savings available to patients and to hospitals and government agencies can range from significant to staggering. The key issue in the great generic controversy has been something else: *Is the quality of generic products as high as that of brand-name products?* Predictably, the makers of generics say, "Yes!" Just as predictably, the brand-name companies say, "You can't count on it."

In this connection, once again, it is crucial to understand that what patients take is rarely a pure active drug. They almost always take a drug *product*. The product includes not only the active drug ingredient but also various fillers, buffers, flavors, coloring matter, and other ingredients. The product may be dispensed as a capsule, a tablet, or a liquid. How rapidly the active ingredient will be absorbed, how high the drug levels will reach in the blood and various tissues, and how rapidly the drug will be excreted will depend on the nature of the various ingredients, the dosage form, and the care with which the product is made. And these factors may also determine whether the drug will be effective, ineffective, safe, dangerous, or lethal.

The question of whether or not a generic product is equivalent to a brand-name one, involving as it does the potential effect on patients, cannot be settled completely without considering three definitions:[12]

- Chemical equivalents, it is now widely agreed, are two or more products containing essentially the same amounts of the same active ingredient in the same dosage form, and meeting all standards set in the *U.S. Pharmacopeia* or other accepted compendia, or specified in FDA's New Drug Application form.
- Biological or physiological equivalents are chemical equivalents which, when administered to the same normal, healthy individuals, will exhibit essentially the same degree of absorption in the body, as measured by blood levels, excretion rates, and the like.
- Clinical or therapeutic equivalents are chemical equivalents which, when administered to patients suffering from the same disease, will give essentially the same clinical effects, such as overcoming the disease or controlling the symptoms.

Ordinarily, chemical equivalency can be readily determined in the laboratory by appropriate and inexpensive chemical or physical tests. Biological or bioavailability equivalence can also be determined relatively easily for most drugs, but at greater expense, by tests on healthy human volunteers. But clinical equivalency is something else. In most instances, tests on patients afflicted with a disease are difficult to perform and even more difficult to interpret. Furthermore, such trials may well be unethical. If it turns out that one product is grossly unequivalent to another, the result may be a dead patient. Accordingly, proponents of low-cost generic products have proposed that, with only a few exceptions, two or more products shown to be chemically equivalent can be accepted as not only biologically but also clinically equivalent.

Such a proposal has not been warmly accepted by most brand-name manufacturers. Since at least the late 1950s and early 1960s, some have hinted darkly or have even proclaimed openly that generic products represent second-class medication, and that any physician who prescribes them—or permits their dispensing by a pharmacist—is risking a patient's life. The brand-name firms insisted in particular that the state antisubstitution laws then in effect or being enacted must be upheld at any cost. At least during part of this noisy dispute, the brand-name drug industry was vigorously supported by spokesmen for the American Medical Association.

One reason for this AMA-drug industry alliance was not hard to find. As we have mentioned earlier, the AMA needed financial support through drug advertising in its journals for its ill-fated attempt to stop passage of the Medicare legislation in Congress, while the industry needed medical spokesmen to testify in favor of brand-name products and against generics.[13] Both efforts obviously failed.

STATE OF THE LAWS

With the implementation of both Medicare and Medicaid programs in 1966, members of Congress suddenly demonstrated an unprecedented interest in generic drugs and drug prices. When hospitalized elderly patients were given drugs under the federal Medicare program, and when medically indigent patients were given drugs under the state-federal Medicaid program, those drugs were paid for by tax funds. In addition, it was realized, the federal government was already paying for drugs used by the Department of Defense, the Veterans Administration, and the Public Health Service, usually obtained on bid at relatively low cost. The total bill in 1967 for prescription drug expenditures by federal agencies was more than $500 million.[14] With such a sum involved, many congressmen and governmental administrators promptly reached the conclusion that the great generic controversy could no longer be left to physicians, pharmacists, and the various segments of the drug industry.

All this added up to an irresistible challenge, for *taxpayers' dollars were at stake!* The result was many years of hearings before various congressional committees. A special task force investigation was started in the Department of Health, Education, and Welfare. Debates flared in medical and pharmacy meetings, in state legislature hearings, and even in newspaper columns. Grisly details of lack—or reputed lack—of equivalency were bandied about. Brand-name manufacturers were denounced for their high prices (and presumably extortionate profits). In turn, these manufacturers defended their prices as reasonable and necessary to support their invaluable research. The HEW Task Force, however, suggested that some of that research wasn't so valuable.

By 1968 or 1969, it became apparent that a few generic manufacturers had committed grievous pharmaceutical sins in the past.[15] They had turned out batches of drugs that were clearly not biologically equivalent to the brand-name versions. Some generics were not even chemically equivalent and were illegally on the market. But there were not many such instances. The failures were far more notorious than numerous. Moreover, there was evidence that successive batches of products turned out by the same brand-name manufacturer were not invariably equivalent.

Perhaps the best conclusion was that presented by the HEW Task Force on Prescription Drugs:

> On the basis of available evidence, lack of clinical equivalency among chemical equivalents meeting all official standards has been grossly exaggerated as a major hazard to the public health.[16]

This conclusion did not end the generic controversy, nor was it expected to have any such immediate effect. The debate still continues, flaring every few years when another instance of real or purported lack of equivalence is published or rumored. But the debate is no longer so hemorrhagic. Currently, generics—where they are on the market—are routinely used in essentially all government programs, major hospitals, union health programs, and Health Maintenance Organizations. About 14 percent—more than double the 1969 figure —of all prescriptions dispensed by community pharmacies are now written generically by physicians.[17] Ten years ago, such a development would have been undreamed-of. At the same time, against the strong protestations of the drug industry, the antisubstitution laws in about forty-five states have already been modified or repealed.[18] In some states, the change in the law has given pharmacists broad authority to select a generic in place of the brand-name product actually prescribed. In others, the pharmacists can substitute only if the generic is listed in a "positive" state formulary, or if it is not listed in a "negative" formulary. Some laws allow substitution, while others require it. In some cases, the pharmacist is required to request the patient's permission to make the substitution; in others, it is necessary for the patient to request the substitution.

In virtually every case, the new laws maintain the physician's right to refuse permission for substitution if the prescribed brand-name drug is clinically necessary for the benefit of an individual patient. This is the so-called "escape clause." In practice, it can be invoked if the physician writes on the prescription such a phrase as "dispense as written," "medically necessary," or "do not substitute." But there are limits: a physician is not allowed to have "dispense as written" printed on all his prescription blanks.

In several states in which substitution is now legally permissible, few physicians have found it clinically necessary to write "dispense as written" on their prescriptions. Only about 4 percent of their prescription orders have utilized the escape hatch.[19]

As a new development, some states are using a standard prescription blank which has two lines for the physician's signature, one above a phrase such as "substitution permitted" and the other above "substitution not permitted." Brand-name proponents have urged that the "substitution not permitted" line be placed in the lower right-hand portion of the prescription, where physicians are accustomed to write their signatures, while generic proponents want it placed in the lower left-hand portion.

Several years ago, in California, we examined the situation in a number of teaching hospitals in which product selection by the pharmacist had long been allowed. We asked pharmacists, "About how many times a year do you see 'do not substitute' written on a prescription?" At one major hospital, the chief pharmacist said, "Well, in the ten years I've been here, I've seen it only about four or five times." At another, the pharmacist told us, "I've never seen it used. But I've been working here for only seven years."

It is important to stress that the new laws do not allow a pharmacist to select an active ingredient different from the one prescribed by the physician. If, for example, the prescription calls for Luminal (Winthrop's brand of phenobarbital), in some states the pharmacist may choose from a large number of phenobarbital products on the market, which are often available at different prices, but he cannot substitute a different active ingredient such as secobarbital or chloral hydrate or aspirin.

There are a limited number of drugs for which bioavailability problems have not yet been completely solved. Where the differences are trivial, in most cases they can probably be ignored. But where "life-and-death" drugs are concerned—as with digitalis and anticoagulants —seemingly minor differences can result in a failure to obtain the desired therapeutic action or in serious or possibly fatal toxic reactions. With these latter drugs, substitution of one brand for another is usually considered to be unwise, especially during the course of treatment, unless the dosage is properly adjusted.

It is important to stress also that, in the states in which substitution has been legalized, pharmacists have been slow to utilize their new authority.[20] The reasons for this are not clear. It may be that, although the American Pharmaceutical Association—but not the National Association of Retail Druggists—has long been a powerful advocate of the use of generics and the right of pharmacists to select the product to be dispensed, some individual pharmacists have a lingering feeling that generics actually *are* second-class products. Or it may be that some pharmacists fear that, if they substitute and the patient then suffers from unhappy results, they may be sued and held liable. For many years, some brand-name drug industry representatives have assiduously fostered this fear in the minds of pharmacists. The record shows, however, that no pharmacist using his legal rights to substitute a generic for a brand-name product has ever been sued.[21] Moreover, it has been claimed that a pharmacist who legally dispenses a generic product has no more—and no less—liability than if he dispensed a brand-name product.

Other factors may also play a role in this situation. For example, State Representative William Marovitz of Illinois charged early in 1979 that while some chains, such as Walgreen and Osco, were making liberal use of the state's new substitution law, the Thrifty chain in the state was running newspaper advertisements proclaiming that it wouldn't even stock generic products. Marovitz gave Thrifty's explanation in these words: "They are concerned about the quality of health care. . . . They would not provide generics to their own family and they will not do it to their customers. . . . Whether or not that . . . is what they really believe, or it was suggested by some higher spirit, I really can't say."[22]

While the various attacks against generics were proceeding noisily, something else was going on quietly in many of the major brand-name companies. One insider, who asked us not to identify him, put it this way:

> Back in the middle or late nineteen-sixties, we were planning our strategies for the seventies. We realized that many of our big money-making drugs were about to lose their patent protection, and could be produced and marketed by our competitors. Our innovative research hadn't been *that* innovative, and we couldn't see many breakthrough products in the pipeline. At the same time, we recognized that essentially the same thing was happening to our competitors. The patents on most of their big sellers were going to expire soon, and we could move in on them. As a result, we figured we'd have to get into the generic business ourselves—and do it in a big way. It was the only way to go.

Accordingly, in the early 1970s, many of the major brand-name firms came out with their own lines of generic products, either under their own name or that of a subsidiary. Ironically, they continued to lambast generics—and some still do.

Another knowledgeable observer adds this comment:

> Some people think that it was the repeal of the state antisubstitution laws and the enactment of the MAC [Maximum Allowable Cost] program which forced us to go into generics. The truth is just the reverse. Since our firms, with their long record of dependability and high-quality products, were marketing generics, it became feasible to repeal antisubstitution and set up MAC.

THE MAC APPROACH

Late in 1973, the Secretary of HEW revealed what was eventually to become the Maximum Allowable Cost or MAC program.[23] The Secretary was then Caspar Weinberger, known in California state government circles for his cost-cutting activities as "Cap the Knife." For beneficiaries of such government-financed programs as Medicaid, the new regulations stated that a pharmacist would be reimbursed according to the lowest of the following:

- The Maximum Allowable Cost of the drug (as set by the government) plus a reasonable dispensing fee. The reasonableness is set by the government.
- The Estimated Acquisition Cost (EAC) of the drug—that is, the price paid by the pharmacist to the wholesaler or manufacturer (as estimated by a government agency)— plus a reasonable dispensing fee.

- The pharmacist's usual and customary charge to the general public for the drug.

The MAC method would presumably apply to multiple-source drugs, while the EAC method would apply mainly to single-source drugs, most of them still protected by patent.

Based in considerable part on California's Maximum Ingredient Allowable Cost (MIAC) program, the MAC approach said essentially that if a physician insisted on prescribing an expensive brand-name product when an inexpensive generic-name product was available for beneficiaries of federal programs, that was all very well. Such was the physician's prerogative. The government would simply not pay for it unless the prescriber stipulated that it was clinically necessary for a particular patient. Otherwise the government would only pay for a relatively low-cost generic version which was "widely and consistently" available. Thus, the government would not base its reimbursement levels on the prices for a product that was on the market in only one or two states, or on special prices set for something like a spring clearance sale.

The concept itself and some of the language of the MAC regulations turned out to be invitations for turbulent rhetoric and a good deal of litigation. The Pharmaceutical Manufacturers Association condemned the basic idea, and pharmacists were sharply divided on whether the acquisition cost should be "estimated," or "actual" (as determined by an examination of invoices), or based on published average wholesale prices. PMA and various drug companies tied up implementation of MAC in the courts for several years. Each attempt of HEW committees to set reasonably acceptable reimbursement levels was bitterly disputed. At the outset, there was no agreement on whether HEW would reimburse pharmacists for the lowest-cost generic, or for any of the *three* lowest-cost products, or for any of the *five* lowest, and so on. Did "consistently available" mean for twelve months of the year, or eleven months, or seven months? Did "widely available" include Alaska and Hawaii? Puerto Rico? The Panama Canal Zone?

Because of such disagreements, many of them taken to court, MAC has not yet been fully implemented. By mid-1980, only about twenty drugs in forty-five different dosage forms had been given official MAC reimbursement levels—or, in governmentalese, been "MAC'd." It was predicted that the number would be close to seventy by the end of the year.[24] To MAC proponents, this has been agonizingly slow. To its opponents, it has been "too damn fast." As one drug company official put it: "Any time we can keep one of our tranquilizers from being MAC'd for one more year, that means an additional fifty million dollars in sales."

One of the most perceptive views of the MAC program has been given by Vincent Gardner, formerly of the Health Care Financing Administration and the man who directed MAC during its first years:

> Important though the MAC program is [he told a conference on national drug insurance], I cannot view it as more than a short-run first step down the long road toward establishing a national health insurance drug benefit that includes effective cost-control provisions. MAC is a short-run solution to the cost-control problem for two reasons.
>
> First, MAC does not do anything about controlling the cost of drugs that are not, because of their patent protection, subject to price competition. While we hope it will not happen, it would be perfectly possible for drug manufacturers to compensate for the impact of MAC on the prices of their multiple-source products by raising the prices on single-source products.
>
> Second, whether the MAC program succeeds or fails, it carries with it the seeds of its own eventual destruction. If it fails, it will have to be replaced by something else, and if it succeeds in reducing the price spread on multiple-source drugs to the point at which significant savings no longer accrue to the Department of HEW as a result of MAC limits, it will have outlived its usefulness.[25]

THE NEW YORK FUROR

Among the disputes over state generic substitution laws, probably none has created such noisy controversy as has the legislation passed by the New York state legislature in 1977. It was developed in large part by William Haddad, newspaperman, indefatigable consumerist, and a longtime major irritant to the brand-name drug industry, which he once denounced as "the last of the robber barons."[26] At the time, he was a staff member of New York's legislative oversight committee.

In congressional hearings and newspaper interviews, he had long and adamantly insisted that there were *no* significant clinical differences between a brand-name product and any of its generic competitors. Many drug experts urged him repeatedly to temper his claims, saying that he was largely though not entirely correct. In this instance, however, cooler heads did not prevail.

The legislation which Haddad and his colleagues eventually had introduced in Albany did not *allow* New York pharmacists to substitute; it *required* them to do so. And it did not call for substitution with a *relatively inexpensive* product; it required substitution with the *cheapest* generic product available.

The reaction was noteworthy. Consumer advocates generally liked the idea, as did the State Board of Pharmacy. But PMA and its member brand-name companies, the American Pharmaceutical Association, the National Association of Retail Druggists, the state medical society and many of its members, and many individual pharmacists were all unified in their outrage. Inexplicably, the New York Pharmacists Association took no stand, announcing publicly that it would neither support nor oppose the measure.

Much of the opposition centered on two points:

- The proposal totally blocked the pharmacist from selecting products on the basis of his expert knowledge and experience. It required the pharmacist to buy a product from a particular firm, even if the company had a miserable record of turning out products that were disagreeably colored or flavored, failing to make deliveries on schedule, mixing up orders, or even marketing inferior products.
- The proposal gave patients no right to protest. If the patient preferred to have a brand-name product dispensed, even if he could afford it, there was no recourse—except for the pharmacist to telephone the physician and request a change in the prescription.

But Haddad and other supporters of the bill, promising substantial savings to patients and taxpayers—and frequently noting the "enormous" profits of the brand-name companies—came out victorious. The bill passed.*

Under heavy pressure from New York officials, FDA was obliged to become involved. FDA experts worked with New York to provide a list of about 800 drugs representing 2,500 generic and brand-name products and then indicate where substitution seemed permissible.[27] Actually, as PMA was quick to point out, most of the 800 drugs were still under patent; less than a third were available in the form of generic products.[28] For that third, under the new law, all a pharmacist needed to do was pick out the least expensive substitute and dispense it.

This marked what was termed the height of consumerist idiocy. "There go all the years I spent learning pharmacy," declared one embittered pharmacist. "A computer could do it just as well." And a

---

*Florida later enacted similar legislation.

medical leader said: "That's about as senseless—and as dangerous—as paying for only the cheapest family doctor or obstetrician or brain surgeon, or the cheapest laboratory test, or the cheapest hospital."

The results were predictable. By early 1979, it was reported by Paul Herdman, New York's Public Health Director, that about 55 percent of the state's pharmacies were ignoring the law. "As a generalization," he told a drug conference in Florida, "we could say the law is really not working very well, although it is to some extent."[29] (Officials of the American Pharmaceutical Association put the figure at closer to 80 or 90 percent.)

At another meeting, John Huck, the president of Merck, was asked to comment on the mystifying support given to the new law by the New York pharmacy board. "That's what the New York State Board of Pharmacy thinks of pharmacists," he said. "'[Pharmacists] simply can't be trusted.'"[30]

THE FDA EQUIVALENCY LIST

The ruckus in New York did not go unnoticed in the rest of the country, and copies of the FDA list of interchangeable drug products were soon requested by other states, and also by hospitals, physicians, and pharmacists.

As far as it went, the list itself was not altogether newsworthy. It consisted primarily of every drug product approved by FDA with the exception of those for which problems of unequivalency were known or suspected. Also excluded were various dosage forms, such as enteric-coated tablets, controlled-release products, certain suppositories, and injectable suspensions other than antibiotics.

The compilation, however, was first called FDA's Therapeutic Equivalence List. This was a particularly lamentable error, which FDA officials quickly admitted in private. In practically every case, nobody knew whether the products were or were not therapeutically equivalent, for the simple reason that nobody had ever tested them scientifically in patients for therapeutic effect. Where equivalence was claimed, it was chemical or pharmaceutical equivalence, or—in some cases—biological equivalence. Later, FDA tried to clarify what it intended to say:

> Drug products are considered to be therapeutic equivalents if they are pharmaceutical [chemical] equivalents and can be expected to give the same therapeutic effect when administered to the patient under the conditions specified in the label.[31]

What the agency seemed to be stating was that there didn't appear to be any reason to expect these products to be therapeutically unequivalent.

As was widely anticipated, the list itself was denounced by PMA and by some of the brand-name manufacturers, usually on the grounds that physicians and pharmacists could not count on the quality of generic products. FDA Commissioner Donald Kennedy, also as anticipated, defended the list.

"FDA concurrence in the New York list," Kennedy wrote in a letter to a state health commissioner, "reflects the Agency's view that there is no consistent difference in quality between drug products sold by large and small firms or between drugs sold under a brand name or 'generic' name. We have a single standard for drugs in this country."[32]

On NBC's "Today Show," the FDA Commissioner was asked whether it was proper for patients to query their physicians who prescribe brand-name rather than less expensive generic products.

"If you, God forbid, got the flu," asked Betty Furness, "and your doctor was about to give you a prescription, would you prefer that he gave you a brand-name, a branded generic, or a generic prescription?"

"The first thing I'd wonder," Kennedy answered, "is why he was prescribing anything, because flu [is caused by] a virus, and he shouldn't be giving me an antibiotic. But if I had a secondary infection, and he wrote me a prescription, I'd be asking just exactly those questions."[33]

THE FTC-HEW MODEL LAW

Despite all the furor, the enactment of the New York substitution law, and the later enactment of what pharmacists and the drug industry assailed as an even worse law in Florida, soon induced other states to consider similar action. In general, it appeared, FDA was in favor of the idea—although with some specific reservations. Also in general, the concept was favored by the Federal Trade Commission, which had long been aware of the lack of price competition in the prescription drug field. Early in 1979, the two agencies unveiled a proposed joint FTC-HEW model for any state that wanted to use it.[34]

The provisions of the model represent what seems to be an eminently sane compromise between wide-open, uncontrolled substitution and no substitution at all:

- The appropriate state agency is to set up a list or formulary of all prescription drugs approved by FDA as safe and effective, and determined by FDA to be "therapeutically" equivalent.

- The list is to be updated at least once a year.
- The pharmacist receiving a prescription for a brand-name drug also available in generic form *may* select an equivalent drug product listed in the state formulary.
- The substitution *must* represent a cost saving for the patient.
- The pharmacist *must* notify the patient of the proposed substitution, and the patient *must* have the right to refuse the substitution.
- Physicians have the right to insist on the dispensing of the brand-name product by indicating that it is medically necessary for the patient.

Also, to get rid of the nagging worry that still bothers some pharmacists, the model law contains this provision:

> A pharmacist who selects an equivalent drug product pursuant to this act assumes no greater liability than would be incurred in filling a prescription for a drug product prescribed by its established name.

By the middle of 1980, the model law had been accepted only by the state of Maryland.

GENERICS AND COST-SAVINGS

In 1969, the HEW Task Force on Prescription Drugs reported on the estimated savings in a proposed out-of-hospital Medicare program that could result from substituting generic-name products whereever such products were on the market. The savings would be substantial, the Task Force said, but they would not be enormous.[35] In theory, it was estimated, the savings would amount to between 5 and 8 percent, depending on how pharmacists set their markup, and not accounting for the costs of administering the program. (In real life, we later calculated, the savings would probably be between 2.5 and 4 percent.)

Proponents of generic substitution were horrified and viewed the Task Force estimate as a stab in the back. "How can you say that," one offended proponent asked, "when you yourselves revealed that some generics are priced 60, or 70, or even 80 percent below the brand-name products?"

Those great price differences did actually exist, but they did not exist for many products. In some cases, use of a generic would provide essentially minor financial benefits. Furthermore, most brand-name drugs—about 75 percent of them—were still under patent, and therefore no generic counterparts could be legally marketed. And, for some drugs, many physicians were already accustomed to prescribe them by generic name, so no savings could be made with them.

The situation now is, of course, different. Since 1969, many drugs have lost their patent protection, and fewer new drugs have been discovered and patented. It is now believed that only about half of the most widely used drugs are still covered by patent, and the percentage seems to be decreasing slowly but steadily. An increasing proportion of physicians is prescribing generically. Under a number of governmental health programs, generic substitution is already permitted or required. And, although there is still a substantial price difference between many or most brand-name and generic products, competition is beginning to be felt, and the price differences in some cases are becoming smaller.

Accordingly, while some enthusiasts are promising enormous annual savings from mandatory nationwide generic substitution—savings in the billions of dollars—it is our belief that such predictions are unrealistic. As a maximum, we feel, the potential savings would be less than 6 percent.

Yet, 6 percent on an out-of-hospital drug program for Medicare beneficiaries, for example, could amount to $240 million a year—hardly an inconsequential sum.

THE END OF THE CONTROVERSY

There is a growing realization that the great generic controversy is essentially over. It may be confidently expected that there will be continuing disputes, most of them localized, as when attempts are made to repeal the few remaining state antisubstitution laws. Similar disputes may occur when, as also seems inevitable, a bad batch of a generic product reaches the market (or when a similarly bad batch of a brand-name product is produced). But the major struggle seems to be over, and the proponents of generics have won. The future will probably see merely mopping-up actions.

A number of factors marked the development of this state of affairs:

- The 1958-1962 hearings chaired by the late Senator Estes Kefauver, which revealed the enormous price differences between many brand-name drugs and their generic competitors.[36]

- The hearings, beginning in 1967, chaired by Senator Gaylord Nelson, which, among other things, showed that the brand-name producers could offer little or no evidence to support their claim that the quality of brand-name products was significantly higher than that of the generic versions.[37]
- The background papers and Final Report of the HEW Task Force on Prescription Drugs in 1968 and 1969, which, also among other things, stated that equivalency could not be guaranteed in all cases, but that the available evidence disclosed that few documented cases of unequivalency had occurred in the past, and that few of these represented any significant hazard to patients.[38]
- The publication of our own book, *Pills, Profits, and Politics*, which expanded and updated the earlier findings and made them widely available to the public and to the Congress.
- A report by the Office of Technology Assessment to the Congress on drug bioequivalency, prepared by a blue-ribbon panel headed by Robert Berliner, dean of the Yale School of Medicine. The first statement in that report—widely publicized by the brand-name drug industry—read: "Current standards and regulatory practices do not insure bioequivalence for drug products." (This was essentially the view expressed earlier by the HEW Task Force.) The drug industry, however, neglected to publicize another major OTA statement: "It is neither feasible nor desirable that studies of bioavailability be conducted for all drugs or drug products."[39]
- Actual bioavailability tests on human volunteers in Tennessee, which failed to turn up any significant problems with most generic products, although they did disclose such differences with a few.[40]
- Perhaps of major importance, the implementation of a California law passed in 1971 but put into effect beginning only in 1973, which required that each firm marketing a drug product in California must disclose the name of the firm which actually manufactured it. The law appeared to be completely innocuous but turned out to be a bombshell.

Until the California law was implemented, it had been generally assumed that the claimed or actual higher quality of brand-name products stemmed from the more sophisticated or tougher quality-control measures utilized by the brand-name companies, and from their general all-around better know-how. This comfortable assumption was rudely exploded when the following facts became public knowledge:[41]

- A.H. Robins' brand of brompheniramine with decongestants, an antiexpectorant marketed under the name of Dimetapp, had actually been manufactured by the generic firm, Strong Cobb Arner.
- The tetracycline products marketed by such brand-name firms as Robins, Smith Kline & French, Parke-Davis, and American Home Products had actually been made by the generic company, Mylan Laboratories.
- Mylan was also listed as the manufacturer of Smith Kline & French's SK-65 brand of propoxyphene compound.
- Ciba-Geigy's brand of the oral antidiabetic phenformin (later forced off the market by FDA as unsafe) was made by K-V Pharmaceutical.
- McKesson's and Pfizer's brands of penicillin V were manufactured by Copanos & Co.
- Chloral hydrate products marketed by Squibb as Noctec, by McKesson as Kessodrate, and by Merck, Parke-Davis, Wyeth, and many other companies, brand-name and generic, were actually all manufactured by the generic firm, R.P. Scherer Corporation.

The cat was out of the bag. Many of these same brand-name companies had charged for years that generic-name products were not to be trusted—"second-class drugs," they called them—and that generic-name firms might be guilty of exercising inadequate quality control. Now it was disclosed that many brand-name companies had in fact been buying some generics themselves and marketing them under their own name.

Even friends and supporters of the brand-name companies were rocked. "When the big PMA firms were denouncing generics, they were fouling their own nest," said an official of the California Medical Association. "How in the name of God can they ever expect us to believe them again?"

A 1975 survey conducted by the Council on Economic Priorities disclosed that there were wide differences in prices charged for different products containing the same drug, all manufactured by the same generic firm.[42]

One hospital pharmacist in charge of drug purchasing said: "The big PMA companies used to insist to me that their product was worth more because the quality was higher. But now they've had to admit that the brand-name product and the generics all came from the same generic house. I've been ripped off, and I don't like it."

Other states have followed California's lead in requiring disclosure of a drug product's manufacturer, and FDA is seeking authority to require it nationally.

There are other signs that the generic war is nearing its end. PMA and its member companies are still working to preserve the remaining antisubstitution laws, and some of their spokesmen are continuing to warn physicians against generics. But the physicians are showing that they are increasingly and singularly unimpressed: where state laws permit substitution unless the physicians object in their own handwriting, roughly 95 percent of the prescriptions carry no "do not substitute" instructions.[43]

Equally eloquent is the fact that the brand-name firms have moved into the generics field themselves. More and more, they are marketing products under their generic names or under the bastardized term "branded generics." The latter represent formerly patented drugs that are now marketed under a new brand-name and usually priced somewhere between the expensive brand-name version and the lowest-cost generic-name product.

"There has been no significant challenge to FDA's position that there are no differences in quality between brand-name and generic drugs," former FDA Commissioner Kennedy told a recent meeting of the New York State Medical Society. Most of the generic products are now marketed by the major firms, he said. And, Kennedy estimated, the PMA member firms have "from 90 to 95 percent of the generic marketplace."[44]

California pharmacist Chester Yee, longtime fighter for generic products, comments: "It's been a long war. Maybe now we can get on to other things."

At least one thing seems evident. In our opinion, the use of FDA-approved generic products and product selection by the pharmacist offer no threat to the quality of health care. Whether this holds for a few generic products recently marketed without FDA approval—a problem that currently represents an acute headache to FDA and to most manufacturers and pharmacists—may be another matter.[45]

One of the more blistering disputes in the field of prescription drug use involves the role of formularies and their value in holding down costs and improving the quality of care.

At the outset, it must be recognized that a formulary is not a compendium. Basically, a compendium is a comprehensive listing of drugs or drug products on the market, usually including a description of the chemical nature, clinical indications for use, warnings and contraindications, side effects, adverse reactions, and potential interactions with foods and other drugs.[1] One example is the widely used *Physicians' Desk Reference*. Rarely if ever does a compendium state or even suggest that product A is better or worse than product B.

In contrast, a formulary is a listing of recommended products.[2] It may be compiled by an individual expert (or non-expert) physician to give his personal recommendations. It may be developed for an individual hospital to indicate the products approved for use in that institution and normally stocked in its own pharmacy. Or it may be developed for an insurance program, a union health program, or a government-financed program to show which products are eligible for reimbursement.

Some of these formularies are voluntary; they offer guidelines which may or may not be followed by the prescribing physician. Others are compulsory; if nonformulary items are prescribed, the program will ordinarily decline to pay for it.

Most compulsory formularies, however, contain an "escape clause." A physician may, under certain conditions, order a nonformulary product if he says that the product is clinically essential for an individual patient.

STATE OF THE CONTROVERSY

Unlike the utilization of a formulary simply to encourage or require the dispensing of low-cost generic drugs, as discussed in the previous chapter, a compulsory formulary can also influence the prescribing and dispensing of brand-name products. Understandably, this is a matter of some interest to brand-name companies, especially when one brand-name product is added to the list while another brand-name product is left off.

It has been held that the proper application of a formulary can yield triple dividends: It can reduce drug expenditures, minimize pharmacy inventory costs, and, of most importance, improve the quality of care by reducing the inducements to physicians to prescribe irrational, questionably effective, or needlessly dangerous agents.

In the eyes of the Pharmaceutical Manufacturers Association and most of the brand-name companies, a voluntary set of guidelines might be acceptable, but a compulsory formulary is an abomination. Drug company spokesmen—and many physicians—have constantly denounced compulsory formularies as a dangerous and unwarranted interference in the traditional right of any physician to prescribe as he and he alone sees fit, even though the "escape hatch" gives him that freedom, subject only to whatever guidance he may accept from his peers. Moreover, it has been claimed that compulsory formularies, notably in some Medicaid programs, do not necessarily minimize costs; they may, in fact, increase expenditures.[3]

There is some truth to this last argument. In Mississippi, for example, when most non-narcotic analgesics like Darvon Compound were removed from the state Medicaid formulary, there was a 75 percent increase in prescriptions for the more potentially addicting narcotic Demerol.[4]

There is an additional reason for the opposition expressed by brand-name companies. Compulsory formularies may nullify all the work of such companies to promote their products. No matter how much money they may invest to convince physicians through drug advertisements, direct-mail campaigns, and enormous detailing campaigns, these efforts are largely wasted if the formulary committee declines to approve the product.

These huge promotional campaigns in themselves have aroused the curiosity of at least some members of hospital formulary committees. One of them asked, "If their drug is as good as they say, why do they have to spend all that money to push it?"

Years of experience in some hospitals, especially in some teaching hospitals, have shown that hospital formularies can actually save sizable percentages of drug expenditures, minimize inventory problems, significantly control the use of products of dubious effectiveness, and minimize some forms of irrational prescribing. Such formularies have been accepted by physicians when (1) the formulary is designed by knowledgeable physicians and pharmacists on the hospital staff, (2) clinical factors are considered to be even more important than cost savings, (3) the formulary is revised and updated periodically, (4) any physician has the right to urge the addition or deletion of a particular product, usually on the basis of his own experience, and (5) the "escape hatch" provision is included.[5] It is essential, of course, that use of the "escape clause" be carefully limited.

So far, it seems, the record outside of hospitals has been less happy. Most of this experience has involved the compulsory formularies used in state Medicaid programs. Many physicians have expressed their displeasure with the decisions of state Medicaid committees, the difficulties in having their voices heard in committee meetings, and some states' habit of slashing the Medicaid list of approved drugs whenever budgets become tight. Too often, it has been charged, when dollars are scarce, the committee will throw out the most valuable drugs and retain only the least expensive.

Unlike the controversy over generics, the debate over formularies shows no sign of early abatement. In fact, with a continuing economic crunch, the formulary dispute may become more intense.

THE OHIO STATE SURVEY

Although it had been accepted that some hospital formulary programs were wisely planned, logical, and effective, it was also commonly believed that this comfortable situation existed in essentially *all* hospitals. This concept was rudely blasted away in 1978 with the release of the findings of a survey conducted by drug economist T. Donald Rucker and pharmacist James A. Visconti of Ohio State University's College of Pharmacy, two of the most respected drug experts in the United States.[6] Supported in part by the Food and Drug Administration, the report was published by the Research and Education Foundation of the American Society of Hospital Pharmacists.

The study showed that some hospital formularies were reasonably good, but that others ranged from barely adequate to disastrous. The study involved fifty-two large private hospitals, each with 500 or more beds. This group, the investigators emphasized, was too small to give a valid picture of the situation throughout the United States. However, the hospitals in the group were supposedly among the best in the country; forty-four of them were affiliated with medical schools, and twenty-three with colleges of pharmacy. The survey findings were startling:

- About 40 percent of large hospitals do not use any formulary at all. The situation is probably worse in smaller hospitals.
- Some formularies listed the drugs only by their brand name.
- In some cases, it was impossible to learn the identity of the active ingredient from the formulary, from standard reference books, or even from the manufacturer.
- Sometimes a company was listed as the manufacturer of the product, but company officials denied that they had made it.
- Although most combination products, consisting of two or more active ingredients, had been seriously criticized by the National Academy of Sciences/National Research Council (NAS/NRC),[7] they were found in large numbers in the formularies. One formulary, in fact, contained *more* combination products than single-ingredient drugs.
- One formulary edition dated 1976 carried a note that it represented the first complete major revision since 1958.
- The three "best" formularies contained an average of 445 drug entities, while the three "worst" contained an average of more than 1,680!

The investigators rated the formularies on the number of inferior drugs that were included. These standards of ineffective or unimportant products included the following:

- Single-entity drugs identified by FDA as possessing little or no therapeutic gain when they were introduced.
- Drugs described by the *U.S. Pharmacopeia* as ineffective or relatively dangerous.
- "Inferior pharmaceutical products," as described by the prestigious publication *The Medical Letter*.

- Products classified as ineffective in the NAS/NRC review but still remaining on the market.
- Combination products failing to meet the criteria of effective or probably effective.

Rucker and Visconti recognized clearly that some of the decisions were not unanimous, and they noted that this lack of agreement usually represented honest differences of opinion among experts. Even with careful study, they said, a few seemingly inferior products might get into a formulary. But in one formulary, those inferior products represented 58 percent of all the entries.

In general, the formularies of hospitals affiliated with medical schools were better than those of institutions without such affiliations.

The Ohio State survey also examined the Medicaid formularies in twelve states. If anything, they were worse than the hospital formularies. One of these state publications included every FDA-approved product listed in a leading price catalogue.

The whole situation, Rucker and Visconti concluded, is "disturbing." We disagree. It is shocking. It may be fervently hoped that most of the inferior products were merely kept on pharmacy shelves—at a considerable economic loss—but were never given to patients.

In attempting to find explanations for the superiority of some hospital formularies, Rucker and Visconti could find only two factors: the formulary system had been in existence for at least eight years, and no drug could be added to the list unless its relative benefits were documented and supported in writing.

Thus, the promise of the formulary system remains. It could serve as an invaluable guide to better health care and a more rational use of drugs. It could help to contain costs. But, to an alarming degree, the promise remains unfulfilled.

The Ohio State team recommended that, to provide hospitals and Medicaid officials with a more objective way to select drugs for their formularies, FDA—in cooperation with the concerned professional associations and program administrators—should study the possible mechanisms for validating comparative information on drugs distributed in this country and for disseminating that information to the people who need it.

HOW MANY DRUGS ARE NEEDED?

There are thousands of different prescription drug products on the market. How many of them are really essential? This question or something like it has been asked for decades—and probably for centuries—by military medical supply officers going into combat areas. It has been asked by leaders of expeditions. It has been asked by drug experts in civilian life. In recent years, the question has been raised particularly in Third World countries with serious health problems and limited supplies of foreign currency.

Some authorities have estimated that perhaps only one hundred or possibly only fifty drugs could be enough. Under ordinary conditions, such bare-bones levels would appear to be completely unrealistic and unapproachable. (For someone about to be stranded on a desert island and told he could take only fifty drugs, fifty would have to suffice!)

A more realistic proposal was recently developed by an expert panel of the World Health Organization, which proposed a basic list of 214 drugs. Of these, 182 were classified as "essential" and 32 as "complementary."[8] In some circles, this, too, was dismissed as unrealistic and unapproachable—but some countries are approaching it.

One of those countries is Mozambique, where a list of fewer than four hundred products was implemented in 1978, and it is predicted that the list will be shortened to less than three hundred. The Mozambique approach is not to select only the most effective and least expensive product but also two or three others as alternatives.

Professor Antonio Ruas, head of the Mozambique Therapeutics Committee, declares that his policy is "good therapeutics at the lowest price." For example, he said, "In ninety percent of cases of pneumonia, penicillin is OK. But you must have other drugs available for the other ten percent."[9]

Similarly, if a drug is determined to be safe and effective in one age group but not in another, suitable alternatives must be provided.

An even more remarkable step was taken in Guatemala, where a list of essential drugs, together with complete prescribing information, was put together by Aida LeRoy as part of a Pan American Health Organization project. Her list of essential drugs contained only 231 drugs in a total of about 300 dosage forms. To the amazement of some of her Guatemalan co-workers, it was approved by the Minister of Health.[10]

The Guatemalan formulary has recently been reviewed by some of our drug experts at the University of California medical center in San Francisco. "With this formulary," a clinical pharmacologist commented, "any competent young physician—if he hasn't been brainwashed by drug salesmen, or by his elders—can give excellent drug treatment to ninety-five percent or more of his patients who require it."

Whether such developments contain a message to industrialized nations remains to be seen. It may be hoped, however, that the message reaches the formulary makers.

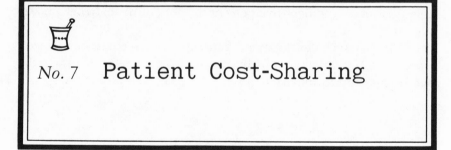

No. 7 Patient Cost-Sharing

In most countries in which a drug insurance program is in operation, only the poor—and, in some cases, the elderly and children—are entitled to obtain prescription drugs without paying something out of their own pockets.[1] These out-of-pocket contributions are intended to reduce program costs, minimize overutilization of the program, or both.

In general, three cost-sharing methods have been employed, either alone or in combination. These are:

- A fixed co-payment (for example, the patient must pay the first $1.00, $1.50, or other sum for each prescription).
- A fixed co-insurance percentage (such as 20 percent, 30 percent, or some other portion) of the prescription price.
- An annual deductible similar to the deductible clause in many automobile or health insurance policies (for instance, a requirement that each individual must pay the first $50, $75, or $100 of his drug costs each year, or that a family must pay the first $100, $150, or $200).

Each of these approaches has drawbacks. The co-payment method has been known to induce some pharmacists to indulge in what is known as prescription-splitting, dividing a single large prescription into four or five small ones, thus enabling them to submit a claim for multiple fees instead of one. The co-insurance or percentage method has served as an inducement for some pharmacists to refuse to substitute a low-cost generic in place of a high-cost brand-name product; in fact, it offers an incentive for them to dispense an expensive brand-name drug when a generic was actually prescribed. The annual deductible method may pose special bookkeeping difficulties. In the case of a serious illness, especially one involving hospitalization, the patient can easily show that he has met the deductible requirement by submitting only one bill from the physician or the hospital. With drugs, however, it may be necessary for the patient to keep records for fifteen or twenty prescriptions to prove that he is eligible for help from the insurance program. Especially for the elderly and perhaps for the indigent, this can prove very burdensome, since many individuals lose their bills or neglect to submit claims, and thus lose benefits to which they are entitled.

Recently, however, it has been found in programs in Canada that many of these bookkeeping problems can be solved or at least reduced by the use of individual coupon books in which the pharmacist affixes a coupon or stamp each time he dispenses a prescription for the patient (see Chapter 10, below). Unfortunately, coupon books, too, can be misplaced, and this system can be abused. This problem could be solved if patients would patronize only one pharmacy, so that the pharmacist could then keep the records.

Probably better than co-payment or co-insurance, the deductible method would make it possible to incorporate a sliding scale, with the deductible amount set according to the financial status of the patient. Thus, a well-to-do beneficiary could be required to pay the full deductible amount, while one on welfare could have a deductible of zero. Admittedly, such an idea would pose problems—perhaps the need for each individual to show a copy of his income tax return each year to some governmental agency, which would then assign the appropriate deductible amount. For those with little or no income, and therefore no income tax return, the requirement could be modeled after that used to prove eligibility for various welfare programs.[2]

To some of us, the concept of fragmenting health care into several portions—physician services with a special deductible, hospital services with a special deductible, prescription drugs with a special deductible, and so on—verges on the ridiculous. It seems far more logical to have a single deductible requirement, probably based on the financial status of the individual, for all covered health services— physician services, hospitalization, prescription drugs, and laboratory tests. Once the patient had met the annual deductible requirement through any one of these services, or any combination, he would be covered for the rest of the year.[3]

Almost any form of cost-sharing—certainly co-payment and co-insurance—may be used as what some independent pharmacists decry as an unfair promotional practice: the offer made by chain pharmacies or discount stores to waive the cost-sharing requirement as a way to attract customers. Those who have used this gambit have defended it as a perfectly proper competitive device.

There is abundant evidence to show that virtually any cost-sharing mechanism will reduce program costs.[4] What is not so clear is whether such reductions have simply reduced overutilization or whether they have caused serious underutilization, keeping patients from obtaining clinically needed drugs.

A partial answer has been suggested by a 1972-73 survey of California Medi-Cal (Medicaid) patients who were observed first during a six-month control period and then during a twelve-month co-payment period. During the latter, each patient was required to pay $1.00 for each of the first two physician visits during any month, and $0.50 for each of the first two prescriptions received in any month. There was a seemingly gratifying drop in both physician visits and in the use of prescription drugs. But there was also a catch: after a brief lag period, the costs for increased hospitalization substantially exceeded any of these savings. The study concluded that higher hospitalization use rates suggest that financial deterrents on excessive use by poor people of ambulatory services such as physician office visits and of such prescription drugs as oral contraceptives are penny-wise and pound-foolish.[5]

What is not known is how much of this increase in hospital costs could be attributed to fewer physician visits and how much to the decreased use of drugs. Almost certainly, both factors played a role.

Somewhat similar results have come from another California investigation, this a two-year study conducted from 1974 to 1976 on about four thousand Medicare-eligible beneficiaries in two counties.[6] Under existing law, out-of-hospital drug benefits are not provided by Medicare. For this investigation, these benefits were made available to four groups:

1. One whose members received their prescribed drugs without any cost-sharing requirement.
2. One whose members were required to pay $1.00 of the charge for each prescription.

3. One whose members were required to pay co-insurance of 25 percent per perscription.

4. One whose members were required to meet an annual deductible of $50 plus a payment of 25 percent co-insurance.

In this pilot study, the drug use by people in the first three groups was not significantly different from one group to the next. If these patients received a prescription, they generally had it filled. In the fourth group, however, some patients tended to let their prescriptions go unfilled; but if they received prescriptions and met the deductible requirement, they used the program to the full. "This suggests that, if a high level of cost-sharing results in patients not having prescriptions filled and, as a result, incurring additional expenditures for covered services [such as hospitalization]," it was said later by Vincent Gardner of the Health Care Financing Administration, "attempting to save money by having high levels of cost-sharing may result in false economies."[7]

The investigators felt that the experimental program had little if any effect on the prescribing patterns of physicians, who were unaware of the program details. But the pharmacists were aware. They knew which patients were in the program, because each one had to present an eligibility card at the time the prescription was handed to the pharmacist. Some of the pharmacists may have had a slight touch of larceny in their hearts.

"Our study," reported Dennis Hefner, "was composed of elderly persons who were accustomed to purchase maintenance medications from the same pharmacy for a particular price. As a result, when a patient who had been paying $1.97 for a nitroglycerin prescription was sent a bill for $4.00, the logical conclusion was to suspect the third party. . . . Once a third party was involved, the patient's previous price, which was the pharmacy's 'usual and customary price,' was abandoned as soon as that pharmacist saw the eligibility card."[8]

Among the several cost-sharing devices considered so far, none seems foolproof or even good.[9] The task seems to be to select the one which is least bad.

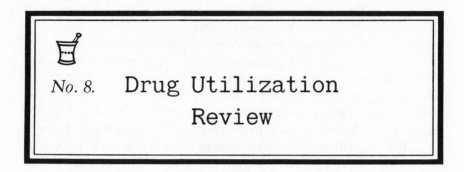

No. 8. Drug Utilization Review

In 1969, in its *Final Report,* the HEW Task Force on Prescription Drugs—in particular, staff member Donald Rucker—probably created the term "drug utilization review." The concept was defined as a dynamic process aimed first at rational prescribing and the consequent improvement of the quality of health care, and second at minimizing needless expenditures.[1] These priorities were in line with the Task Force's basic philosophy: the major goal of any drug program should be not cheap drugs but good health.

Later, the concept was more specifically spelled out by Donald Brodie in these words:

> Drug utilization review is an authorized, structured, and continuing program which reviews, analyzes, and interprets patterns (rates and costs) of drug usage in a given health care delivery system against predetermined standards.[2]

The drug utilization review (DUR) system must be authorized or legitimized. It must be a component of an organized system—a hospital, a state or regional Medicaid or Medicare program, or the like. It cannot be a one-time operation but must be continuous. It should develop or adopt reasonable standards of rational prescribing and then see how actual prescribing patterns measure up to those standards.

Back in 1969, no one seemed to know whether the prescription should be analyzed prospectively (before it was dispensed to the patient) or retrospectively. No one seemed to know how or by whom the patterns were to be reviewed—that is, by physicians, by pharmacists, by both, or by somebody else. No one was prepared to say how confidentiality could be protected. And no one was ready to propose what should be done about physicians who regularly or even occasionally failed to follow the established standards. Since then, as will be noted later in this chapter, we have come—if not a long, long way—at least a long way.

The Task Force was by no means the first to consider an analysis of prescribing patterns. In the United States, among the first such reviews were those published by Furstenberg and his colleagues in 1953,[3] Charlotte Muller in 1965,[4] Leighton Cluff in 1967,[5] and Paul Stolley and Louis Lasagna, also in 1967.[6] These and other early investigators clearly demonstrated that the prescribing habits of at least some physicians were open to serious question and probably unacceptable: many of their prescriptions were potentially dangerous, involved the use of the wrong drug to match the patient's diagnosis, were unnecessarily expensive, or were not needed in the first place. Corrective steps were presumably indicated.

THE LAC-USC PROGRAM

One of the first and most dramatic demonstrations of the potential values of DUR in hospitals came from an extensive project at the Los Angeles County-University of Southern California (LAC-USC) Medical Center, one of the largest hospitals in the United States. Using a complex computer system, Robert Maronde and his associates uncovered a degree of irrational prescribing that amounted to a pharmacological horror story:[7]

- A number of drugs—particularly tranquilizers and sedatives—were being prescribed for individual patients in nearly unbelievably large quantities.
- A few drugs, such as antibiotics, were being prescribed for some patients in quantities so small that the patients' lives could be endangered.
- Two or more different drugs were prescribed together for the same patient, even though there was the risk of a possibly dangerous or deadly drug-drug interaction.
- There were stunning examples of an individual patient being given prescriptions for the same drug by several different physicians, sometimes on the same day. (In

theory, such a situation could not arise, since each physician would look at the patient's chart. Nevertheless, it did happen.)

- Expensive products were prescribed when the use of a less costly product would have almost certainly yielded the same clinical results.
- Drugs were prescribed for patients whose records showed that they were allergic to the products.

Retrospective studies at the Los Angeles center disclosed that most of the staff physicians were unaware of their irrational performance or misprescribed only rarely. When they were shown computer printouts documenting their patterns, most of them were stunned at first, but were then quick to improve. There was, however, a small core of offenders, representing perhaps 4 percent of all the staff physicians, who refused to mend their ways; they refused to have their prescriptions questioned by the Medical Center pharmacists, and they ignored the advice of clinical pharmacologists and other medical experts. Although the 4-percent group was small, it accounted for as much as 35 percent of the use of some drugs.

Once the irrational prescriptions had been identified by the computer-based DUR process, action could be taken. In some cases, the physician's prescriptions would not be accepted by the pharmacy unless they were countersigned by the head of the department concerned. In other instances, the uncooperative physicians were simply not reappointed to the staff.

It also appeared that there was a limited number of drug products on the hospital formulary which were most likely to be misprescribed and which were not considered by drug experts to be vital for good health care. They were dropped from the formulary, often over the anguished protests of drug company representatives and even of some physicians.

The LAC-USC data processing system was so designed that it could be used retrospectively to survey any damage after the fact, but also prospectively to prevent the damage. In the two large outpatient pharmacies, the pharmacists, by pushing the appropriate buttons, could get an instant picture of a patient's prescription record, an indication of any known drug allergies, a record of all prescription drugs currently being used and a listing of potential drug-drug interactions, and a disclosure of drug quantities being obtained that might signal a potential suicide attempt or diversion to the street market.

Once a pharmacist had intercepted a possibly irrational prescription, he could telephone the prescribing physician and pose such questions as these:

"Are you aware that the patient is allergic to the drug you prescribed?"

"Do you know that another doctor has prescribed the same drug for your patient during the past week?"

"Do you really want to prescribe an adult dosage for the youngster?"

"For this lady with a urinary tract infection, do you actually want us to give her only a three-day supply of an antibiotic?"

In most instances, the successful application of such a DUR program depends not only on drug knowledge but also on public relations. Physicians are most likely to cooperate if they know why the program was started and what its objectives are—not so much to cut costs but to improve the quality of drug therapy—and if they recognize that they have the right to order an apparently irrational prescription if this is in the best clinical interest of a particular patient.

For example, a physician may be summoned to meet with the DUR committee and asked such a question as this:

"Doctor, every one of your colleagues in your department feels that the drugs of choice in the treatment of uncomplicated pneumonia are penicillin, ampicillin, or tetracycline. You order Keflex—which is far more expensive—for practically all your pneumonia patients. Maybe you know something that we don't know. Will you tell us what it is?"

Most often, it has turned out, the physician is unable to defend his unique position. Sometimes, however, he can make a case for his views, and the DUR standards are altered accordingly.

Another key point is that the DUR program must be aimed wherever possible at physician education and not physician punishment. Understandably, most physicians do not relish having their knuckles rapped, even in the relative privacy of a DUR committee meeting, with only physicians and pharmacists involved. They would probably be even less inclined to cooperate and change their prescribing practices if these were challenged in the presence of patient or public representatives. On the other hand, some consumer spokesmen have insisted that it is vital for public representatives to participate, if only to keep everybody honest.[8]

The LAC-USC drug utilization review system has now been extended for both inpatients and outpatients to all hospital and other health care facilities under the direct control of the Los Angeles County Department of Health Services.[9] Some other hospitals have followed the lead of the LAC-USC program, but most have not. The major objections have been partly financial and partly physician resistance. It is costly to install a sophisticated computer system similar to that used in Los Angeles, especially one able to conduct virtually instantaneous prospective DUR review and intercept irrational prescriptions before they are dispensed. The expenses of this kind of program may be justified on clinical grounds but not alone on financial grounds if the system is applied exclusively for DUR. If, however, the DUR operation accounts for only a portion of the expenses of the data processing system, while the same system is also applied for cost-accounting, bookkeeping, inventory control, and other important functions, the DUR costs may be acceptable.

One unexpected dividend from the LAC-USC operation came when the system was used to compare the invoices showing the quantity of a particular drug product ordered from a wholesaler or manufacturer, the quantity known to have been dispensed to patients, and the quantity still remaining on the pharmacy shelves. One such comparison revealed that the quantities dispensed plus the quantities still in stock did not equal the amounts originally ordered. That comparison disclosed that one larcenous pharmacist had been cheating the program by selling—at a 30 percent discount—hundreds of thousands of dollars worth of drugs to various Southern California pharmacies, whose own ethical standards were possibly not of the highest. The LAC-USC pharmacist was indicted, tried, convicted, and sent to prison.

The amount of this variety of pilferage in hospitals is not known. At the Los Angeles medical center, it has been estimated that the value of stolen drugs had been between $250,000 and $1 million a year.[10]

"It appears," Maronde concluded in a 1977 paper, "that prospective and retrospective drug utilization review can decrease the expenditures for prescription drugs by at least 20 percent and at the same time improve patient care. The additional cost savings that may be realized from inventory control, decreased drug abuse, and improved patient care itself are not included in this figure. Certainly the savings will be much greater when peer review has more fully developed and its sophistication has increased."[11]

Comparably gratifying results have been achieved with another sophisticated DUR program developed in 1974 for Group Health Cooperative of Puget Sound (see also Chapter 11, below). It was set up when officials of this Seattle-based Health Maintenance Organization (HMO) recognized that the state of Washington was about to require the maintenance of patient prescription records in every pharmacy.[12]

"Early in our assessment," says Sue Madsen, who now directs the HMO's pharmacies, "it was determined that just to keep the profile by manual methods would require twenty-six additional full-time equivalent [employees]."

Those twenty-six additional people would be able only to keep records. Without additional staff and procedures, there would be no way to extract data required for DURs or to conduct urgently needed inventory studies at short intervals.

"And," Madsen added, "as pharmacists often do without profile systems, we were relating to each patient as if the only thing we ever knew about that patient was the prescription that was being filled at the moment."

When a patient gives a prescription to a Group Health Cooperative Pharmacy, Madsen told a 1977 conference, it is checked briefly by a pharmacist for any gross errors and then handed to an operator who types the information into the data processing system. The first report flashes on the screen in front of the operator in four seconds. Madsen told the conference:

> I want you to know what the system has done in those four seconds. It has checked first to see that the medical history number is on file—that the patient is one of ours—that the drug is in the formulary, and that the patient's coverage status is current. It has already checked for allergies which that patient may have disclosed to us, and for major, agreed-upon health-threatening or life-threatening drug interactions. If either an allergy or potential drug-drug interaction of a serious nature were detected in the patient's record, . . . the process is stopped at that point . . . and the pharmacist takes appropriate action.
>
> The system has checked to see that there is an adequate supply of the drug on hand. In addition, the profile has already been reviewed to determine when, if ever, the patient last received that drug on either the same prescription number, or—which is more important—under any other prescription number [which may indicate that two or more physicians are prescribing the same drug for the same patient]. The screen report gives the patient identification, the name, age, and sex, the contract status, and the allergy data; the prescription number has been assigned, the mnemonic [a code identification of the drug] has been decoded for verification, and the inventory unit displayed.

Data related to the last date of issue are provided so that compliance may be monitored and duplication of therapy be avoided. If there is special information that the pharmacist should be aware of related to the patient [such as being likely to become drug-dependent, known to use alcoholic beverages to excess, etc.], a warning begins to flash, and the pharmacist goes to the appropriate hard-copy document advising of the special monitoring procedure needed. If this is a pediatric or geriatric patient, the age flashes as an additional cautionary measure.

If all has gone well up to this point, more buttons are pushed, the system automatically prints the label, the prescription is filled, and the pharmacist consults with the patient to answer questions and give whatever additional instructions or advice may be needed. At the same time, there is an automated inventory deduction; if the amount remaining on the shelves is too low, an order is sent to the warehouse for a new supply.

The Group Health Cooperative system is not inexpensive. Over a four-year period, development, maintenance, manpower, and programing time totaled about $300,000. But over that period, the system saved about $300,000 a year in salaries, speeded up the whole dispensing process, minimized errors, intercepted what could have been irrational or needlessly dangerous prescriptions, made possible rapid inventories—daily if necessary—and yielded information essential for utilization review.

The DUR procedure at Group Health Cooperative has been somewhat unusual. It is voluntary and confidential. Each month, in private, each physician is shown his own prescribing pattern, along with a statistical analysis of the patterns of his peers. He may or may not elect to go along with the others. Whether or not he decides to conform is now under study.

Another recent study has strongly suggested that peer review by itself may not be very effective in improving prescribing patterns unless an irrational drug is made unavailable through the use of a formulary.[13]

THE SCANDAL: DURs AND NURSING HOMES

The use of prescription drugs in extended care facilities or skilled nursing facilities (SNFs) has been associated since at least the late 1960s with an exceptionally unpleasant aroma.

SNF patients—many of them Medicare or Medicaid beneficiaries—have reputedly been plied with unnecessary drugs in unnecessarily large amounts. They have been kept in what have been described as chemical straitjackets, mainly sedatives and tranquilizers, to keep the wards quiet and reduce the number of staff members required on duty. Adverse drug interactions have been inordinately common, and many SNF patients have had to be hospitalized or rehospitalized at substantial expense to themselves or their third-party programs.[14]

This dismal picture may have its origins in a variety of factors:

- It could be that the process of institutionalization, along with the removal of familiar surroundings and friends, is so disorienting that psychoactive drugs are needed.
- It could be that the elderly patients requiring psychoactive drugs are the most likely to be institutionalized.
- It could be that the lack of widely accepted, clear-cut medical guidelines for the prescribing of these drugs leads physicians to use them more often than is clinically indicated.
- It could be that these patients insist on psychoactive agents, particularly tranquilizers and sedatives, for the simple reason that they are accustomed to use them.
- It could be that the attitude, knowledge, and status of nurses play a critical role, especially their attitude toward the elderly and their belief in the value of psychoactive drugs.

There remains much disagreement about the extent of psychoactive drug misuse in nursing homes. Very few large-scale epidemiological studies have been undertaken on this problem. In one recent study of two hundred such homes, no evidence of drug misuse was noted in 25 percent, but significant overprescribing was found in 10 percent.[15]

A number of investigations have revealed a wide range of problems:

A General Accounting Office review of one month's records of 106 Medicaid patients in fourteen nursing homes in California showed that 311 drug doses were given in amounts larger than had been ordered by physicians, and 1,210 prescribed doses had not been administered at all.[16]

In a recent study by Lee Morse and Aida LeRoy, it was found in surveys conducted in Arkansas, California, and Minnesota that, of 489 patients hospitalized presumably because of an adverse drug reaction, 113—or 23 percent—had been transferred from a nursing home.[17]

Medical supervision in nursing homes, it has been asserted, has been inadequate because patients may be visited by their physician once a day, once a week, once a month, or even only once every several months. Much of this unsavory situation was brought out in hearings conducted by the late Senator Frank Moss of Utah. Those hearings likewise disclosed that few of the nursing facilities maintained their own pharmacies but, instead, obtained the drugs on bid under contract from a local community pharmacy. To obtain those often juicy contracts, many local pharmacists testified that they were required to provide rebates or kickbacks ranging from a few cents or a few dollars per prescription to free color television sets or free trips to Hawaii for the nursing home operators. The costs for these presents, of course, were added to patient drug bills.[18]

The operators expressed their horror at such charges. There was nothing compulsory or contractual about these "kickbacks," they insisted. The gifts were entirely voluntary.

As a result of the Moss hearings, widely reported by the media, HEW enacted new regulations in 1974 which required utilization review in all SNFs providing care for Medicare and Medicaid beneficiaries.[19] Included was a requirement for drug review, specifying that a pharmacist must review all patient drug records at least monthly.

There could be little doubt that such DUR could be effective in both improving the quality of care and holding down costs. One of the most impressive accounts of such improvements came from a Los Angeles study conducted by pharmacists Alan Cheung and Ronald Kayne in cooperation with several expert physicians.[20] The investigation involved three proprietary nursing homes in Los Angeles, each containing from 80 to 99 beds, and each certified by the Medicare and state Medi-Cal (Medicaid) programs.

In all of the homes, after a control or observation period, a clinical pharmacist attempted to get a drug history of each patient (preferably upon admission), set up a drug profile, evaluate the patient's response or nonresponse to drug treatment, monitor for the possibility or actual occurrence of an adverse drug reaction, recommend changes in drug therapy where this seemed advisable to the patient's physician, instruct patients on discharge how to use their prescribed drugs at home, and provide drug information to the physicians and to members of the SNF staff. Among the results were these:

- Medication errors—wrong drug, wrong patient, wrong dose, wrong route (for example, by mouth instead of by injection), missed doses, or inappropriate dosing interval (for example, a drug ordered to be given ten minutes before a meal being actually administered two hours after a meal)—were reduced from 20 percent to 8 percent.

- About 120 adverse drug reactions were detected, usually in their early and controllable stage, or potential adverse reactions were avoided or prevented. Of these, slightly more than half were considered by the consulting physicians to have been potentially so serious that, if not detected early or prevented, they could have resulted in hospitalization.
- The number of medication orders or prescriptions was reduced by about 18 percent, from an average of 6.8 to 5.6 prescriptions per patient per month.

"This service," the investigators said, "was well received by the patients' physicians because they knew, for the first time, that their therapeutic goals would be properly and expertly carried out."

Finally, the annual cost-savings—not counting the savings through prevented adverse drug reactions—were estimated for the three SNFs to be roughly $80,000. (And these calculations were made at a time when the average charge for a prescription was only $5.00 and that for a typical day of hospitalization was only $100. By 1979, the averages had gone up to more than $6.00 per prescription and approximately $200 per hospital day.) The potential savings nationwide for Medicare and Medicaid were estimated to be between $3 million and $37 million a year, depending on the practices of the various homes.

The results of the Los Angeles study, and others that confirmed it, should presumably have led to widespread adoption of this form of clinical pharmacy by most if not all SNFs. There was one major reason for failure: lack of money.

Under the terms of the new federal regulations, SNF operators could add a reasonable cost for DUR to the bills they eventually submitted to the government. It was believed that this additional sum would be used to compensate the pharmacists who actually performed the reviews. Many operators did not see it that way; they indicated that the pharmacist should be pleased to conduct the review as part of his contract to provide drugs, and they merely put the additional funds into their own pockets.[21] Among other things, this practice is a violation of federal law and carries a penalty of up to a $10,000 fine, a year in prison, or both.[22]

The reaction of most pharmacists seemed to be, "No, thank you!" They continued to provide the SNF with the drugs that were purchased under contract, but they refused to contribute any DUR services for free.

It may be noted that if this had been a wartime operation, patients entering at least some nursing homes would have been entitled to combat or ultrahazardous duty pay.

UNKNOWN TERRITORY: DURs IN COMMUNITY PRACTICE

Unlike DUR programs in hospitals, such reviews have so far received only minimal acceptance in the outside community, where physicians prescribe for ambulatory patients. There are some obvious reasons for the difference.[23] Community pharmacists rarely have access to complete patient records and are usually unaware of the patient's diagnosis. The methods of maintaining patient drug profiles may vary from one pharmacy to the next. Ambulatory patients may use several different pharmacies, and their record in any one pharmacy is accordingly incomplete. There is no standardized mechanism for collecting data. Computer facilities are seldom available. In addition, while hospital-based physicians are accustomed to having their surgical and medical treatments reviewed by their peers (although they may not be wildly enthusiastic about it), their non-hospital-based colleagues are apparently far more sensitive to criticism and do not like to have others looking over their shoulders. It may also be important that community physicians are relatively more accessible to drug company detail men, who have been decrying generic-name products and drug formularies for decades.

In spite of these and other difficulties, DUR has been attempted —and attempted successfully—in some communities. One of the earliest examples was a Lawrence County, Pennsylvania, program developed in the mid-1960s by Joseph McEvilla.[24] Another was a four-county program in California·headed by Marcel Laventurier of Paid Prescriptions and involving nearly 42,000 Medicaid patients covered under a contract with the San Joaquin Foundation for Medical Care.[25] Both programs revealed shocking cases of irrational prescribing.

Another Paid Prescriptions project involving Medicaid patients was developed in Florida. In that state, project representatives Aida LeRoy and Lee Morse called on physicians who were found to be (1) prescribing apparently lavish amounts of drugs for individual patients, (2) calling for the wrong drug for the diagnosis, or (3) ordering costly brand-name drugs when equally effective generic-name products were available.[26] In order to induce the erring physicians to change, the representatives merely showed each prescriber a printout of his own prescriptions in comparison with the prescribing patterns of his colleagues. Or, if necessary, they would put in a call to Bethesda, Maryland, from the physician's office—although not at his expense—and let him get the latest objective evidence directly from the computerized reference service in the National Library of Medicine. The technique proved to be so effective in changing prescribing patterns in the Florida Medicaid program, Morse said later, that drug company officials attempted to torpedo it.[27]

In Utah, drug use by Medicaid patients has been reviewed since 1975. Physician Alan Nelson described the program in this way:[28]

> The Utah program uses the information from the physician billing claim, which has the patient identification, the diagnosis, the procedures that were done, the treatment that is being given, and then, of course, the information is linked to the drug claim. The patient profile thus has the diagnosis, laboratory tests, and procedures in a chronologic system that also includes medications.
>
> The computer system is programmed to kick out exceptions—combinations of drugs which we wish to look at, volume of drugs over a certain time, and special projects—for example, tetracycline in patients under the age of 12, or medications that may be hazardous [during] a pregnancy.
>
> We have a continuing flow of physicians doing the review work. They also look at the prescriber's profile to see if a pattern of abuse emerges. If it does, he is sent a graded series of letters, the first of which says, sort of, "Gee, Doctor, did you know such-and-such was happening?" And at the other end, one that may say, "Doctor, you should change your behavior or else." It appears to work.

One less delicate physician described that last of the series of letters in these words: "We say, 'Look, turkey, cut it out or we'll bust you!'"

Still another DUR program for Medicaid outpatients was carried on in New Mexico, with particular attention focused on the administration of injections—usually of antibiotics—when oral treatment would have been equally effective and less expensive. After an intensive educational campaign, the use of these injections dropped by more than 60 percent, from an astounding 41 per 100 patient visits down to 16. Even of the remaining 16, more than a third were judged to be medically unnecessary.[29]

Most of these projects, generally involving large numbers of patients and drug claims, were carried out by means of computers. Whether the cost-savings justified the expense is unknown, although the beneficial effects for patients almost certainly warranted the cost.

Where small numbers of drug claims are to be reviewed, manual procedures can be used instead of computer processes. One approach, developed by David Knapp and using cards punched by hand, has been tested and found effective.[30] The cost of this method, far less than computer processes, appears to be economically acceptable.

If the ball game remains the same, the prospects for DUR remain uncertain. Probably more and more hospitals will introduce formal DUR programs. Unless they are forced to do so, skilled nursing homes will probably not. Outside of such institutions, the prospects for expanded DUR seem bleak. But if national drug insurance is implemented, there will be a new and different ball game. If only to cope with a deluge of drug claims, most of the nation's pharmacies and third-party agencies will almost certainly be required to develop automatic or computerized data processing networks. And if such networks are developed, the retrieval of the data essential for utilization review will become a relatively inexpensive segment of the operation.

One final point deserves consideration. Of all the various methods devised to improve the quality of drug therapy and contain costs—use of generics, formularies, patient cost-sharing, and the like—only utilization review has received the endorsement of physicians (including the American Medical Association), pharmacists, patients, insurance companies, governmental agencies, and the drug industry. (This agreement across the board may stem from the fact that few companies and few physicians have yet had much experience with DUR. So far, they do not feel threatened by it.)

Such unanimity—especially including the approval of the industry—has been upsetting to some slightly paranoid individuals. "If the drug industry is in favor of drug utilization review," said one consumer spokesman, "what's wrong with it?"

Drugs and Cost-Saving

The proposal to cover prescription drugs under national health insurance seems to raise this key question: *How can we cut down on drug expenditures?* Inevitably, such a query leads to consideration of price controls, limited formularies, and patient cost-sharing.

But there are other questions which may be far more significant: *How can drugs be used to cut down on total health care expenditures? How can they be used to minimize costly physician visits, costly surgery, and even more costly hospitalization?*

In the case of two drug classes—vaccines and anti-infectives— the answers to all these questions have been evident for many decades.

In the industrialized nations, and in many of the developing countries as well, it is clear that the use of vaccines to prevent disease will not only prevent needless suffering, disability, lengthy hospitalization, and needless deaths, but such applications are also almost unbelievably cost-effective. Certainly this has been shown to hold for such infectious diseases as smallpox, diphtheria, tetanus, mumps, measles, rubella, whooping cough, typhoid fever, typhus fever, bubonic plague, yellow fever, cholera, influenza, and polio. In the case of polio, for example, one authority has calculated that, for the United States between 1955 and 1961, approximately $653 million were spent on the polio vaccine program, including government-financed research and field trials. Without the vaccine, the direct and indirect costs for polio would have been more than $1 billion per year. In terms of 1980 dollars, the amount would have been far higher. During the 1955-61 period, as based on the records for the immediately preceding years, the use of polio vaccine in this country prevented 154,000 cases of paralytic polio and 14,300 cases of total disability, and saved 12,500 lives.[1]

The cost-effectiveness of such vaccines has been so readily demonstrable that many governmental agencies have financed enormous vaccination programs.

A similar situation exists in the case of antibiotics and other anti-infective agents, which often make prolonged physician care and hospital care unnecessary, minimize the need for expensive surgery, and have come close to transforming once-dreaded plagues into relatively minor nuisances. So far, it has not been possible to vaccinate against such diseases as streptococcus or staphylococcus infections, gonorrhea, syphilis, or even leprosy, but these can be inexpensively controlled (except where drug-resistant strains have appeared), often in the period of a relatively few days.

But vaccines and anti-infective agents do not exhaust the instances in which the use of drugs—sometimes at the expense of taxpayers—cannot only prevent suffering, disability, and needless death, but also reduce health care expenditures. Some of the applications of prudent drug use which offer exciting challenges for the future are discussed in this chapter.

TUBERCULOSIS

The classic example of achieving such cost-savings is the case of tuberculosis. The history of the developments in this field has been related in the excellent monograph by R. Y. Keers.[2] For century after century, the "white plague" remained a major cause of death and one of the most feared of all illnesses. In good times and bad, in cities and villages, in rich and poor countries, it defied all attempts by researchers to find an effective and specific treatment. For patients who could afford it, physicians recommended a regime of nutritious food, sunbaths, and enforced bedrest in a sanatorium for many months. Few victims survived.

In the United States, the TB death rate had been going down since at least the beginning of the twentieth century, presumably as the result of improved sanitation, the pasteurization of milk, better nutrition and housing, and the use of lung collapse and other surgical procedures, but the rate remained above 40 deaths per 100,000 population.[3]

Then, in 1944, Selman Waksman of Rutgers University isolated a new antibiotic and found that it was effective against TB organisms in the test tube. The antibiotic was named streptomycin. By the end of that same year, William Hugh Feldman and Corwin Hinshaw at the Mayo Foundation discovered that the new substance worked against TB in guinea pigs. In September 1945, the Mayo workers issued a guarded preliminary report on the treatment of their first thirty-four patients. Their announcement was marked by what Keers has described as "admirable caution and restraint":

> It appears probable that streptomycin has exerted a limited suppressive effect. . . . It is to be ardently hoped that if these results are noticed by lay persons, they will interpret the results in the same cautious frame of mind that the scientific investigators have endeavored to maintain. . . . No one as yet knows what the final judgment will be concerning the effect of streptomycin on clinical tuberculosis.

The effects of this first anti-TB drug were often striking. Temperatures dropped, appetites improved, coughing lessened, and patient morale improved. But there were problems: some patients lost their sense of equilibrium, and a few lost their hearing. More serious, the beneficial effects usually lasted for only a few months, at which point streptomycin-resistant strains made their appearance and the disease flared again.

The main value of streptomycin, it appeared, was to "cool down" patients with active disease so that they could be considered acceptable risks for lung collapse or other surgical intervention.

At almost the same time, a second anti-TB drug was introduced by a Swedish scientist working at the University of Göteborg. Finding that the respiration of TB bacilli could be stimulated by benzoic or salicylic acid, Jorgen Lehmann found that a related but toxic substance, para-aminosalicylic acid (PAS), could inhibit the growth of the organisms. In January 1946, he reported favorable results in most of twenty patients. But PAS, too, had its unpleasant side effects—notably gastrointestinal distress—and its use was sooner or later marked by the rise of PAS-resistant TB strains.

Better results could be achieved, and the appearance of resistant strains delayed, by using streptomycin and PAS in combination, but many physicians were convinced that sooner or later most patients would need surgery.

In 1951, a third new agent was developed: isonicotinic acid hydra-zide, or isoniazide (INH). It was tested first at the Sea View Hospital, in New York. Its results, too, were impressive. But before the investi-gators could make their first report, the sanatorium was invaded by reporters—probably tipped off by visitors who had come to see their friends or relatives—who described previously dying patients actually "dancing in the wards." Relatively inexpensive, effective when taken by mouth, and marked by few serious side effects, it represented another major advance, especially when it was given in combination with PAS tablets and streptomycin injections.

By 1955, there was growing agreement that these three drugs, given in one combination or another, could serve not merely to "cool down" patients in preparation for surgery, but that they alone, with-out surgery, could control most uncomplicated cases of TB. But it was still felt that prolonged rest for a year or two in a sanatorium was essential. (In some early cases, new types of surgery—especially the removal of a lobe of the lungs or even a small segment of a lobe, to get rid of the focus of infection—could shorten this sanatorium stay to perhaps six months.)

During the 1950s and 1960s, still other new anti-TB drugs made their appearance, of which ethambutol and a semisynthetic antibiotic, rifampin, were probably the most important. But perhaps the most dramatic development was what became known as the Madras experi-ment. This study, conducted by British, Indian, and World Health Or-ganization scientists, involved two groups of TB patients, both treated with the same combination of drugs. One group was kept in a hospital for many months, with the usual hospital hygiene and a nutritious, balanced diet. The second group of patients was treated at home, which usually meant an overcrowded, unsanitary hovel in the poorest section of Madras, and kept on the usual inadequate Indian diet. Both groups were observed for a period of five years. At the end of that time, 89 percent of those given their initial treatment in the hospital and 90 percent of those living at home in squalor had apparently recovered from TB.

The lesson seemed clear: In most cases of uncomplicated TB, prolonged treatment in a sanatorium is not necessary. As one expert put it, "The striking unimportance of bed rest had been shown."

In the United States and many other countries, the special TB sanatoria began to go out of business.

The economic effects of all these developments were stunning.

In the late 1940s, for example, it was accepted that the standard sanatorium treatment, for as many as fifteen to twenty months, could cost
the patient—or the taxpayers—as much as $5,000 per case. (At 1980
price levels, it would cost at least four to ten times as much.) With the
out-of-hospital treatment applied to most patients for eighteen to
twenty-four months—or now, in many cases, for only nine to twelve
months—the total drug cost may be as low as $40 to $60 a month if
the drugs are obtained from a county clinic or similar tax-supported
institution, although it may be somewhat more if a community pharmacy is used.[4]

The significance to taxpayers of such changes may be illustrated
by what happened over a decade in the state of Pennsylvania.[5] In 1968,
Pennsylvania maintained two state TB sanitaria which cost the taxpayers $5.2 million in that year, increasing to $6.4 million in 1971.
The state began to phase out its special TB institutions in 1973. If
patients needed brief hospital care, they could be treated in specially
designed units in general hospitals. The results:

- The average TB patient stay in any institution dropped
  from 250 days in 1965 to 104 days in 1974, and to 17 days
  in 1975-76.
- Between fiscal years 1971-72 and 1975-76, the state's annual tuberculosis control budget dropped from $10.9 mil-
  lion to $5.4 million.
- Added to such savings were reductions in losses resulting
  from lost earnings, minimizing pain and suffering, and
  preventing premature death.

Such changes as these have been so dramatic that many counties
and states in the United States have decided that providing anti-TB
drugs free of charge to any patient who needs them represents a most
happy way to save money. Men and women whose TB infection is
quickly controlled and who can once again earn wages, it may be
noted, will also pay taxes.

GLAUCOMA

With an estimated prevalence of roughly 2 million patients in
the United States, glaucoma can usually be detected easily and controlled by simple, inexpensive drug therapy. Tragically, it is often not
diagnosed in time and treatment not begun until the mounting pressure within the eye has permanently damaged the eye structure and
the optic nerve. Thus, of the estimated 2 million victims, only about

1.4 million have been diagnosed—most of them over the age of 45. Glaucoma ranks second only to diabetes as the leading cause of blindness in this country.

Of those patients who have been diagnosed, 160,000 are described as suffering severe and irreversible visual impairment. About 60,000 are listed as legally blind. The social and economic costs to the patients and to society are enormous.[6]

In 1977, direct medical care costs totaled nearly $436 million—approximately $49 million for physician visits, $33 million for hospitalization, $54 million for surgery, $237 million for care in a nursing home or other institution, and $63 million for drugs purchased by patients.

For those with impaired vision because of glaucoma between the ages of 55 and 64, the indirect costs—loss of earnings and unemployability—are estimated to be $1.9 billion per year.

What makes such financial costs—not to mention the grievous physical and emotional problems of the victims—so shocking is the fact that, if the disease is detected in its early state and appropriate treatment begun promptly, glaucoma can almost always be stopped before it leads to blindness or even interference with vision. And this can be achieved with drugs like pilocarpine[7] that will cost most patients less than fifteen cents a day. (This figure is based on the use of four drops per day in each eye of a 2-percent pilocarpine solution, with a retail price of about $4.65 for a 15-cc bottle, and assumes that 1 cc is equivalent to twenty drops.)

HIGH BLOOD PRESSURE

The toll taken by hypertension as measured by pain, disability, needless deaths, and dollars is enormous:[8]

- This condition, usually developing insidiously, is a major factor contributing to the 500,000 strokes and 175,000 stroke deaths reported annually in this country.
- It plays an important role in the 1,250,000 heart attacks and the 650,000 fatal attacks reported each year.
- In lost productivity, lost wages, and direct medical care costs, its annual price to the United States is an estimated $8 billion.

It now appears that these staggering losses could be markedly reduced by the appropriate use of antihypertensive drugs which American physicians now have—and have had for years.

According to Robert Levy, director of the National Heart, Lung, and Blood Institute (NHLBI), thirty-five million Americans have definite hypertension, and twenty-five million others have "borderline" hypertension. But as recently as 1972, the situation was complicated by some disturbing factors.

"In 1972," said Levy, "half the Americans with high blood pressure did not know that they had the disease. Only one-eighth were on effective treatment, and physicians were not aggressively taking advantage of the knowledge we had at that time in treating their hypertensive patients."[9]

Largely as a result of clinical trials carried on in Veterans Administration hospitals, physicians knew that drug therapy was effective in moderate to severe hypertension in preventing stroke, kidney failure, or heart failure. (Generally, diastolic blood pressures of 90 to 104 are classed as mild, of 105 to 114 as moderate, and of 115 or above as severe.) The VA studies were conducted primarily on middle-aged men with advanced manifestations of hypertension and its complications. It was not clear whether or not the findings would also apply to women, to the young and the elderly, and to the community at large.

In 1972, the NHLBI embarked on a double-barreled program with two important goals:

- To set up the National High Blood Pressure Education Program to inform both physicians and patients of the facts and opportunities on hand. (Since the start of this campaign, deaths from stroke alone have plummeted by more than 5 percent each year.)
- To undertake a five-year study to measure total deaths from all causes in patients with mild to moderate hypertension, one half given the typical treatment provided (or not provided) generally in the community, and the other half treated in an aggressive, intensive, systematic program in special cooperating hypertension centers.

This was not a replay of the VA project, in which good care was measured against no care. The NHLBI project—called the Hypertension and Detection Follow-up Program—was designed to compare normal care in the community, where many physicians were uncertain about the need to treat mild hypertension, with aggressive "stepped care"—the use of one drug or a combination to bring the pressure down to the desired level and then keep it there.

Although each patient in the "ordinary care" group was referred to his own physician, or asked to select one, the patients in the "stepped care" group were provided every possible incentive, including free drugs, free transportation, and free physician services, and were asked to report for a follow-up examination every four months. A total of 10,940 patients participated in the two programs.

At the end of five years, the scientists reported these findings:[10]

- For all degrees of hypertension, deaths from all causes were 17 percent fewer in the intensively-treated group.
- For mild hypertension, the intensive treatment reduced the death rate by 20 percent.
- The lowered death rates were particularly striking in the case of black women, black men, and white men, though there was less difference in the comparable groups of white women.[11]

It is not clear yet what part of the results in the "stepped care" group could be attributed to the drugs themselves and what part to other features in the intensive care program. Levy concluded, however, that "To the millions of Americans who have high blood pressure, this study says: 'Get on treatment and *stay* on treatment. It will mean a much longer life—more years to spend with your loved ones.'"[12]

There appears to be an additional message: Improving the access to modern outpatient prescription drugs and to appropriate therapy may also play a vital role in saving lives.

Further evidence of the value of treating mild hypertension has recently been reported from a four-year Australian study in which one group of patients received antihypertension drugs while a second group received a placebo or "dummy" medication. The death rate in the treated group was two-thirds lower than that in the control group.[13]

DUODENAL ULCER

One of the most daring gambles in recent pharmaceutical history —and one viewed most skeptically at the outset by many authorities— paid off handsomely when a new drug, cimetidine or Tagamet, was introduced for the control of gastric acid secretion as found in duodenal ulcer and other gastrointestinal diseases.

The search started in 1964 in the English laboratories of Philadelphia-based Smith Kline & French (SKF), when James Black, William Duncan, Roger Ganellin, and their associates sought a chemical that might block the action of histamine in the stomach. It was histamine, they believed, that was largely responsible for the release of excessive gastric acid. It was well known that this excess acid plays a role in ulcer. Block the acid, they theorized, and the ulcer might heal itself.

After five years of intensive research, the SFK scientists had failed to turn up a useful compound. "We were within an ace of calling it quits in 1969," recalls company chairman Robert Dee. "We then decided to go one more year."[14]

In 1970, just as the project was about to be abandoned, the scientists hit on the first promising lead. It was a substance they named burimamide. It showed a modest effect in controlling gastric acidity, but it had one unfortunate flaw: it was inactive when given by mouth, and had to be administered by frequent intravenous injections. Soon the scientists developed a second effective chemical, and this one could be taken by mouth. It proved that the theory was right: duodenal ulcers would heal if the stomach's acid production were reduced. Unfortunately, it caused blood damage in some patients, and its use in clinical trials was stopped.

Meanwhile, trials were already under way on what eventually became 700 other products. Among these was cimetidine. It worked when taken by mouth and was remarkably safe in patients studied for a year or more. It was approved for marketing in Great Britain in 1976 and in the United States in 1977, after an expedited nine-month FDA review of the animal and patient data. As a matter of fact, FDA had been reviewing the preliminary data for several years and was in an excellent position to decide quickly. Cimetidine has since made unprecedented profits for the company, and it has come close to revolutionizing ulcer treatment.[15]

"Also," claims one of our British medical colleagues, "it has damn near put the stomach surgeons out of business."

Gastroenterologists seem to agree that, for most duodenal ulcer patients, cimetidine is not much more effective than large doses of antacids used to neutralize stomach acid, but the new cimetidine tablets are substantially less expensive than those large antacid doses. Moreover, many ulcer patients won't take the usual antacids; these medications, they complain, taste horrible, they must be taken in inconvenient liquid form many times a day, and some cause diarrhea and other digestive disturbances.[16] But such patients—by the millions, it appears—will take their prescribed cimetidine. Its side effects seem to be minimal, but it must be emphasized that the consequences of very long-term use are still being investigated.

In one unusual step, SKF agreed to conduct a voluntary postmarketing surveillance study to detect any unanticipated adverse reactions. That surveillance, coupled with additional clinical trials, has recently led FDA to approve the drug not only for the treatment of an acute duodenal ulcer attack but also for the prevention of an ulcer recurrence.[17]

In another unusual move, the company supported a wide variety of research projects to determine the probable economic impact of cimetidine. Among these were studies by the Stanford Research Institute in Menlo Park, California;[18] the Netherlands Economic Institute in Rotterdam;[19] Robinson Associates in Bryn Mawr, Pennsylvania;[20] a group at the University of Wisconsin;[21] and a British team at York University.[22]

Based on the assumptions of expert gastroenterologists that the new drug would probably be used by 80 percent of ulcer patients, and using 1977 data, these were the key findings and predictions:

- The national cost of duodenal ulcers in 1977 was nearly $2.2 billion for more than 2 million patients.
- With the use of cimetidine, costs for hospital care could be reduced from $732 million to $474 million per year.
- Surgeons' fees could be reduced from $74 million to $44 million per year. Perhaps the most striking advantage of cimetidine was its value in minimizing the need for surgery.
- The costs of physician visits and related services could be reduced from $112 million to $95 million per year.
- Short-term absenteeism costs could be reduced from $455 million to $307 million per year, and long-term disability costs from $476 million to $295 million.
- For the United States, the total annual price tag for duodenal ulcer could be cut from $2.2 billion to $1.5 billion, for a reduction of about 30 percent. If the drug were used by only 50 percent of ulcer patients, the cost-savings would represent about 18 percent. (Comparable percentage savings were predicted by the above-cited study in the Netherlands.)

For the average individual patient, the studies showed that the total annual cost could be slashed from $1,040 to $732, even though the annual costs of medication would rise from $40 to $57. Or, to put it another way, the average duodenal ulcer patient could spend an extra $17 a year on drugs and still save approximately $300 on his total bill.

PNEUMOCOCCAL PNEUMONIA[23]

Recently, Edward Cohen of the University of Illinois estimated that the treatment of a typical case of pneumococcal pneumonia *without* antibiotics—involving perhaps thirty days of hospitalization, physician fees, respiratory therapy, surgical chest drainage, special nursing, and all the rest—would cost slightly more than $16,000. Treatment *with* antibiotics, he calculated, including only two days in the hospital, would cost $750.[24]

For Medicare beneficiaries, most of the costs in either case—except for out-of-hospital drugs—would be covered by the program. But probably in at least 80 percent of the elderly—generally those at most risk—the disease could be prevented by a newly introduced vaccine which would cost an estimated $11 per person. Yet, the Medicare program does not now cover the use of any preventive vaccine. In many instances, government funds are used to provide vaccination against such diseases as measles, mumps, rubella, diphtheria, tetanus, pertussis or whooping cough, and polio. Pneumonia has never been included in this category.

In spite of the sulfa drugs and antibiotics, pneumonia has not yet been conquered, and is now the fifth leading cause of death in the U.S. It should be noted that there are many different microbes which can cause pneumonia. One of the most important of these is the pneumococcus. Pneumoccocal pneumonia is responsible for only about 15 percent of all cases of pneumonia, but this type causes the most severe form of the disease, especially in the elderly.[25] Its victims are more likely to need hospitalization, and often more prolonged hospitalization. What is making the situation increasingly troublesome is the fact that many of the causative strains are becoming antibiotic-resistant.

Since the 1940s, it has been known that a vaccine could be prepared to control one or more of the approximately eighty strains of pneumococcal organisms that are known to exist. Of these, twelve strains may account for more than three-quarters of all cases. Until the early 1960s, however, most physicians showed little interest in such vaccines and instead relied on penicillin and other antibacterial agents. By then, however, it was becoming increasingly apparent that the anti-infective drugs were losing their punch, especially when the organisms invaded the bloodstream and caused a pneumococcal bacteremia. For patients over the age of 50 who were struck with such a complication, the death rate was close to 20 percent.

One of the most concerned researchers was Robert Austrian,

now at the University of Pennsylvania. Largely because of his insistent campaigning, the National Institute of Allergy and Infectious Diseases —one of the National Institutes of Health—agreed to provide funds to support both basic and applied research to develop an effective and practical pneumococcal vaccine. Eventually, between 1968 and 1976, NIAID invested about $6.5 million in this project.

Financial support for vaccine development went originally to Eli Lilly, but in a few years the company decided to drop nearly all of its vaccine work. By that time, enough pneumococcal vaccine had been prepared for the first major trial on workers in South African gold mines who suffered from an inordinately high rate of pneumonia. In this first trial, directed by Austrian, 4,000 subjects were vaccinated and 8,000 were used as controls. The rate of the dreaded pneumococcal bacteremia in the vaccinated group was cut by 82 percent.

Although Lilly dropped out of the picture, two other American firms, Lederle Laboratories and Merck Sharp and Dohme, decided to enter on their own, without any direct governmental financial aid. Expanded field trials were set up, again in South Africa and also in New Guinea, in Chile, and in a few special groups in the United States. By the end of the premarketing trials, approximately 23,000 individuals had received the vaccine. The effectiveness of the new preventive was dramatically obvious. Its side effects were relatively infrequent and usually minor in nature.

The Merck vaccine, known as Pneumovax, was licensed by FDA in November 1977 and put on the market three months later. The Lederle product, Pnu-Imune, was first marketed in 1979.

Because of the newness of the antipneumonia vaccine, the duration of its effect is not known. Preliminary findings suggest that the immunity it produces in human beings will last for more than three years, probably for eight years, and possibly for even longer.

Also, because of the newness of the vaccine, its effects on costs are yet unknown. According to figures for 1976, all forms of pneumonia together represented direct medical care costs of $1.4 billion, of which $1.1 billion were for pneumococcal pneumonia.[26] Whether any appreciable portion of this can be saved will depend not only on the effectiveness of the vaccine but also on how many individuals—especially the elderly and others who are considered to be in the high-risk pneumonia category—will be willing to accept vaccination and to pay for it.

In the instances cited above—and many others could be added—the costs of outpatient prescription drugs and vaccines are not covered under the existing Medicare program nor under many private health insurance policies. (Efforts are now being made to amend the Medicare law to cover the costs of antipneumococcal vaccine and perhaps other preventive vaccines for the elderly, but the results of these efforts are yet to be seen.)*

With the present situation, Medicare beneficiaries have only two real options:

- To pay for the drugs out of their own pockets, if they can afford to do so.
- Not to buy the drugs, thus taking a chance on more illness, more serious illness, more physician visits, more hospitalization, more disability, and perhaps needlessly early death. For most of *these* costs, Medicare *will* pay.

The solutions now available do not appear to be any significant bargain.

*Late in December of 1980, the President signed into law P.L. 96-611, which permits reimbursement for the new pneumonia vaccine under the Medicare program.

Part IV   The Public Purse

Prologues to
National Drug Insurance:
The Foreign Experience

With the exception of the United States, every major industrialized country in the world—along with many nonindustrialized or developing nations—has provided a program of national health insurance for many years or even decades. In most of these insurance plans, the cost of prescription drugs is covered in one way or another.

It would seem foolhardy for the architects of any national health insurance program for the United States to proceed far without being aware of at least some of these foreign approaches, the wide variety of systems that have been employed, and their major advantages and disadvantages. It is evident, of course—or at least should be—that an approach which works effectively in, for example, Great Britain, Sweden, the Netherlands, or New Zealand may fail disastrously if transplanted to this country. Similarly, an approach that was unacceptable to the British or the Swedes might well be approved by Americans.

During 1979, it became possible for us to examine the drug insurance programs in fourteen foreign countries, including six different provincial programs in Canada. In most cases, we were able to make on-the-spot studies, working with officials of the various ministries or departments involved, and with practicing physicians and pharmacists, drug experts, and economists. A relatively brief account of our findings is presented in the following sections.[1]

It will be evident that, in the countries we observed, the major consistent finding was inconsistency. There was no complete agreement on which patients should be considered beneficiaries of the various plans or on which drug products or drug classes should be covered. There was little agreement on whether the selection of covered drugs should be based on their relative cost or their therapeutic value, or on some combination of cost and benefit. Some countries provided drugs at no cost, while others required patients to pay part of the cost, but there was no agreement on whether any cost-sharing should be based on (1) the age or financial status of the patient, (2) the nature of the illness, (3) the nature of the drug, (4) whether the patient was treated in or out of a hospital, or (5) whether the treatment was prescribed by a family physician or a specialist. In some countries, the governmental agency paying the bills has the right to examine individual patient records or physician prescribing patterns, and drug utilization review is therefore possible. In other countries, notably in Europe, any such examination would be considered an immoral or illegal violation of privacy, and would be viewed with outrage or horror.

Perhaps the one common finding during the economically distressed year of 1979 was the growing attention paid to cost-containment. Not only in the case of drugs but also involving physician fees and hospital bills, there were visible efforts to hold down expenses which would eventually have to be paid by taxpayers. These efforts were not received by physicians, pharmacists, hospital administrators, and the drug industry with visible joy, and there were vigorous protests—including strikes by physicians.

One observation that startled us was the range in the numbers of drugs approved for marketing in the different countries. For example, the health care system in Iceland seems to cope very well with only 1,100 prescription drugs, including all dosage forms and strengths, and Norway maintains excellent health care with about 1,900, while there are an estimated 13,700 drugs on the market in Italy and 15,000 or more in Great Britain and Germany. The British and German figures would be far higher if the large numbers of herbal and single-pharmacy remedies were also included. (See Table 4.)

This situation has been most recently and most carefully analyzed by Graham Dukes of the Central Inspectorate for Drugs in the Netherlands, and Inga Lunde of the National Centre for Medicinal Products Control in Norway.[2] Their studies were focused primarily on

TABLE 4. *Estimated Numbers of Prescription Drugs (All Strengths and Dosage Forms) Marketed in Selected Countries*

Country	Number of Drugs
United Kingdom	15,000*
West Germany	15,000*
Italy	13,700*
Japan	13,600†
United States	12,500†
Canada	12,000†
Switzerland	8,900†
Greece	8,000†
Belgium	7,900*
France	7,800*
Ireland	7,400*
Luxembourg	7,300*
Australia	7,000†
Finland	3,700*
The Netherlands	3,400*
New Zealand	2,900†
Sweden	2,700*
Denmark	2,100*
Norway	1,900*
Iceland	1,100*

SOURCES: Numbers marked with a dagger (†) are semiofficial governmental figures. Numbers marked with an asterisk (*) are taken from M. N. Graham Dukes and Inga Lunde, "Controls, Common Sense, and Communities," *Pharmaceutish Weekblad* 114: 1283 (1979); and Dukes and Lunde, "Measuring the Effects of Drug Control—An Emerging Challenge," *Pharmaceutical Journal* (London) 223:511 (November 17, 1979).

the so-called Nordic Council nations—Denmark, Norway, Sweden, Finland, and Iceland—and most of the then-members of the Common Market or European Economic Community (EEC). They note that the figures they present differ—sometimes markedly—from those reported officially or semiofficially by governmental agencies. The governmental figures, they emphasize, are not comparable in many instances, since each government decides on its own how it will count its approved drugs. The Dukes-Lunde figures, on the other hand, developed with the aid of drug experts in each country, are believed to be comparable.

The differences in the numbers of approved drugs in the various countries, they say, rest in part on the toughness of the drug regulatory agency involved and of the laws and regulations it implements. A rigid or hard-nosed agency, for example, will not accept most fixed-ratio combination products or drugs with only minimal therapeutic value; drug companies know this and will not waste their time and money requesting approval for such products. In the same way, companies will usually elect not to market a drug in a country which offers only limited sales possibilities.

Of perhaps equal importance are historical, cultural, and religious factors. These factors may have played a strategic role in determining the attitude toward drugs in the Nordic Council countries (along with the Netherlands) on the one hand, and in the rest of the EEC countries on the other.

The link between religion and attitudes toward drugs and the practice of medicine, Dukes and Lunde suggest, may seem farfetched. But, they add:

> One must remember how profoundly the Reformation, and in particular the teaching of Calvin and Luther, both reflected and affected the mentality of whole populations.
>
> North European man is, broadly speaking, a sober (if not sombre) individual, with a handsome acknowledgement of the need for law and authority. When it comes to it, he is frugal in his ways; if he has a cold in the head, he will tell himself that it must run its course, and perhaps he will take some camilla tea, being aware of the adverse reactions to anything more potent. His fellow-sufferer in the sunnier south of Europe will, in a similar situation, probably betake himself to the doctor or the pharmacist to request (and to obtain) a medley of antibiotics, antihistamines, and analgesics. We may be exaggerating slightly for the sake of argument, but only slightly.
>
> Certainly the mentality of populations plays a role in determining the way in which drug control functions. The further north one goes into the zone where the puritan ethos . . . dominates, the more restrictive does drug control tend to become; yet in these northern countries, the attitude of the manufacturer and the drug controller to one another is generally one of mutual respect. The manufacturer is likely to regard the drug controller, like the tax inspector, as an official who can be expected to make rigid and reasoned demands on objective grounds and according to the letter of the law. In the more relaxed atmosphere of Europe's Catholic south, the drug controller (again like the tax inspector) is a sparring partner whose more exotic demands may well be

tempered by a little sporting argument, and the law itself may in parts even be unenforced or unenforceable, however impressive it looks in the Statute Book.[3]

The additional thousands of drugs available for prescription by southern European physicians—along with those in Britain and West Germany—Dukes and Lunde emphasize,

> do not indicate that such doctors have any significant advantage in treating the ills of their patients.
>
> Most of the specialties to be found on any longer list represent mere alternatives having at best marginal advantages in terms of efficacy or tolerance over those on the basic list. It follows that in a country with 13,000 drugs on the market, this factor alone is not likely to result in any pronounced difference in public health statistics as compared with those of a country where only some 1,100 drugs are on sale.

They likewise add one disquieting note: "One has the impression that there is something of a parallel between the liberality of a drug market and the nature and number of [adverse drug] accidents."

Finally, it must be noted that the drug lag—the unavailability of drugs in one country that are on the market in another—is far more severe in many of the European countries than it is in the United States. Yet, while the drug lag in the United States has been built up—in considerable part by the drug industry—as a serious threat to health and an intolerable interference with high-quality health care, it is generally viewed in Europe as a minor inconvenience or no problem at all. In most instances, European experts agree, if one drug is not allowed on the market, a suitable alternative is readily available.

One reason for the no-problem status of the drug lag in many European nations may be the provision in the law enabling a physician or pharmacist to import an unapproved drug from a country where it is available if this is necessary for the care of a particular patient. Even if such a provision is at hand, however, it is rarely used. Whether this legal loophole should be written into American drug laws appears worthy of consideration.

As noted in Chapter 1, the delay in having a new product approved for the United States market is usually, but not invariably, greater than in other countries. Some new drugs are approved by FDA before they are passed by regulatory agencies in foreign nations.

AUSTRALIA[4]

Of the 7,000 prescription drugs available in Australia—the overwhelming proportion of them imported from abroad—somewhat less

than a third are included as benefit items in the Pharmaceutical Benefits Scheme list. It spite of this apparently limited list of approved or
reimbursable drugs, they account for more than 90 percent of all prescriptions and make possible a wide range of products for drug therapy.

Drug costs now account for about 7 percent of total health care
costs.

The listed drugs are supplied without cost-sharing to pensioners
and their dependents, who make up roughly 12 percent of the population but account for about 45 percent of all prescriptions. For the rest
of the population, there is now a required co-payment of $2.75 (about
$3.10 U.S.) per prescription.*

The pharmacist receives payment from the government for the
remainder of his acquisition cost, plus a percentage markup and a
professional fee to cover his services.

Australian physicians infrequently order drugs by their generic
name, and pharmacists are not permitted to substitute a low-cost generic product where one is available.

For a number of years, it has been Australian policy, in determining whether or not to place a product on the approved list, for the
government to weigh price against therapeutic value. Among the factors considered by an advisory committee in making its recommendations to the Minister for Health are quality, safety, efficacy, and a
drug's availability at a "satisfactory" price.

The advisory committee may likewise recommend that an accepted product be marketed for unrestricted use—that is, be available
for any patient for the treatment of any disease or condition—or be
restricted to the treatment of a specified disease or condition, or for
the treatment of a particular group of patients, such as pensioners, or
in larger than normal quantities for certain clinical conditions. Fixed-
ratio combination drug products are rarely acceptable. Where possible,
the maximum quantity of a drug that may be dispensed is that which
would provide treatment for the normal course of an acute illness, or
one month's treatment plus two refills for a chronic disease.

A drug may be removed from the list under a number of conditions: when another drug is discovered that is less toxic; when the
demonstrated or suspected toxicity outweighs the therapeutic value;

---

*The U.S. dollar equivalents shown in this section and those that follow
are based roughly on international exchange rates as they existed during the
latter part of 1979.

when the drug has fallen into disuse; or when therapeutically comparable alternative drugs at lower cost become available.

Through a computer system, which has been in operation for a decade and a half, it is possible to analyze the prescribing patterns of individual physicians. When prescribers continue to disregard restrictions, even after counseling, they may be given an official letter of warning or a governmental reprimand, they may be required to repay the value of items wrongly or excessively prescribed as benefits, or their permission to write prescriptions for drug benefits may be suspended or revoked. Apparent fraud may be made the subject of court action. Similar penalties may be invoked against pharmacists.

Australian physicians and pharmacists are aware that some products available in other countries are not approved for marketing in Australia. This is considered to be only a minor problem. It has certainly not set off the storm of controversy that has been observed in the United States.

BELGIUM[5]

The compulsory illness and disability insurance program in Belgium, originally regulated by a 1963 law and later expanded by royal decrees, now covers the entire population of the country. The amounts of reimbursement depend in part on the socioeconomic status and income of the individual.

Special attention is given to what are commonly called the VIPOs —widows (les veuves), invalids, pensioners, and orphans, all below a maximum income level.

So far as drugs are concerned, government officials note, reimbursement applies only to certain listed pharmaceutical specialties. The costs of other drug products are borne completely by the patient. Inclusion in the reimbursable list is based on well-defined and accepted criteria.

For prescription drugs on the reimbursable list, patient cost-sharing may be required, with the amount determined by the nature of the product and the economic status of the patient. A lower amount is charged to the VIPOs. The patient contribution is paid directly to the pharmacist, with the remainder paid by the sickness fund to which the patient belongs.

Under the present system, the general public—not including the VIPOs—is required to pay 70 Belgian francs (about $2.45) for each standard prescription, a multiple of 70 Bf for a drug needed to treat an acute disease, and 40 Bf for one needed in a chronic illness. For preparations specially compounded by a pharmacist, a charge is made to the general public, but VIPOs are exempt from this requirement.

Prescriptions must be dispensed as written by the physician. No substitution is allowed. However, pharmacists have a virtual monopoly to dispense drugs. Only in a very few instances are drugs dispensed by physicians, and this practice is expected to disappear in a short time.

Before any drug may be marketed in Belgium, it must be approved and registered by the Minister of Health. The price of all prescription drugs is determined by the Minister of Economic Affairs on the advice of the price commission for pharmaceutical specialties. Setting these prices is based on criteria set by law. A markup of 31 percent by the pharmacist is permitted.

For a prescribed drug not registered in Belgium but approved in another country, the pharmacist may import and dispense it on his own responsibility, on the condition that he immediately notifies the appropriate office in the Ministry of Health.

The present system of reimbursement is now undergoing revision. Under one proposal,[6] reimbursable products would be divided into three categories with different reimbursement levels:

- Category A would include products which would be dispensed with no charge to the patient. Among such drugs would be insulin and anticancer agents.
- Category B products would require a 25 percent cost-sharing for patients (15 percent for VIPOs), up to a maximum of 300 francs (200 for VIPOs). In this group would be placed such drugs as antibiotics and anti-asthma agents.
- Category C products, including such drugs as vasodilators and antihistamines, would require patient cost-sharing of 40 to 50 percent (25 percent for VIPOs), up to a maximum of 500 francs (300 francs for VIPOs).

For drugs not in any of these categories, including other prescription drugs and all over-the-counter products, the patient would be required to pay the full price.

Total drug costs accounted for nearly 19 percent of total health care expenditures in 1979. Many widely prescribed drugs—among them oral contraceptives, tranquilizers (including Valium), and antidepressants—are not on the approved list for reimbursement. Gaining acceptance to the approved list entails lengthy procedures and the risk of government pressure on prices. For this reason, for certain products of average-to-low prices, some companies prefer not to apply for inclusion on the list. In the case of Valium, it appears that sales remain brisk even though the patients must pay for the drug themselves.

Belgian drug experts note that the drug insurance program is facing serious financial problems. At least part of the blame has been placed on abuse of the program by the VIPOs. Almost certainly, the VIPOs use an inordinately large number of prescriptions, but it is not clear whether this amounts to program abuse or reflects the greater drug needs, especially among women and the elderly.

By early 1980, although the government's proposals for modification of the drug insurance program had not been formally introduced, they had drawn bitter criticism.[7] The proposed changes, it was charged, would be needlessly complex and confusing, excessively expensive to administer, and excessively costly to the VIPOs, who had the greatest need for drugs and the least ability to pay for them.

Various alternatives have been proposed. The Belgian drug industry, for example, has accepted the concept that some drugs should be provided at no cost to patients while others should require payment in full. All other prescription drugs, industry spokesmen have urged, should require patient cost-sharing based primarily on one factor: the price of the prescription. The patient payment should be set relatively high for low-cost prescriptions and low for expensive prescriptions. The patient payments by the VIPOs would be set lower than those for the general public.

The possibilities for the use of low-cost generic products in the future are uncertain. Some hospitals already stock generic products in their pharmacies and include them in their own formularies. Attempts are now under way to create a nationwide hospital formulary, listing both generic and brand-name products.

Drug utilization review is essentially unknown in this country, and the very concept is unacceptable. Neither the government nor any of the sickness funds has the power to control irrational prescribing, although prescribing abuses may be checked by the various medical specialty associations. To curb drug expenditures, the government is increasingly resorting to tighter reimbursement criteria and to the removal of products from the reimbursable list.

CANADA[8]

For most beneficiaries, outpatient prescription drugs are not covered in any national Canadian program, although they may be covered nationwide in some private nonprofit insurance plans. Drug reimbursement is provided by the provincial and territorial governments, and a wide variety of approaches has been used.

As will be noted below, Canadian physicians are being increasingly urged or required to prescribe generically, and pharmacists in many of the provinces are obliged to substitute a low-cost generic product in place of a more expensive brand-name product.

It is estimated that about 12,000 different drugs are now marketed in Canada. Unlike the situation in most European countries, there are no provisions except in emergency situations for a physician or pharmacist to import into Canada an unapproved drug that may be available elsewhere. Although physicians recognize that some drugs not approved in Canada are available in a number of other countries, this drug lag is considered to be only a minor problem and has attracted little attention. In general, new drugs are available on the Canadian market before they are available in the United States.

For Canada as a whole, government officials believe that prescription drug costs represent about 5 percent of total health care costs. Between 1970 and 1974, the average prices of certain drugs still under patent dropped by an average of 39 percent, while those for the same drugs in the United States dropped by only 1.4 percent. The products involved were those particularly affected by Canada's new compulsory patent licensing legislation. Also contributing to the change in Canada was a government program to provide physicians and pharmacists with data on the quality of brand-name and generic products in order to demonstrate the suitability of generic products for substitution. Information on comparable product prices is likewise provided by the government. Provincial laws have been amended to permit pharmacists to select a less expensive form of a prescribed drug and to pass on the savings to patients.

The highlights of some of the provincial programs are as follows.

Manitoba

The Manitoba drug benefit program began with coverage for only the elderly, but the program proved to be so successful (with widespread benefits and low program costs) that it was expanded to all residents. For persons 65 years of age or older, there is a $50 deductible per family unit, with the province paying 80 percent of the cost over that amount. For persons under 65, the plan is the same except that the deductible is $75 per family unit. The patient must submit a claim for reimbursement, usually twice a year; in many cases, pharmacists maintain and complete the prescription claim forms for their patients.

In the case of a small number of brand-name drugs, the pharmacist must substitute a low-cost generic product selected from those listed in the Manitoba Drug Standards and Therapeutic Formulary. The pharmacist may not charge more than the lowest price figure listed, nor may he exceed the maximum dispensing fee ($3.50 as of July 1, 1979).

Saskatchewan

In this province, all residents are covered by the Drug Plan. Cost-sharing involves payment by the patient of a sum up to $2.45 for each prescription (the pharmacist may charge the patient less if he chooses to do so). The provincial government will then pay the pharmacist the remaining portion of the dispensing charge plus the acquisition or ingredient cost. Pharmacists have negotiated a maximum dispensing fee of $3.25. This is divided between the patient, who pays up to $2.45, and the province, which pays the balance.

A formulary is issued twice a year listing covered drugs and reimbursement prices. For some of the drugs in the formulary, the government invites bids for the supply of a product at a fixed price for a six-month period. These drugs are supplied to pharmacies from wholesalers who act on behalf of the government. The use of a formulary, while restricting the choice of drugs, has had the effect of eliminating products of dubious value, particularly fixed-combination products.

Ontario

Through a fusion of earlier provincial and municipal programs, Ontario now covers drug costs for the elderly and for people who are recipients of social assistance. A drug benefit list is used. Pharmacists are required to substitute the least expensive among the multiple-source products listed, and the program provides for full coverage of the listed items without any patient cost-sharing. The products to be listed are evaluated for quality and therapeutic merit by a Therapeutics Committee, and the price is negotiated with the suppliers. Product selection is allowed only within these guidelines. The program assumes legal liability for any damages occurring as a result of product selection. The present maximum dispensing fee is $3.27.

British Columbia

A universal program has now been implemented for all residents. For those 65 years of age or older, those in long-term care facilities, and those receiving social assistance, prescribed drugs are covered without any patient cost-sharing. For the remainder of the population, there is a $100 deductible per family unit, with the province paying 80 percent of the cost over that amount. The pharmacist must indicate the cost of ingredients and the dispensing fee separately on the prescription label. The maximum dispensing fee cannot exceed the average fee of the province by more than 15 percent. That average fee is now $3.44.

Alberta

In Alberta, drug programs for the elderly and for social assistance recipients are operated through Blue Cross. The elderly must pay 20 percent of the cost of each prescription, with a minimum of $1.00. Pharmacists charge Blue Cross for their acquisition cost plus a dispensing fee of up to $3.45. Full drug coverage, with minor exceptions, is provided for social assistance recipients at no charge.

Quebec

The Quebec program involves an extensive drug benefit list prepared by an Advisory Council on Pharmacology, on the basis of criteria which enable it to assure therapeutic effectiveness, the compliance of manufacturers with Manufacturing Facilities and Control Regulations, and the overall quality of drug products. The list also enables health professionals to prescribe or dispense drugs with the knowledge of the price of comparable brands of the same drug. Without patient cost-sharing, the program covers all those over the age of 64, all social welfare recipients, and all those over 60 who receive a government low-income pension or a guaranteed income supplement. The pharmacist is reimbursed for the cost cited in the list plus a negotiated dispensing fee ($2.75 as of October 1979). Refusing to dispense a prescription that the pharmacist considers to be irrational is recognized as a professional service, and a fee of $2.75 is paid for this service by the program.

In addition, a $5 fee is paid for a pharmacist's opinion, provided in writing to the patient and physician, on the therapeutic value of prescribed medications. The opinion must be based on records maintained by the pharmacist.

DENMARK[9]

Health care in Denmark is nearly free for all inhabitants of the country. Hospital care and physician care are provided without charge. For an employed worker, a sickness benefit of 90 percent of the weekly wage is paid, up to a maximum of 1,569 Danish kroner (about $314 per week). The same benefit is granted in connection with childbirth, and there is a maternity leave of fourteen weeks.

Anyone living in the country is entitled to Public Health Security benefits, including part of the cost of prescribed drugs, providing these are listed as reimbursable by the Ministry of Social Affairs. Most of the drugs approved for marketing in Denmark are included in the reimbursable list.

Patient cost-sharing is dependent primarily on the nature of the drug. For those drugs categorized by the program as of particularly great therapeutic value—such as antibiotics, antihypertensives, and antidiabetic agents—the patient is obliged to pay 25 percent of the cost. For those of less therapeutic value—such as analgesics, iron preparations, and estrogens—the patient must pay 50 percent of the cost. In cases in which the patient has insufficient funds to pay even a share of the costs, the charge may be paid from public funds under other social legislation.

Drug costs account for about 10.6 percent of total health care costs. On the average, Danes obtain roughly 6.9 prescriptions per capita per year.

Drug utilization review to detect irrational prescribing by physicians or drug misuse by patients is not attempted.

Danish physicians prescribe by brand name rather than by generic name in almost all cases. Generic substitution by a pharmacist is not allowed.

Drugs not approved in Denmark but on the market elsewhere may be imported by either a physician or a pharmacist for use with particular patients.

FRANCE[10]

National health insurance in France covers virtually the entire population and includes nearly any drug that may be prescribed. For hospitalized patients, drugs are covered on essentially the same basis as other elements of hospital care. An ambulatory patient, on the other hand, will generally pay the charge in full to the pharmacist and then apply to the health insurance system for reimbursement.

Recently, the program was modified so that, for prescriptions costing 30 French francs (about $7.20) or more, the patient may show his eligibility, pay the required co-payment, and then ask the pharmacist to apply to the health program for the remainder. This new modification has so far not been viewed with great enthusiasm by most pharmacists and has not yet been widely applied.

The co-payment depends on both the nature of the drug and the diagnosis:

- In the case of twenty-five specified illnesses, all of them serious chronic diseases, no patient cost-sharing is required.
- For certain drugs that are of demonstrated value but are available only at a relatively high price, such as certain anticancer agents, no cost-sharing is required.
- For so-called "minor drugs," such as prescribed vitamins, the patient's share is 60 percent of the retail price.
- For nearly all other prescription drugs, the patient's share is 30 percent of the retail price.

About 9 percent of all prescriptions are dispensed at the 60-percent cost-sharing level, 89 percent at the 30-percent level, and less than 2 percent without any cost-sharing.

Some private insurance companies may reimburse patients for that portion of drug costs not covered by the national program. Now under consideration by the government, however, is a proposal to limit coverage under any private plans to 95 percent of the cost.

Price controls are exerted by the government before a drug is put on the approved list for reimbursement. Both the price and the therapeutic value are considered. Manufacturers may be asked to disclose their costs for research, production, distribution, and the like. Most of them have been willing to comply, but some governmental officials have questioned the reliability of the company information.

The number of prescription drugs on the French market is difficult to assess. Some authorities put the number at about 4,500 different drugs in 11,000 different strengths and dosage forms; others estimate that there are about 7,800 drug products on the market. Approximately 4,300 individual drugs are on the approved reimbursement list for the health insurance program.

All drugs carry a fixed price set by the government for all of France. There is no need for a patient with a prescription to shop at various pharmacies to get the best price.

In 1970, drug costs represented 27 percent of all health care expenditures. By 1978, that figure had been dramatically reduced to 19 percent. The reduction was brought about not by any significant reductions in drug use or drug prices but by a cut in the Value Added Tax (VAT) and even more by a soaring increase in hospital costs. Physician charges under the national program, at least so far, have been more rigidly controlled by the government. Physicians have been visibly irritated by these controls, and in late 1979 they staged a brief but largely ineffective strike.

The so-called drug lag is of no concern to French physicians. In those few instances in which a drug has been approved elsewhere but not in France, a French physician may order it if he feels it is essential for certain individual patients. The special importation process, however, is described as so cumbersome and complex that it is used only infrequently.

French physicians practically never prescribe by generic name. They usually order by brand name, or if they want the patient to have such a drug as penicillin, they prescribe it as the penicillin product marketed by a specific company. Price competition between brand-name and generic-name products is close to nonexistent. As a result, the efforts of drug companies to influence the prescribing habits of French physicians by means of detailing or other methods is believed to be particularly intense—and effective.

In recent years, the government has demonstrated some interest in reducing program costs by stimulating the introduction of low-cost generics on the market and inducing physicians to prescribe them. Substitution of a generic for a brand-name product by the pharmacist is, so far, unthinkable.

Another recent development is the growing willingness of pharmaceutical companies to restrict the claims of effectiveness of their products and make more complete disclosure of hazards. During the last two years or so, the promotion of some of the most widely-used products in the standard French drug directories has come to be close to that presented to U.S. physicians in the *Physicians' Desk Reference*. Among the reasons offered for this change is pressure exerted by the press and, informally, by the government.

To achieve economies and perhaps simplify the work of pharmacists, most prescription drugs are now prepackaged by the manufacturer in the number of units most frequently prescribed—for example, a 10-day or 20-day supply. But if a physician wants a particular patient to have only a 5-day supply, and the smallest prepackaged container on the market holds a 10-day supply, the patient will receive —and the program will pay for—a 10-day supply.

Because of the traditional insistence on personal privacy in France, even the notion of maintaining or divulging patient prescription records or physician prescribing patterns—even divulging them to the governmental agency that must pay for the drugs—is considered scandalous. Drug utilization review is, in general, unknown. A pharmacist inclined to alert physician B that physician A is simultaneously prescribing the same drug for the same patient, or that a drug-drug reaction might result from two different prescriptions, would have to possess considerable courage to reveal the situation.

In the past few years, efforts have been made to provide informative package inserts with the drugs patients receive. Most of these patient package inserts, however, can apparently be understood only with great difficulty by laymen.

As in other European countries, the economic well-being of the French health insurance program—as well as other social programs— is being seriously questioned. "It is, of course, a matter of to whom one listens," says a Parisian physician, "but the talk of bankruptcy is in the air."

If unemployment should rise substantially, it is noted, contributions to the program by workers and employers would drop, with devastating effects. The apparent alternatives—to raise general taxes, reduce program benefits, or scrap the program entirely—are equally unpalatable.

GREECE[11]

The Greek social security system began in about 1937. Health insurance was included from the outset in one form or another, and the forms were and are numerous, often depending on the nature of one's employment. One type covers farmers and farm workers, another provides care for civil servants and their families, and still another covers workers in industry. Currently, about 92 percent of the population are beneficiaries.

Any prescription drug legally on the market is qualified for reimbursement.

Drug costs account for about 35 percent of total health care costs.

Patient cost-sharing varies widely among the different types of coverage. For example, some beneficiaries have no cost-sharing requirement, while others are obliged to pay from 10 to 15 percent. Civil servants obtain drugs for themselves at no cost, but they must pay from 20 to 25 percent of the cost of drugs for their families.

Government officials note that there is an odd attitude toward drugs in Greece. The word "pharmacy" comes from *pharmakon*, the Greek word for poison, yet Greek patients are as eager as those in other countries to obtain a prescription.

"Some Greek physicians," a Ministry of Social Services official observes, "prescribe the most expensive drug, and some patients demand it because they think the most costly product is the most effective. If the physician doesn't prescribe the most expensive drug, people will think he's not a very good doctor."

Dispensing by physicians is uncommon, and is allowed only in remote areas where there are few or no pharmacies.

No patient drug records are maintained as such in pharmacies. Instead, in most programs, each patient carries an individual Personal Health Care Record in which are listed each office visit to a physician, each home visit, each hospitalization, each diagnosis (usually given in code), and each prescription. For drugs, one copy of the prescription is kept by the patient, one is taken to the pharmacy, and one is forwarded to the insurance program. By consulting this record, a physician can quickly determine which drugs have previously been prescribed by other physicians for the patient. Program officials can likewise detect irrational prescriptions, such as chloramphenicol for "flu" or the common cold.

"If we find a patient has been misusing drugs, we can discuss the matter with him," a government expert says. "If he refuses to change his behavior, under the law we can take him to court. If we find a physician who frequently writes irrational prescriptions, we report him to the medical association for whatever education or sanctions may be necessary."

In most instances, a patient obtains drug information only from a physician. With some prepackaged products, an information sheet prepared by the manufacturer is attached. In certain cases, the physician may ask the pharmacist not to give the information to the patient. "These instructions," it is said, "are understandable by many patients but certainly not by all of them."

Drug prices, as in West Germany, are controlled at the pharmacy and wholesaler level but not at the manufacturer's level. Retail prices for each product are identical throughout the country.

As in other nations, it is the long-standing custom for physicians to prescribe by brand name. Pharmacists are not permitted to substitute a less expensive generic product.

To date, largely because of pressure from physicians and the drug industry, the government has not been able to find effective methods to control drug expenditures. Price is not considered when a new drug product is presented for approval. Under consideration, however, is a proposed formulary system under which needlessly expensive products would not be approved for reimbursement.

There is no apparent concern about any drug lag. A physician needing a nonapproved drug for an individual patient can get governmental approval to import it from any country in which it is available. Such importation, however, is very rare.

A major problem to drug experts in the government is the inadequate promotion carried out by some companies. "Some manufacturers," one of these experts notes, "have taken a responsible position, especially in limiting their claims of efficacy and in disclosing contraindications and possible adverse reactions. Others have not. These irresponsible firms—especially their detail men or 'drug visitors'— have given inadequate information to physicians. In such circumstances, we have the legal authority to stop their sales for six months, or twelve months, or permanently. We are just beginning to use this authority."

ITALY[12]

On January 1, 1980, the Italian health care system was changed from the earlier medical care (or Italian Blue Cross) insurance program to the new National Health Service program. The new approach was authorized by legislation enacted in December 1978.

The National Health Service is aimed at "caring for health through interventions covering prevention, care, and rehabilitation."

The provision of prescription drugs is made possible on an equal basis for all citizens, regardless of income, financial status, employment, age, sex, or type of illness.

For out-of-hospital patients, reimbursable prescription drug products are those listed in a national Therapeutic Handbook. These are classified in two categories:

- Class One drugs are "indispensable" products for the treatment of conditions that are viewed as clinically and socially important. Included are most antibiotics, anticancer agents, digitalis and other cardioglucosides, antihypertensives, beta-blockers for the treatment of angina and also hypertension, anticoagulants, insulin, and anti-parkinsonism agents. These are provided free of any charge to patients.

- Class Two drugs are those considered to be useful but not indispensable. Among them are vasodilators, antacids, "digestives," naturally occurring organ extracts, anti-anemia agents, and most sedatives. These require what would appear to be relatively modest patient cost-sharing.

For each prepackaged container of prescription drugs costing up to 1,000 lire (about $1.20) at the retail level, the patient must pay 200 lire (about $0.24). For each package with a price between 1,000 and 3,000 lire ($1.20 to $3.60), the patient must pay 400 lire (about $0.48). For each package with a price higher than 3,000 lire, the patient must pay 600 lire.

Patients are required to pay the complete cost of nonprescription or over-the-counter products.

In the case of hospitalized patients, reimbursable drugs are those listed in hospital handbooks authorized for each of the various regions of Italy. These are similar to the list for ambulatory patients but provide somewhat broader coverage.

Prices are government-controlled at every level—manufacturer, wholesaler, and pharmacist. Of the retail sales price, approximately 5.6 percent represents the Value Added Tax, 23.6 percent goes to the pharmacist, 7.5 percent goes to the wholesaler, and 63.2 percent goes to the manufacturer. The manufacturer's price is set by the Interministry Price Committee as determined by two factors, one based on an analysis of the cost of raw materials, direct labor, and packaging materials, and the other an all-inclusive lump sum covering all other manufacturing expenses, including indirect labor, administration, research, royalty payments, marketing, public relations, advertising, taxes, financing costs, and profits. An additional amount may be added in the case of innovative new products.

Some manufacturers have objected to the rigidity of the system, which they claim makes it unprofitable for them to manufacture some of their products. They have reacted by limiting the production of these drugs.

The National Health Service, a part of the Ministry of Health, is financed in part by employee and employer contributions and in part by general tax revenues.

Except for narcotics, Italian pharmacies do not keep patient drug profiles or records. There is no regular system of drug utilization review to detect irrational prescribing by physicians or drug misuse by patients.

The substitution of low-cost products for a prescribed brand-name product is not permitted in community pharmacies but is allowed in hospitals, where physicians usually order a drug by its generic name or by its active principle and where pharmacists purchase products on the basis of competitive bids.

There is no significant concern over any "drug lag," although there has been criticism of the time it takes to get some new products approved for use. For drugs not approved in Italy but available in another country, Italian physicians may import small supplies but only for experimental purposes and at their own risk.

Since 1927, the prepackaged containers of prescription drugs have included patient package inserts that are prepared by the manufacturer and approved by the government.

JAPAN[13]

The national health insurance system in Japan was basically established in 1922 and gradually expanded. Since 1961, it has been a nationwide program covering the entire population.

Employees are covered in one of four different programs: Health Insurance (company- and government-managed), Seaman's Insurance, Day Laborers' Health Insurance, and Mutual Aid Associations. Those who are self-employed, such as farmers, fishermen, and physicians, are covered under community health insurance, which is called simply National Health Insurance.

Prescription drugs are reimbursable if they are listed in the official Drug Tariff established by the Minister of Health and Welfare. Most prescription products on the market, however, are on the list. Most drugs are provided with a small cost-sharing charge to patients. The Drug Tariff likewise sets the sales price for each product.

A drug can be removed from the Drug Tariff list primarily if, on reevaluation, it is judged to lack substantial evidence of efficacy or its unanticipated side effects outweigh its therapeutic value.

Japanese physicians customarily prescribe by brand name rather than by generic name. Pharmacists are not permitted to substitute a generic version for a brand-name product.

The government is permitted to examine physician and patient records to detect irrational prescribing or patient misuse.

There are now estimated to be about 13,600 prescription drugs on the market, including all strengths and dosage forms. The use of such products represents approximately 17 percent of total health care costs.

In recent years, Japan has become a major producer of pharmaceutical products. Total production in 1978 was about 2,794 billion yen ($12.7 billion) at the manufacturer's level. Of this amount, approximately 84 percent represented prescription drugs. The use of over-the-counter preparations has been visibly diminishing over the past few years, especially as more effective—or supposedly more effective—prescription drugs are developed, and especially since the latter are available at low cost while OTCs require payment by the patient.

THE NETHERLANDS[14]

The provision of prescription drugs in the Netherlands is marked by several unusual features:

- Each patient must elect one pharmacy or dispensing physician from whom he or she will obtain all prescription drugs during the year.
- The number of such drugs on the market is one of the smallest among all industrialized nations.
- Drug expenditures represent only about 8 percent of total health costs in the nation.
- The annual number of outpatient prescriptions, about 4.5 per capita, is among the lowest in Europe.

About 70 percent of the population is covered for ordinary medical care by the general sickness insurance program, which generally provides free care for any needed medical service. An insured person must have prescriptions filled at the pharmacy or by the dispensing physician with which he is registered—the so-called capitation system. In 1978, some seven million persons covered by health insurance were registered with a pharmacist, and about 2.4 million were registered with a dispensing physician. There is no charge to the patient. The pharmacist or physician is paid an annual capitation fee for each patient on his list. The fee is negotiated annually. In addition, the pharmacist or physician is reimbursed for the acquisition cost of the drug plus an amount to cover the costs of doing business and to give the pharmacist or physician a reasonable profit.

In remote rural areas where pharmacists are scarce, physicians dispense drugs under the capitation system. Prices set for pharmacists and dispensing physicians are approximately the same. In many large pharmacies, much use is made of technical assistants, with one pharmacist supervising an average of seven technicians.

Most Dutch physicians are accustomed to prescribing drugs by their brand names, and pharmacists in community practice do not substitute even though less expensive generic-name products may be available. Nevertheless, there appears to be a growing proportion of community physicians who are now prescribing by generic name, and the authorization of pharmacists to substitute generically is currently under study. The situation in hospitals is, however, far different. Many hospital formularies list generic products which are kept in stock, and hospital pharmacists are allowed to dispense these in place of the brand-name products that were actually ordered.

There appears to be little or no concern among physicians, pharmacists, or the general public over possibly unequivalent generics. If there is even a suspicion that a bioavailability problem exists—or may exist—the product is simply not allowed on the market. Where it seems necessary, actual bioavailability studies are conducted on human subjects.

Dutch authorities are now investigating methods of providing more and better drug information to patients. Revising the present package inserts for physicians so that they would be more oriented to patient needs and more understandable to laymen is under consideration, as is the development of special patient package inserts or labels.

Dutch pharmacies do not keep patient drug records on file, and information on the drug-prescribing patterns of physicians or the drug-using patterns of patients is not divulged.

As in most other European countries, knowledgeable physicians and pharmacists are well aware that certain drugs may be available in some nations but not in others. In the Netherlands, this appears to be a matter of little or no concern. "If one drug is not available here in Holland," a health official says, "almost always a suitable alternative is available."

There appears to be general agreement among drug experts that most often the decision of a drug company to seek approval of a new drug or to market it in a particular country is influenced less by bureaucratic policies than by the economic facts of life. "Such decisions," it was stated, "may serve as an indication of how a company evaluates the relative toughness of the various regulatory agencies. If they think the agency in one country is tough, they're not going to turn in applications for borderline products. If they know from the record that we don't think highly of combination products, they probably won't ask us to approve a new combination."

In the Netherlands, and perhaps in other countries, there seems to be a concerted move to convince the public, and especially physicians, that national drug regulatory agencies are no longer necessary, and that each company would produce and promote the same drugs with the same quality regardless of governmental regulation. "That view," according to a top drug authority, "was badly damaged when we found how some of the companies in Europe and the United States were selling and promoting their products in developing countries which had no effective drug regulation."

Like all countries caught in the present economic pinch, the Netherlands is seeking to cut drug expenditures. A statement issued by the Dutch Ministry of Health in 1979 disclosed that consideration is being given to weighing the proposed price for any new drug to be introduced on the Dutch market. If the price for the Netherlands is higher than that in the country of origin and in other Common Market countries, the product may be turned down. "Products with unreasonably high prices should not be approved for reimbursement," said a Ministry spokesman. "There should be improved communications among physicians, pharmacists, and representatives of the sickness funds, especially on the matter of drug prices. This is particularly important in cases in which a less expensive generic may be available, or a different drug offering the same therapeutic effect at lower cost. . . . Efforts must be made by physicians, pharmacists, and the sickness funds to counter the intense promotion efforts of the industry. . . . Even patients must be made more aware of the economic factors of drug use. . . . If such voluntary steps are unsuccessful, some form of price control may be inevitable."

NEW ZEALAND[15]

Most prescription drugs in New Zealand are obtained at no cost to the patient. If, however, a drug is unduly expensive, or if a physician prescribes a brand-name product when a low-cost generic is available, there may be a "part-charge" to the patient. In some therapeutic groups, the most expensive products may also incur a part-charge.

When a drug is no longer under patent and is available under its generic name, New Zealand physicians sometimes prescribe generically. Pharmacists are not allowed to substitute for whatever products are prescribed.

Drugs are usually obtained from privately operated pharmacies but may be secured from outpatient pharmacies of the larger hospitals if patients are under the care of the hospital. In some isolated areas, drugs are dispensed by physicians. Certain drugs, because of their high cost, or because they are still considered to require surveillance in the postmarketing phase, or because they are not deemed to be the drugs of first choice, are available only from hospital pharmacies. Still other drugs can be obtained only on the prescription or recommendation of an appropriate specialist.

Pharmacists are reimbursed directly by the Department of Health, with the reimbursement based on the wholesale price of the product plus a dispensing fee and a container charge. Hospital pharmacies are funded out of the annual grant made to each hospital by the central government.

Drugs available free under the Social Security legislation are listed in a Drug Tariff that is amended three times a year. The list, together with its various restrictions on availability, is formulated by the Department of Health on the recommendations of the Pharmacology and Therapeutics Advisory Committee.

Maximum prices charged by manufacturers and wholesalers are controlled directly by the Department of Trade and Industry, but the Department of Health negotiates lower prices whenever possible. If prices are considered to be excessive and the manufacturer is unwilling to accept a lower price, the drug can be removed from the approved list, or it can carry an extra charge that must be paid by the patient. "Either action," it has been noted, "serves to lessen the drug's appeal to the public."

The fact that some drugs not available in New Zealand are on the market in other countries has aroused little interest among physicians, pharmacists, and the public. It is generally felt that if one drug cannot be obtained, there are alternatives which are readily available and clinically adequate.

Drug benefits represent about 11 to 12 percent of total government health expenditures.

NORWAY[16]

National health insurance in Norway, first implemented on a limited scale in 1911, has been expanded and now covers everyone in the country. A modest patient cost-sharing is involved in physician services, but hospital care is provided without cost.

For ambulatory patients, prescription drugs are available free of charge to those with specified long-term chronic diseases. These maintenance drugs, along with all drugs for hospitalized patients, represent about 60 percent of Norway's total drug bill.

The operations and even the exact location of each pharmacy are closely regulated by the government. The prices that a pharmacy charges—both product cost and dispensing cost—are set by the government. In the case of remote areas in which a small pharmacy would not have enough business to survive, a special tax subsidy is provided.

In the early 1960s, approximately 50 percent of all drugs in Norway were produced by Norwegian firms. In the period 1975-77, the figure was about 25 percent. Since 1930, the government has required that all drugs be demonstrated to be safe and effective. A drug can be banned if there are duplicate or comparable products already on the market, or if it possesses no clinical or economic advantages. Norway has one of the smallest lists of approved drugs for any country in Europe. Nevertheless, there is apparently no concern in Norway about any drug lag. If a physician requires for a particular patient a drug that is not on the market in Norway but is available in another country, he may obtain permission from the government to import a small quantity for the treatment of that patient.

Substitution of a low-cost generic-name product for a brand-name drug ordered by a physician is permitted.

Drug utilization review of the prescribing patterns of physicians or the possible drug misuse by patients is not undertaken.

When a new drug is approved and registered, its use may be restricted to physicians with special qualifications.

All advertising for prescription drugs and over-the-counter products must be approved in advance. Drug advertising through radio, television, theaters, or billboards is prohibited.

Prescription drugs costs represent about 6 percent of total health costs in the nation. Government officials estimate that the annual use of these drugs is about 3.5 prescriptions per capita.

Price control may be exercised by the National Center for Medicinal Products Control at the time a product is registered or at any time thereafter, especially when substantial differences become apparent between the price of one product and that of a comparable product in Norway, or between the price of the product in Norway and that of the same product in other countries.

SWEDEN[17]

Sweden has a long tradition, going back to the seventeenth century, of providing medical care by government-employed physicians.

Currently, the overwhelming majority of physicians are employed by the government.

Uniquely, since 1971, all pharmacies in the country are owned, controlled, and operated by a government-dominated corporation, Apoteksbolaget, the National Corporation of Swedish Pharmacies.

National health insurance was established in 1955. All citizens in Sweden are covered, as are noncitizens who live and work there.

Prescription drugs are covered under the program and are supplied at pharmacies free or at reduced prices. Those provided without charge are drugs needed by patients with any one of about twenty specified serious chronic diseases. In the case of hospital inpatients, drugs are provided at no cost.

For all other drugs, a patient is required to pay in full for the first 10 Swedish kroner (about $2.30) and then 50 percent of any amount between 10 and 40 Skr. Thus, the maximum co-payment for any prescription order is 25 Skr (about $5.75). This cost-sharing arrangement holds not only for a single prescription but also for a prescription order—that is, all prescriptions written by the same physician for the same patient at the same time. Accordingly, if a physician writes an order for one, or five, or ten prescription drugs at the same time for the same patient, the maximum cost-sharing by the patient is still only 25 Skr.

In 1978, the total cost of the drug benefits in Sweden was roughly 1,750 million Skr ($400 million), accounting for approximately 10 percent of total health care costs. Of this amount, about half was for drugs imported from other countries. Of the domestic production, roughly 25 percent was for drugs produced by government-owned firms.

The output by these government-owned firms may appear to be relatively trivial. However, at least some representatives of privately-owned companies, both foreign and domestic, see in these firms an everpresent threat. "At any time the Swedish government feels our prices on drugs no longer under patent are too high," says a Swiss company official, "they can expand the production in their own factories, reduce prices, and force us out of the Swedish market."

At the moment, Swedish officials have given no indication that the government intends to make use of these potential powers. They have stressed the need for "reasonable" rather than "lowest" prices, and they clearly recognize the need for drug companies to make reasonable profits in order to support future research.

The number of available products has been held down by a rigid approval procedure. A proposed new product is studied first for safety and efficacy by experts of the National Board of Health and Welfare. If the Board endorses the product as safe and effective, the company must then enter into negotiations with Apoteksbolaget to agree on a "reasonable" price which will be set nationwide for all pharmacies.

If Apoteksbolaget suspects that the proposed price is unjustifiably high, it may ask the manufacturer to open its books for inspection. The price proposed for Sweden may be compared with prices in other countries in which the same drug is already being marketed.

"If the proposed product has no apparent advantages—if it is a 'me-too' drug that is no safer, no more effective, and no less expensive than products that can be used for the same purpose," says an Apoteksbolaget official, "we can turn it down simply on the grounds that we don't need it."

In the case of a breakthrough drug, one for which no suitable alternative is known, real price negotiations are essentially impossible. The company's proposed price must be accepted.

If the sales of a new product, and thus the profits, turn out to be substantially more or less than anticipated, the negotiations may be reopened and the price changed accordingly. In the case of a drug for which extremely small sales can be foreseen—usually a drug for use only in the treatment of a rare disease—the company may be allowed to charge higher than normal prices.

Swedish physicians are well aware that there are many hundreds or even thousands of drugs being used elsewhere that are not normally available in Sweden. "This drug lag has caused no problem for us or our patients," one physician claims. "Of course, it may have caused some problems for the drug industry." If a physician feels that a drug not approved for regular marketing in Sweden is needed for a particular patient, there are provisions to have the product specially imported. However, these provisions are rarely used.

In the twenty-odd counties of Sweden, there are now approximately one hundred drug committees, mainly hospital-based. From the drugs approved by the National Board of Health and Welfare and marketed through Apoteksbolaget, the committees can select the products—including low-cost generics—to be listed in their regional formularies.

A pharmacist may not substitute a generic for a brand-name product without prescriber approval, but he may request such approval or suggest an alternative product.

In recent years, the Apoteksbolaget pharmacies have been working in close cooperation with drug committees and individual physicians to improve drug therapy in general. Apoteksbolaget itself had a shaky start, with warnings that it would greatly increase drug prices and expenditures and act as a drain on government funds. For the first year or two of its operations, there were problems. Because of the insurance provisions, some physicians seemed to be overly enthusiastic about prescribing vitamins, especially in the form of expensive products. Some prescribed many drugs on a single prescription order, requiring the patient to make only a single co-payment. Since, then, however, such difficulties have largely disappeared. Drug prices have risen, but far less rapidly than prices in general. The program is apparently solvent.

A new computer network, which analyzes drug use by sex and age of patient, now links most Swedish pharmacies, but it reveals nothing about the drugs prescribed by an individual physician or those dispensed to an individual patient. By strict Swedish law, such data cannot be disclosed or even entered into the computer. In Sweden, sensitivity toward matters of personal privacy is believed to be as great as in any other country in the world. As a result, drug utilization review as applied to individual physicians or patients is almost unknown. If, however, a physician is believed to be engaged in irrational prescribing—especially if a patient is supposedly injured by such a practice —the National Board may receive complaints from the patient, the patient's relatives, or another physician, and the appropriate local drug committee may be asked to investigate and recommend corrective action.

Apoteksbolaget has already developed an impressive series of pamphlets for patients on the indications, hazards, potential side effects, and proper use of selected groups of drug products, and these pamphlets are now being distributed to the public in Swedish pharmacies. Pharmacists are encouraged to discuss each prescription with individual patients in order to encourage the most appropriate use of drugs, but without causing needless worry or weakening the patient's confidence in his physician. Under a new policy recently adopted by the organization, work has begun on the preparation of special patient information sheets for selected individual drugs, especially those most likely to be misused. The information is to be prepared independently, without "guidance" from industry.

At its inception, the Apoteksbolaget system was denounced as completely socialistic. To an outsider, it now appears to be less socialistic than Swedish—streamlined, efficient, and effective. Whether such a system could be successfully transplanted to any other country is, of course, impossible to predict.

SWITZERLAND[18]

Health insurance is the oldest of all Swiss social security programs, having begun around 1912. Approximately 95 percent of the population is covered.

Although the federal government has the authority to establish a national health system, no such program exists. Instead, the authority has been delegated to the twenty-three cantons into which Switzerland is divided. In five of these cantons, health insurance is not required, while in the others it is more or less compulsory. In general, the compulsory aspects apply particularly to persons with low incomes. Federal law requires that every citizen be eligible for coverage, and it provides regulations assuring at least a minimum of protection.

There are now more than 550 sickness funds operating in the country. To receive a government subsidy, each fund must meet minimal coverage requirements, including the provision of physician services, hospitalization, drugs, and a daily sickness allowance during the period of disability. Beneficiary contributions and the scope of benefits may vary widely from fund to fund.

There is a two-tier system for drug approval, one for general marketing and one for listing on the health insurance formulary. For products on the insurance plan list, the funds pay 90 percent of the cost. For unlisted drugs that are otherwise approved for marketing, many funds pay as much as 50 percent. The pharmacist is reimbursed in full by the sickness fund, which then calls on the patient for the appropriate share of the cost.

Drugs account for roughly 22 percent of total health care costs in the nation.

Swiss physicians rarely prescribe drugs by their generic name, and pharmacists are not allowed to substitute a low-cost generic for a brand-name product.

There are no price controls as such, but expenditures are controlled by means of the formulary listing system. If a price appears to be too high, the manufacturer may be asked for an explanation. If the explanation is inadequate and the price is judged to be unjustifiably high, the product may be kept off the formulary list. The judgment is usually based on the normal costs of other brands of similar drugs already on the list.

There are about 8,900 prescription drugs (in all strengths and dosage forms) on the market. Although an unapproved drug may not be imported for use on any individual patient, Swiss physicians do not seem to be particularly concerned by any drug lag.

UNITED KINGDOM[19]

For most patients in the United Kingdom, a co-payment of £0.70 (about $1.40)—raised from £0.45 in April 1980—is required. There is no cost-sharing, however, in the case of prescriptions for children below the age of 16, expectant or nursing mothers, the elderly, or persons with certain specified diseases.

Pharmacists are paid by the National Health Service according to the provisions of the Drug Tariff. Prices are based on current whole-sale prices agreed upon by the government and the pharmacists' national association. Payments cover the wholesale cost of drugs, an "on-cost" allowance, a container allowance, and a professional fee.

In isolated rural areas, physicians may dispense their own drugs. Remuneration procedures usually follow a capitation approach or the Drug Tariff as a basis for determining the amount to be paid.

Throughout the United Kingdom, physician prescribing costs are surveyed by the government. If the prescribing costs of a physician substantially exceed the average in his area, he may be asked for an explanation by the Department of Health, and penalties may be levied. In general, the prescribing patterns of an individual physician are examined only for inordinately high expenditures.

The Department of Health also monitors pricing by manufacturers, along with their financial statements, through the Pharmaceutical Price Regulation Scheme. If the Department considers a company's profits to be excessive, it negotiates price changes.

British physicians have been urged by the government to prescribe by generic name, and generic prescribing is already appreciable and slowly increasing. At the same time, patients—if only to save their own money—have been urged to purchase low-cost over-the-counter preparations for such common conditions as coughs and colds, headaches, indigestion, and constipation. Often, it is noted, these non-prescription products will cost the patient less than would the co-payment required to obtain a "free" prescription drug.

In the United Kingdom, the impact of any drug lag has been minimized by provisions enabling a physician to import and administer an unapproved or unlicensed drug from another country if he certifies that the product is to be used for a particular named patient. The drug lag is therefore not a source of any serious frustration.

In community pharmacies providing pharmaceutical services under contract with the government, the pharmacist may not substitute a generic product for a brand-name drug actually prescribed. If, however, the physician orders a drug by its generic name, the pharmacist may fill it with any version, brand-name or generic, but the pharmacist will be paid on the basis of the least expensive preparation available.

National Health Service hospitals purchase their drugs on competitive bid and normally select the least expensive product, provided that the quality of the preparation and the reliability of supply are acceptable. The lowest price may in fact be offered by a brand-name rather than a generic-name manufacturer. The product that is selected will be the only one used in the hospital, and will be substituted where this is appropriate for any particular brand ordered by a physician. It will be known in the hospital only by its generic name. All patient records refer only to the generic name of prescribed drugs.

Drug costs are estimated to account for about 10 percent of the nation's total health care costs.

WEST GERMANY[20]

First established in 1891, the statutory health care delivery system in West Germany provides mandatory coverage—including drug coverage—under some 1,500 sickness funds. More than 92 percent of the population is now covered. Others may obtain coverage through private insurance companies.

A co-insurance feature was involved until recently, with a patient required to pay about 20 percent of the cost for each prescription, up to a maximum of 2.50 Deutschmarks (about $1.43). Since mid-1977, the cost-sharing amount has been a flat $1.00 DM ($0.57) co-payment per prescription. This requirement may be waived for persons living on pensions or for so-called hardship cases, such as those requiring prolonged or lifelong drug therapy.

Until recently, prices and markups were set by the government, but only at the pharmacy level. Such price controls have now been extended to wholesalers. Only the drug manufacturers are still allowed to set any prices they like, thanks to the government's belief that company prices will be kept down to reasonable levels by the "ordinary competitive forces in the marketplace."

Observers seem to agree that the German drug industry, either alone or as part of the even larger chemical industry—second in size only to the German steel industry—continues to wield profound influence on how drugs are prescribed, used, and priced. The number of drugs available in Germany is one of the largest in any country, probably in excess of 15,000, not including thousands of different prescribed herbal teas and "single-pharmacy specialties."

While most American physicians manage the drug therapy of most of their patients with perhaps eighty or ninety different drugs, many German physicians may prescribe as many as three hundred in their practice.

In the various sickness fund programs, drug costs are estimated to represent approximately 15 percent of the nation's total health care costs.

In order to reduce program costs, pharmacies are now required to give a 5-percent discount—recently reduced from 7 percent—on all prescription drugs for program beneficiaries.

Not all drugs on the market are approved for reimbursement, but most of them are. The reimbursement list is established, and changed as necessary, by representatives of government, medicine, pharmacy, the sickness funds, and the drug industry.

German physicians are not accustomed to prescribing generically, and pharmacists may not substitute a generic for a brand-name product. As one expert put it, "The whole matter of generics has been unemphasized here. There is no strong consumer or taxpayer group demanding the use of low-cost drugs."

Under the law, the sickness funds are allowed to review prescriptions to see if they are "economically justifiable." Physicians found to be prescribing more prescriptions and more expensive prescriptions than their peers may be asked for an explanation. Apparently, however, there is little or no formal utilization review on purely clinical grounds, such as determining when a prescribed drug was not actually justified by the diagnosis, or if any drug was indicated in the first place.

Some German pharmacists have expressed strong feelings that they are treated by physicians and the government as second-class professionals. Many complain that they are caught in an increasingly serious financial bind, and some are predicting that a growing number of pharmacies will be forced out of business. They likewise declare that they are unable to take advantage of their knowledge of drugs; they are rarely asked for consultation by physicians, and their advice on drugs is largely ignored. It is not customary for pharmacists to advise patients, and any advice they may offer is usually disregarded.

One major problem in the German program has been the custom

of manufacturers to distribute their prepackaged drug products in inexplicably large quantities. Thus, a patient needing only a 5-day supply of a particular drug is obliged to take a 20-day supply—and the program is obliged to pay for it—because the smallest prepackage contains a 20-day supply. Or a physician may prescribe an enormous supply—carrying only a 1 DM co-payment—rather than a small supply with the possibility of ordering refills, each with a 1 DM co-payment, simply to save money for the patient. "As a result of this and other factors," it has been claimed, "the loss to the sickness funds for drugs that are not used or are thrown out costs two billion Deutschmarks a year." Government officials are currently planning to implement a new law which will require manufacturers to prepackage their products in smaller numbers of tablets or capsules.

With the large number of drugs now on the German market, there is no evident drug lag problem. Furthermore, under the present law, if a physician believes that a drug which is not available in Germany (of which there are a few, including some on the market in the United States!) is needed for a particular patient, it can be imported from another country. This provision of the law is apparently only rarely applied.

For this chapter, no attempt was made to examine the drug reimbursement programs and other aspects of drug use in Eastern Europe. Such a study has been undertaken by Albert I. Wertheimer in eight nations: Bulgaria, Czechoslovakia, East Germany, Hungary, Poland, Romania, the Soviet Union, and Yugoslavia.[21]

No. 11 The American Experience

Although the United States has not yet mounted a full-scale program of national health insurance, this country is not without experience in paying for health care, including prescription drugs, with tax funds. Some of these programs cover as many beneficiaries as the populations of entire nations which have their own health insurance schemes.

This chapter presents brief descriptions of a few selected American drug insurance systems, governmental and private. Most of these have functioned over the past years or decades with reasonable success and a minimum of controversy.

Particular attention should be paid to two governmental programs, Medicare for the elderly and Medicaid for the economically disadvantaged. Most aspects of Medicare have worked without serious dispute. In contrast, most aspects of the Medicaid programs have been under constant attack. Although both Medicare and Medicaid have unquestionably provided quicker and easier access to good medical care for the elderly, the disabled, and the poor, this accomplishment has not met with universal approval.

Especially where the poor are concerned, it is strongly felt in some circles that these individuals are not deserving of governmental support. The poor, some critics claim, are pushy; they overcrowd physicians' waiting rooms; they take up too many hospital beds; they demand too many prescriptions; they abuse the program; they are malingerers; they are malodorous; they do not pay taxes; and—the most grievous sin of all—they do not display proper gratitude.

Such attitudes—which, incidentally, may also be observed currently in other countries—represent a throwback to the not-too-distant days when the poor were supposedly entitled to only second-class health care, to charity, and to the demeaning, dignity-stripping treatments provided (when proper gratitude was shown) by county clinics and hospitals.

We strongly believe that it is not our responsibility to determine if or how poverty should be punished. Rather, we are concerned with how health care can be best delivered—to everyone.

VETERANS ADMINISTRATION[1]

As part of its program of providing health care to veterans, the Veterans Administration furnishes drugs and medical supplies to eligible beneficiaries, now numbering more than twenty-nine million.

Drugs are supplied at no cost to patients hospitalized in a VA facility. For outpatients, three major procedures are utilized: (1) the patient may receive a prescription from a VA staff physician and have the drug dispensed by a VA pharmacy; (2) he may receive the prescription from a local or hometown non-VA physician and have it filled by a VA pharmacy, directly or by mail; or (3) he may obtain the prescription from a local non-VA physician and have it filled by a local non-VA pharmacy. Even if a local pharmacy is used, there is no cost-sharing by the patient. The pharmacy is reimbursed directly by the VA, on a "usual and customary charge" basis.

A Central Purchasing Program buys 80 percent of the drugs used by VA pharmacies. These purchases are made when the volume purchase price represents a saving of more than 15 percent over local wholesale prices.

Each VA medical facility develops its own formulary, using the American Hospital Formulary Service as a basis. The formularies are developed individually by the Therapeutic Agents and Pharmacy Review Committee of each facility. The committee includes representatives of the medical staff and the nursing service, together with the chief pharmacist and the supply officer. In addition to serving as a means of inventory control, the formulary provides the medical staff with a reasonable range of medications with which to implement rational drug therapy.

Utilization review is undertaken both to control costs and to minimize irrational prescribing.

VA policies generally allow pharmacists to substitute a generic version for a prescribed brand-name product. According to 1978 figures, about 34 percent of prescriptions dispensed call for a generic product—nearly three times the rate for community pharmacies.

Prescriptions for acute conditions are usually limited to a 30-day supply. For approved maintenance drugs, a 90-day supply may be provided.

CHAMPUS[2]

Since 1966, outpatient drug coverage has been provided by the Civilian Health and Medical Program of the Uniformed Services (CHAMPUS). Participation is available for spouses and children of members of the uniformed services, and for retired members, with their families, of those services. Approximately seven million persons are enrolled in the program.

Outpatient pharmaceutical services are limited to drugs available only on prescription, together with insulin and compounded drugs. Prescriptions may be filled by any licensed pharmacy.

Reimbursement is usually made to the patient or family after a specified annual deductible—$50 per person or $100 per family—has been reached. In addition, a co-payment or co-insurance charge must be paid by the patient to the pharmacy at the time of purchase. In a few cases, the vendor submits the bills and is reimbursed directly.

No formulary is employed, and there is no requirement to prescribe or dispense generic products, but the pharmacy is required to dispense the least expensive product consistent with the physician's orders. Generic substitution by the pharmacist is permitted. The quantity on any single prescription is limited to a 100-day supply. Claims surveillance is conducted to detect and control program abuse and overutilization, but not to monitor for other kinds of irrational prescribing.

For bills submitted directly by a pharmacy, reimbursement is limited to the acquisition cost plus a fixed dispensing fee. For bills submitted by a patient, reimbursement is based on "usual and customary" charges.

The administration of the drug benefits program is handled by nine carriers, including Blue Cross, Blue Shield, and one commercial insurance carrier.

INDIAN HEALTH SERVICE[3]

The Indian Health Service (IHS), part of the U.S. Public Health Service, provides pharmacy services to about 760,000 beneficiaries at 48 hospitals, 101 health centers, and more than 1,000 part-time clinics which the IHS operates. Where there is no IHS facility, the service has contracts with 230 community pharmacies in sixteen states. These contract pharmacies will fill prescriptions written by contract physicians who see patients in their own offices. The pharmacy contracts are negotiated annually through the nine IHS area offices.

In the case of non-IHS pharmacies, reimbursement for drugs is based on the acquisition cost plus a professional fee which ranged between $2.35 and $2.95 in 1979. No patient cost-sharing was required. The pharmacy contracts stipulate that the government cannot be charged more than is the general public for any drug dispensed. IHS pharmacists review all prescription bills for price to make sure that each contract pharmacy is in compliance with the contract. IHS pharmacists likewise list each contract pharmacy prescription in the patient's IHS medical record so that this document will reflect a complete account of the patient's drug treatment.

As a relatively recent development, the IHS contract with pharmacies states that the government will not pay more than the maximum cost for drugs shown in HEW's Maximum Allowable Cost (MAC) program listing, unless the physician states in writing that an unlisted brand-name product is needed by a particular patient for clinical reasons.

IHS encourages but does not require that generic-name products be dispensed by contract pharmacies. In IHS hospitals and clinics, all drugs are dispensed by generic name.

Each IHS hospital and health center has a Pharmacy and Therapeutics Committee and uses a formulary. The formulary is followed except when nonformulary drugs are medically indicated.

IHS pharmacists review prescriptions and drug orders for the appropriateness of the prescribed drug, the dosage, the dosage schedule, and the possibility of adverse effects. If there is a question involving any of these points, the pharmacist will discuss the problem with the prescriber before the drug is dispensed or administered. IHS pharmacists have immediate access to a patient's health record. They also have private offices for patient-pharmacist consultation and counseling, as well as for some forms of primary care.

As part of this program, IHS pharmacists—working under the

general supervision of a physician—are given the responsibility for providing primary care to patients with minor acute diseases and to some who are under long-term drug therapy, such as those with stabilized diabetes, mild hypertension, and pernicious anemia. In fiscal year 1979, pharmacists provided this kind of care in 395,000 patient visits, representing more than 18 percent of all visits to IHS facilities. This new use of trained pharmacists has not only helped to make up for some of the shortages of physicians and saved federal funds, but it has given patients easier and faster access to the health care system.

MEDICARE[4]

Since 1966, under Title XVIII of the Social Security Act, Medicare beneficiaries—mainly those aged 65 or more—have been entitled to receive hospital care, including the provision of necessary drugs while they are inpatients.

Under a special provision, beneficiaries can also obtain physician care out of the hospital by paying a quarterly premium, an annual deductible (now $60), and a percentage of the bill (now 20 percent), but outpatient drugs are not covered. For these drugs, patients must pay out of their own pockets.

Unlike the Medicaid programs, which are joint state-federal operations, Medicare is entirely a federal program. In most instances, details of drug coverage are determined by each hospital, using its own formulary and its own pricing structure. Hospitals bill Medicare for drugs on the basis of costs.

In 1978, the hospital portion of Medicare expenditures was about $18 billion. Of this, an estimated 8 to 10 percent represented the cost of "drugs and drug sundries" and drug services.

Almost since its inception, the Medicare program has been criticized for its lack of coverage of out-of-hospital drugs. The elderly, it has been pointed out, comprise only about 11 percent of the population, but they account for roughly 25 percent of prescription drug costs.[5] At the same time, the elderly are among the least able to meet these costs. Usually they have limited incomes, minimal savings, and little or no coverage under other health insurance policies unless they can qualify for Medicaid coverage as medically indigent (see below). In some cases, this problem has been so acute that a patient will be hospitalized—at perhaps $200 or more a day—merely to obtain costly drugs covered under Medicare.

During the past few years, attention has been drawn to another flaw. Under the existing law, outpatients cannot be covered for vaccines or other preventive agents. With the recent introduction of a new vaccine to prevent pneumococcal pneumonia—always a particular menace for the elderly—efforts are under way to reappraise the Medicare law and perhaps to make appropriate changes.[6]

MEDICAID[7]

Under Title XIX of the Social Security Act, all states are permitted—but not required—to make reimbursements for outpatient prescription drugs provided to patients receiving welfare benefits or legally defined as medically needy—that is, those who are aged, blind, or disabled, and who fit into the welfare category, but who, for whatever reason, are not receiving cash assistance. All but three states have now implemented this approach. Alaska and Wyoming have adopted Medicaid programs which do not cover drugs. Arizona, after long court battles, has no Medicaid program at all.

Unlike Medicare, Medicaid is a joint program, with costs shared between each state and the federal government.

In general, nearly all prescription drugs required for the treatment of hospitalized Medicaid patients are covered, with the details of the formulary and the price usually determined by the individual hospital. For Medicaid outpatients, drug benefits may vary widely from state to state, and, even within the same state, from month to month. The formulary of drugs approved for reimbursement may be altered depending on the state of medicine, the state of pharmacy, and the state of the budget. In many cases, state budgetary restrictions have brought about drastic slashes in the drug list.

The federal government bases its share of the reimbursement on whichever of the following is the lowest:

- The Maximum Allowable Cost (MAC) set for certain multiple-source products no longer under patent or available from two or more firms under a licensing arrangement, plus a "reasonable fee."
- The estimated acquisition cost plus a "reasonable fee."
- The "usual and customary" charge to the public.

The matter of the "reasonable fee," set by each state, has been a target for particular criticism. Many if not most pharmacists charge that it is entirely unreasonable.[8] The fee was set too low in the first place, they insist, and has not been increased to make up for the rising costs of doing business. In some states, many pharmacists have flatly refused to participate in the program, sending their potential Medicaid customers to other pharmacies. Still other pharmacists have grudgingly accepted the state fee but have compensated for this by raising their prices to the general public.

Since about 1970, medical care costs under Medicaid have been taking an increasing portion of all public assistance funds. In that year, all Medicaid programs accounted for $4.3 billion, or 39.7 percent of all public assistance funds, of which nearly $0.4 billion went for drugs dispensed mainly by community pharmacies. Since then, total Medicaid expenses have risen steadily to $14.2 billion in 1976, $16.3 billion in 1977, and $18.1 billion in 1978. It is estimated that total Medicaid costs in 1978 exceeded 58 percent of all public assistance program expenditures. At the same time, Medicaid drug costs slowly increased to about $1.1 billion in 1978, but they represented a slowly decreasing percentage of all health care costs—in 1978, about 6 percent.[9]

While the Medicare program has been subject to moderate criticism, primarily on the grounds of permitting needless or needlessly prolonged hospitalization and unnecessary surgery, the Medicaid programs in the various states have been under far more heated attack. There have been denunciations of excessive hospitalization. Physicians have been accused of operating "Medicaid mills" that provide unnecessary services or charge for office care, laboratory tests, or X-ray studies that were never performed. Pharmacists have been accused of engaging in fraudulent "prescription splitting," dividing a large prescription into five or six small ones and then charging the program for five or six dispensing fees. In many states, investigations have revealed that ineligible patients were being treated under Medicaid at the expense of the taxpayers.

BLUE CROSS AND BLUE SHIELD[10]

In the United States, Blue Cross and Blue Shield—along with a large number of private insurance companies—offer a wide assortment of third-party programs for the coverage of out-of-hospital prescription drug expenditures. Unlike government programs, these private plans can usually provide whatever coverage an employed group —or, in some cases, an individual beneficiary—desires. As one union official put it, "We tell them what kind of coverage we want, and they tell us how much we'll have to pay in premiums."

Among the various Blue Cross and Blue Shield plans offered in different parts of the country, details of the basic program may be modified to fit the needs of the group which it serves in the community. Some plans exclude certain products, such as oral contraceptives, but these may be obtained on a special rider. Medical devices are usually excluded, as are over-the-counter products.

A subscriber is free to choose any "participating pharmacy," where he will pay a nominal co-payment if one is required. The pharmacy is usually reimbursed for the actual acquisition cost plus a dispensing fee established by the plan, less whatever co-payment is made by the patient. If the prescription is filled at a nonparticipating pharmacy, the patient must pay in cash at the time he receives the prescription, and he is later reimbursed for 75 percent of the usual and customary charge.

Most programs will cover not more than a 34-day supply of any prescribed medication except for specified chronic conditions in which a 100-unit quantity may be allowed. A few drugs may be supplied in 200-unit quantities. Most plans do not use a formulary except in the case of these long-term maintenance drugs.

In general, generic prescribing by the physician and generic selection by the pharmacist are not required, encouraged, or discouraged.

Depending on the plan, patient cost-sharing may include a co-payment of up to $3.00 per prescription, co-insurance of up to 20 percent, or an annual deductible of up to $25.00 per person.

Some plans now involve some form of utilization review, with the sophistication of this surveillance varying with the size, location, and benefits offered.

Illustrative of the above-described national policies are the details of programs administered by Blue Shield of California, involving some 520,000 beneficiaries. Patient cost-sharing includes co-payment and co-insurance but no annual deductible. Pharmacists are authorized to substitute a low-cost generic product where this is permitted or required by state law.

In general, physicians, pharmacists, and patients have found it comfortable to live with these and similar third-party programs. Physicians are free to prescribe virtually any drug they believe is needed by their patients. Although pharmacists may be irked by some features of the reimbursement formula, they seem to find it easier to work with these private programs than with such a government program as Medicaid, which is notoriously slow to pay and is marked by low dispensing fees. Patients—most of them actively employed workers—can cope with the cost-sharing provisions. The drug industry apparently approves the lack of restrictive formularies.

Perhaps the most serious criticism leveled by outsiders against

Blue Cross, Blue Shield, and private insurance company programs is
that they have few if any built-in incentives to contain costs. Utilization review is rarely applied to detect or prevent irrational prescribing.
If there is irrational prescribing, especially overutilization or the use
of needlessly expensive drugs, the third-party carrier will simply raise
the premium rates. In some states, however, there are growing complaints from pharmacists that the fees are too low—lower, in fact,
than Medicaid fees.

PUGET SOUND[11]

A particularly innovative Health Maintenance Organization,
Group Health Cooperative of Puget Sound, was organized in Seattle,
Washington, in 1947 to provide its members with a wide assortment
of health services. The provision of prescription drugs was included
from the start. A consumer-owned and operated organization, it now
includes about 280,000 beneficiaries.

The cooperative consists of ten primary clinics, each with a full
range of services, located over a 90-mile span, together with two hospitals with about 360 beds, and a small extended care facility. There
are 250 prescribers on the staff; most are primary care professionals.

To a considerable extent, officials say, its drug program represents the out-of-hospital version of an in-hospital service. Prescription
costs are about half of those in community pharmacies.

Within the plan, there is freedom of choice of physician. A closed
formulary is used which includes only about 600 to 700 prescription
drugs in a total of 2,600 strengths and dosage forms. Tranquilizers,
mental illness drugs, and dietary supplements are not covered. Neither
are anti-TB drugs, which are provided by the state. Infrequently, a
staff physician will order a nonformulary product needed for a particular patient. Prescriptions are filled only in the group's own pharmacies.

Pharmacists are required to substitute low-cost generic products
when these are available on the market.

There is no co-payment, co-insurance, or annual deductible. The
premium for drugs is part of the monthly premium paid by each member for full health care.

The closed formulary is used to control both the quality and the
cost of drugs. Major savings are also made possible by the direct purchase of drugs in large quantities and by using competitive bidding.
All listed drugs are evaluated and approved by the Pharmacy and
Therapeutics Committee, composed of members of the medical and

pharmacy staffs. Drugs of similar clinical characteristics are periodically reviewed, and inferior products are removed from the formulary.

The group's computer system, described in a previous chapter (see Chapter 8, above), is one of the most advanced in any pharmacy operation. It is used not only to process prescriptions, provide inventory control, and automatically warn of possible allergic or drug interaction hazards, but also to provide data essential for drug utilization review. This review, voluntary and confidential, is not based on any rigidly preset criteria. No prescription is branded as "right" or "wrong." Instead, each physician is shown a monthly record of his own prescribing pattern and enabled to compare it with the patterns of his peers. No one else is permitted to view the data for an individual physician. If unusual patterns are noted by any means, no punitive action is taken. Pharmacists, however, may discuss with the physician what seem to be irrational prescriptions.

KAISER (CALIFORNIA) [12]

Originating during the 1930s to provide care for a construction crew building the Los Angeles aqueduct in the Southern California desert, the Kaiser-Permanente medical care program was one of the first of the direct-care prepaid group practice health programs known today as Health Maintenance Organizations. Kaiser-Permanente provides care to 3.7 million members in six states: California, Oregon, Washington, Hawaii, Ohio, and Colorado. Most of the members are enrolled through employed groups. In Texas, the Kaiser/Prudential Health Plan operates as a joint endeavor between Kaiser-Permanente and the Prudential Insurance Company of America.

Various types of standard coverages are offered, each with a different prepaid rate. Optional benefits are also available, and, depending on the particular type of benefits selected, out-of-hospital drugs may be provided with a minimal co-payment or no charge at all. Drugs prescribed for hospital inpatients are included in all standard coverages.

Various options of outpatient prepaid prescription drug plans are available in the Northern California and Southern California regions of the Kaiser-Permanente program. These options are representative of prepaid prescription drug plans offered in the other Kaiser program regions. As of January 1, 1979, approximately 1,065,000 members in the Northern California region and 701,000 members in the Southern California region were covered under prepaid prescription drug programs.

In the Northern California region, five options are available: one provides drugs for which a prescription is required by law (and such accessories as syringes and needles for insulin injections) at the wholesale price, with no limit on the number of days' supply; another provides benefits at half the wholesale price, with no limit on the size of the prescription; a third provides up to a 34-day supply (or the smallest prepackaged size), with a $1.00 co-payment; a fourth provides the same benefits for up to a 100-day supply; and a fifth requires no co-payment unless the prescription exceeds *both* a 100-day supply and the smallest prepackaged size.

In the Southern California region, five different coverages are available: one provides up to a 100-day supply of drugs without any co-payment; another provides up to a 100-day supply with a $1.00 co-payment; a third provides up to a 100-day supply at half the wholesale price; a fourth provides up to a 100-day supply with a $2.50 co-payment; and a fifth provides a special program covering both prescription and nonprescription drugs at no charge to the patient.

The greater the benefits incorporated in the drug coverage and the less the cost-sharing by the patient, the higher are the monthly rates paid by health plan members or employers.

None of the California programs involve the use of a restrictive formulary. Since the inception of the drug coverage programs, pharmacists in the program pharmacies have been authorized to substitute lower-cost generic products unless the prescriber bans substitution for a particular prescription.

No formal program of drug utilization review has been instituted. A system of automatic data processing is in effect, but is now used only for inventory control.

To control costs, the Kaiser-Permanente program pharmacies buy drug products wherever possible on competitive bids.

UNITED AUTO WORKERS[13]

In 1967, the UAW successfully negotiated a nationwide prescription drug coverage program with the major auto manufacturers. Put into effect in October 1969, the program has served as an important pattern for UAW members employed elsewhere, as well as for other third-party programs.

Covered products include prescription drugs, together with insulin. To be a "covered drug," the product must be dispensed in quantities for which the charge is at least $3.00. Some local plans utilize a formulary.

For each separate prescription order and refill, a member must contribute a $3.00 co-payment. Certain long-term maintenance drugs may be dispensed in 300-unit quantities or in a 34-day supply, whichever is larger. Other maintenance drugs are restricted to 100-unit quantities or a 34-day supply.

Participating pharmacies enter into a contract with a local plan to provide covered drugs at a cost to the member not to exceed the $3.00 co-payment. The participating pharmacy then bills the local plan for the difference between the prescription charge and the co-payment. The prescription charge is based on the acquisition cost plus a dispensing fee.

If a covered drug is obtained from a nonparticipating pharmacy, the member is required to pay the full charge by the pharmacy. Upon submission of a claim to the plan, the member is then reimbursed 75 percent of the usual and customary charge, less a $3.00 co-payment.

In general, the UAW program does not cover over-the-counter products, contraceptive drugs, or medical devices. In 1975, however, the program instituted a broad benefit for prosthetic appliances and durable medical equipment, with no patient cost-sharing required. In negotiations conducted in 1979, coverage was extended to syringes and needles needed for the injection of insulin.

Also as a result of the 1979 negotiations, it was agreed to implement drug utilization review programs in several geographic areas. The review is intended to improve the quality of drug therapy as well as to control costs and minimize abuse of the program.

Generic substitution of drugs by pharmacists is neither required nor authorized.

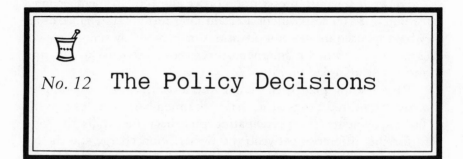

No. 12 The Policy Decisions

When, it is asked with increasing annoyance, is the United States ever to get a national health plan? When will it get national health insurance? Will this nation continue to be the only industrialized country in the world without such insurance?[1]

"We already have a national health plan," notes Robert Ball, of the Institute of Medicine and for many years Commissioner of the Social Security Administration. "We've had it since 1965. And, since 1966, we've had national health insurance, at least in the Medicare and Medicaid programs."[2]

Neither the plan nor the programs may be accepted as complete or even adequate. They were never intended to be. But neither the plan nor the programs, which now provide substantial coverage and better access to better care for more than 40 million Americans, can be dismissed as trivial or unimportant.

THE POLICY GOALS

In the design of any drug insurance program, every effort must be made to achieve certain goals:

- The primary goal must be improved health. The quality of health care must not be sacrificed needlessly just to realize economy.
- The costs of any national drug insurance program must nevertheless be kept at reasonable levels.

- Patients must be given protection against catastrophic costs of illness.
- The program must aim for simplicity, with a minimum of regulations and paperwork.
- The drug industry must not be deprived of incentives to support productive research.
- Pharmacists must receive reasonable reimbursement for not only their goods but also their services.
- Wherever possible, patients must take part in the decision-making process that concerns which drugs they will (or will not) use and how they will use them.

In addition, the Congress and the administrative agencies must make policy decisions on a number of specific matters that would presumably be involved in almost any drug insurance program.[3] In most of these instances, a failure to make a decision would in itself be making a decision by default.

SELECTION OF BENEFICIARIES

One of the thorniest problems will be deciding at the outset who should be covered by the program.[4] One approach—universal coverage of everyone for whatever drug prescribed—would presumably be impossible to implement in the foreseeable future. It would probably entail unacceptably high program costs, since it would stimulate many patients to demand and many physicians to prescribe drugs which are not required. Instead, attempts should be made first to provide coverage for relatively small groups: the elderly (those aged 65 or more), persons with a serious chronic disability, and the poor or medically indigent.

Covering the elderly and the disabled would entail an expansion of the present Medicare program; providing more adequate drug coverage for the poor would involve modifying state Medicaid programs. In the latter case, drug coverage could be federally required rather than an optional benefit. (See Chapter 11.)

All of these groups face the greatest economic and clinical risk. All three have an inordinate amount of illness and a need for drug treatment. Most of the patients have limited savings and fixed incomes, or may be unemployed. Under the present Medicaid program, there are provisions in most states for drugs to be provided at no cost to poor patients, in or out of the hospital. But for the elderly and those disabled patients of any age who may qualify for Medicare coverage, the situation is distressingly different. They are covered for prescription drugs while they are hospitalized, but they have virtually no protection against the cost of out-of-hospital drugs. In some instances, having a costly prescription filled may force them to cut down on other necessities, such as adequate food.

The present Medicare system, which pays for the visit to a physician who prescribes a drug but not for the drug itself, seems to be senseless. It is like paying for a diagnosis and the recommendation of a surgical operation but declining to pay for the surgery.

In contrast, extending Medicare coverage to out-of-hospital prescription drugs would represent a moderate increase in federal expenditures, but these might be significantly offset by reduced federal payments for physician visits and hospitalization.

To contain costs under this out-of-hospital drug coverage for the elderly, it has frequently been proposed that the coverage be limited to elderly patients who are suffering from certain specific diseases—for example, cancer, heart disease, arthritis, or asthma. Such a system is being utilized in a number of foreign programs, but it has obvious weaknesses. It offers an invitation to program abuse, fraud, patient pressure to physicians to report a "covered" diagnosis, and pressure on Congress by special interest groups to include their special diagnosis category in the law.

> For a start, we believe that in-hospital drug coverage for both Medicare and Medicaid patients should be continued, that out-of-hospital drug coverage under Medicaid should be improved by setting up minimum, federally-mandated nationwide standards, and that coverage under Medicare should be expanded to cover out-of-hospital drugs.

In the future, if this approach proves successful, coverage may well be considered for other groups who are not now included in the Medicare or Medicaid programs, particularly nonpoor children up to the age of 1 year, or 6, or 18, and perhaps patients of any age with cancer or other illnesses whose drug expenses may be very high. It is conceivable that pressures will be exerted on behalf of coverage for certain minority groups, or Republicans, or Democrats, or people with green eyes. Members of the Congress are not unused to such pressures. It is to be fervently hoped, however, that no additional incentives will be instituted to increase drug usage of any kind by pregnant women;

with few exceptions, most prescription drugs during pregnancy are deemed irrational because of potential fetal damage or death.

DRUG COVERAGE

Another policy decision that could have significant importance in controlling costs and, directly or indirectly, in selecting the patients to be protected and in minimizing irrational prescribing, would involve selecting the classes of drug products to be covered. It would likewise stir up brisk controversy.[5]

One method would be to provide comprehensive coverage for all prescription drugs (plus insulin, which does not require a prescription) and all essential pharmaceutical services rendered by pharmacists to all eligible beneficiaries, such as the elderly or the poor. This comprehensive approach, too, like universal coverage of all Americans, would be relatively simple to devise. It would probably be endorsed by physicians, pharmacists, and patients. Some elements of the drug industry would probably oppose it, however, in the fear that the resultant high program costs might lead to rigid price controls.

A second method would be to provide coverage for certain therapeutic classes of drugs but not for others, a technique that has been adopted in a number of foreign countries and in some state Medicaid programs. Thus, such products as all anticancer drugs, all anti-arthritis products, and all agents to reduce high blood pressure might be covered but not anti-obesity agents or multi-vitamins. One version of this procedure would be to cover only those groups of drugs needed for the treatment of "serious, chronic, disabling illness"; unfortunately, it would be difficult to reach agreement on a precise definition of this concept. Also, it is important to consider that most of the drugs used by the elderly are so-called long-term maintenance drugs. Furthermore, as Irwin Lerner of Roche Laboratories has stated, restricting coverage to maintenance drugs, no matter how these might be defined, would discriminate against patients who have high drug expenses during an acute illness.[6]

A third approach would be to cover only selected drugs within all or nearly all classes, presumably by means of a voluntary or compulsory formulary (see the following section). Donald Beste, of the University of California in San Francisco, states that

> Those who favor such a system [as the British] over systems that impose some restriction frequently beat the drum of second-class medicine and interference in the free enterprise system and interference in

the practice of medicine. I'm speaking in favor of limiting the number of drugs available for use in any pharmacological classification. I seriously doubt that many physicians in teaching hospitals feel that they are practicing second-class medicine or being significantly interfered with when prescribing within the confines of a well-executed formulary system. I have never seen a drug company go under when a few of its products are not included or are replaced in such a formulary system.[7]

Still another technique would be to require the dispensing of low-cost generic or branded-generic products in place of any expensive product actually prescribed. This could be accomplished by means of a formulary system or by writing requirements in the law, or by both. Strong protests against this approach may be expected from many physicians, although probably not from those in most hospitals where formularies and substitution have long been accepted. Opposition may also be expected from many brand-name manufacturers, but it would probably not be as vehement as might have been predicted a decade ago, since many of these companies are already moving into the generic drug business. (See Chapter 5.)

> *It is our feeling that when the program is paying the full cost of the prescribed drugs, coverage should be provided for only a limited number of drug products in each therapeutic class.*
>
> *Preventive vaccines should be covered.*
>
> *The selection of covered products should be based on considerations of efficacy, safety, and relative cost.*
>
> *In the case of multiple-source products—that is, when there is one brand-name version available, together with various generic or branded-generic versions, often at different prices—the pharmacist must have broad authority to select a low-cost product of equal quality in place of any expensive product actually prescribed.*
>
> *Any resultant cost-savings must be passed on to the patient or the insurance program. They should not be pocketed by the pharmacy.*
>
> *Physicians must have the right to require the use of a nonlisted product when this is clinically necessary for a particular patient.*
>
> *Similarly, patients must have the right to refuse substitution, but, if this becomes a factor, they must agree to pay any difference in cost.*

No product should be included if it is classified by FDA as "ineffective" or "possibly effective," or if there are reasonable grounds to believe that there are or may be clinically significant differences in bioavailability. Differences which may be statistically significant but clinically trivial should be ignored.

Except in unusual circumstances, over-the-counter products, even when prescribed or recommended by a physician, should not be covered.

There may be a demand that some classes of drugs, such as the minor tranquilizers and the anti-obesity agents, should not be included in any reimbursable list, since their use has been frequently associated with drug abuse. But as the experience in Belgium has shown, if a tranquilizer like diazepam (Valium) is stricken from the list, physicians will continue to prescribe it and patients will pay for it themselves. We believe that, to keep the program design as simple as possible at the beginning, representatives of all drug classes should be included. Therapeutic classes found to be unnecessary or too costly in relation to their benefits could be dropped later.

The question of physiological or therapeutic equivalence will undoubtedly continue to plague the drug industry, health professionals, and consumer groups, but the furor is already diminishing. Until the equivalency debate is entirely resolved—if it ever will be—FDA or some comparable governmental agency will continue to have the responsibility for requiring the submission of the necessary scientific evidence to settle each controversy. In this connection, it must be emphasized that if there is scientific evidence of clinically significant nonequivalency, the inferior product should not merely be removed from a drug insurance list; it should be taken off the market.

FORMULARIES

Discussions of formularies tend to become acrimonious, often because they fail to focus on the real problems. As discussed in Chapter 6, voluntary formularies that serve mainly as suggested guidelines have incited only minor difficulties. In contrast, compulsory formularies—especially if they severely limit the choice of drug products—have been involved in more bitter controversy.[8]

In any future national drug insurance program, a voluntary formulary would undoubtedly win the enthusiastic support of most physicians, pharmacists, and drug companies, but we do not believe it would have much impact in holding down expenditures or minimizing irrational prescribing. At the same time, we believe that a single compulsory national formulary could be a disaster.[9] It would be bitterly opposed by many health professionals and by much of the drug industry, and we believe the potential benefits would not compensate for the many problems it would cause. As noted earlier, the companies have finally found that they can live with a system of many hospital formularies; if they cannot have their products accepted in one hospital, they have a chance to compete for acceptance in another. Many companies also live with compulsory formularies in individual state Medicaid programs. But with a single national formulary, especially if large population groups were covered, some firms seem convinced that they would be severely damaged.

> *We propose, therefore, the use of a system of state compulsory formularies meeting minimal national guidelines if drug coverage is enacted.*
>
> *These guidelines must be established primarily to lead to more rational prescribing, and also to contain program costs.*
>
> *Each formulary committee should include practicing physicians representing selected medical specialties, along with clinical pharmacologists and clinical pharmacists, and should make appropriate use of expert consultants.*
>
> *As we emphasized in the section on drug selection, the products listed in each formulary must be selected on the basis of efficacy, safety, and relative cost, and possibly also on particular clinical and socioeconomic factors within the state.*
>
> *Within each drug class, the physician must have a reasonable choice of products, since rarely will the "drug of choice" be the best drug for all patients.*
>
> *The physician must have complete freedom to insist on an unlisted drug if, in his professional opinion, this is essential for an individual patient.*
>
> *Serious efforts must be made to see that the various formularies are not so rigid that they cut drug expenditures at the price of requiring more physician visits or hospital care.[10] Similar efforts are needed to see that the lists do not represent the results of political trading, with one member of a formulary committee telling his colleagues, "I'll vote to include your favorite product if you people will vote for mine."*

It is our belief that the inclusion of such artificial restrictions as allowing only two prescriptions per patient per month, simply to reduce expenditures, does not justify all the frustrations they have caused to patients, physicians, and pharmacists alike.[11]

We strongly suspect that much of the need for a formulary, and much of the dispute over formularies, would be obviated if more physicians were cost-conscious and had a realistic awareness of what prices their patients have to pay in their community pharmacies. With that kind of knowledge, physicians might elect to prescribe less expensive products. It is possible that many physicians will acquire and make proper use of the price information now being furnished to them periodically in the Health Care Financing Administration's new *Guide to Prescription Drug Costs*.[12] As yet, it is too early to tell.

UNAPPROVED DRUGS

In several foreign countries, a drug not approved in one country but approved and available in another may be imported by a physician if he informs the appropriate government agency that this is needed for the treatment of a particular patient (see Chapter 10). Even where this provision is allowed, it seems to be utilized infrequently.

> *We propose that the Congress enact legislation making it possible for a prescription drug that is approved in another country with a drug regulation system satisfactory to FDA, but not approved—or not yet approved—in the United States, to be imported from abroad (or supplied by a manufacturer in this country) if a physician declares that it is essential for the treatment of a particular patient.*
>
> *The cost of such an unapproved drug should not be reimbursable under any form of U.S. drug insurance program.*

REIMBURSEMENT FOR DRUG PRODUCT COST

One major element in the reimbursement to the pharmacist for any covered prescription drug is the acquisition cost which the pharmacist must pay to the manufacturer or wholesaler.[13] A heated debate has raged over whether this cost should represent the Estimated Acquisition Cost (as developed by periodic surveys in a particular state or other area) or the Actual Acquisition Cost (as stated by the pharmacy and verified when necessary by audits of invoices).

With the approval of some pharmacists but the opposition of others, HEW elected to use the Estimated Acquisition Cost approach in the Medicaid programs. This decision is still being protested.

> *We recommend that the reimbursement of pharmacists for their drug acquisition cost be based on the Actual Acquisition Cost as reported by each pharmacy, and that it be modified as needed to reflect annual or other discounts.*
>
> *It will be necessary to conduct periodic invoice audits of many and perhaps all pharmacies, and to provide for heavy penalties when program abuse or fraud can be demonstrated.*
>
> *For those multiple-source products with a Maximum Allowable Cost (MAC) set by the government, the acquisition cost should not exceed the MAC level.*

It may be safely predicted that the use of this approach will not win unanimous approval, and that in the long run it may be more expensive for the program. Nevertheless, it appears to be more equitable.

REIMBURSEMENT FOR DISPENSING COST

The second major element in reimbursement to the pharmacy will reflect the dispensing costs—the expenses of doing business plus a reasonable profit.[14] In this case, a "reasonable profit" might be set by determining the proceeds that could be obtained by putting the same amount of capital in stocks, bonds, real estate, savings accounts, or other common investments.

> *It is our belief that the dispensing fee for pharmacists should be established, area by area, on the basis of uniform cost-accounting procedures.*
>
> *Adjustments should be considered to account for volume of business, 24-hour or weekend operations, rent and salary scales, and the like, and the provision of full pharmaceutical services.*
>
> *Only in exceptional instances should dispensing physicians be reimbursed for dispensing costs.*

FULL PHARMACEUTICAL SERVICES

Many clinically-oriented pharmacists are convinced that they can make a substantial contribution to drug therapy by providing what may be termed full pharmaceutical services.[15] Included would be the following:

- Maintaining patient drug profiles containing records of all prescription and nonprescription drugs used by the patient and all other members of the household, known drug allergies or idiosyncracies, and known information on illnesses previously or currently involved.
- Consulting with patients to reinforce physician instructions involving the proper use and storage of the drug, when and how it is to be administered, which foods or alcoholic beverages should be avoided, whether or not the patient should drive an automobile, what side effects may be expected and what to do about them, and what to do if a dose is forgotten.
- Consulting with physicians when a potentially irrational prescription is intercepted, as when there is a possibility of an adverse drug-drug interaction, or when the prescription calls for a drug to which the patient may be allergic.

It is our belief that such servies would be a benefit to patients and that many clinical pharmacists are eager to furnish these services and are competent to do so. If they provide such assistance, they are clearly entitled to compensation. We believe further that most patients would be willing to pay for these services.

Pharmacists actually providing full pharmaceutical services should document the fact and receive appropriate reimbursement.

Pharmacists not providing these services should not get additional compensation.

With only rare exceptions, the prescription should include an indication of the diagnosis.

Some physicians may object to this last point, insisting that the patient receiving the prescription should not be told the diagnosis. In most instances, however, the patient is fully entitled to know the diagnosis of his illness. Some physicians may declare that the first diagnosis may be only tentative, but we believe that the patient is entitled to know that, too. And some physicians may be convinced that the patient's diagnosis is none of the pharmacist's business and that divulging it would violate patient privacy. This last view is archaic. Many prescribed drugs are immediate giveaways of the diagnosis: an order for chlorpromazine or trifluoperazine, for example, strongly suggests schizophrenia, one for phenytoin usually signals epilepsy, and one for busulfan, chlorambucil, or uracil mustard almost certainly indicates cancer. Furthermore, pharmacists can render the greatest assistance to both patients and physicians when they have access to the diagnosis, as they do routinely in many hospitals.

PAYMENT TO PHARMACIST OR PATIENT

In all but one of the national drug programs that we have examined (see Chapter 10), reimbursement is made to the pharmacy. Only in France is reimbursement made to the patient. In the United States, with any national program designed initially to help the elderly and the poor, any requirement for the patient to pay out-of-pocket would seem to be needlessly burdensome.[16]

Reimbursement for drugs prescribed for eligible beneficiaries should be paid to the pharmacy.

THE CAPITATION APPROACH

Except for some Health Maintenance Organizations (HMOs), the United States has had little experience with drug coverage under a capitation system, such as that used for many years in the Netherlands (see Chapter 10). Under this method, a patient would sign up with one pharmacy from which he would agree to obtain all of his prescription drugs. The pharmacist, paid a fixed sum for each person on his list, plus a small amount for each prescription, would have a strong incentive to dispense the least expensive product meeting the prescriber's specifications.[17]

HEW should be encouraged to investigate the advantages and disadvantages of covering prescription drugs by means of a capitation approach, either through HMOs providing physician and possibly hospital care as well as pharmacy services, or through pharmacies directly.

DATA PROCESSING

Depending on the details of its coverage, any out-of-hospital drug insurance program—even if it provided coverage for only the elderly —could involve the processing of several hundred million claims each year. Unless a suitable electronic data processing (EDP) network were established to connect pharmacies with national or regional computers, pharmacists would be suffocated under a mountain of paperwork. Moreover, there would be delays in payment that many pharmacists would find intolerable.[18]

In contrast, an EDP system could simplify the claims process and speed reimbursement. It could also play a strategic role in preventing drug-drug interactions, minimize fraud and program abuse, and demonstrate drug use and drug prescribing patterns for utilization review. In the long run, it could help reduce program costs.[19]

> *Long before any national comprehensive drug insurance program is implemented, an EDP system should be designed, developed, and thoroughly field-tested.*
>
> *The system must be able to verify patient eligibility and the identity of both the prescriber and the pharmacist, determine whether the prescribed drug is reimbursable, and calculate the reimbursable acquisition price and the pharmacist's dispensing fee.*
>
> *Both community and hospital pharmacies should be integrated into the system.*
>
> *If feasible, the same system should be utilized in all governmental drug insurance or third-party programs.*

Although the data processing system should be designed and operated to provide maximum privacy, it must be recognized that absolute privacy in any drug claims process, manual or electronic, is probably impossible to guarantee at the present state of the art. Even under the present system of claims processing, physicians, nurses, pharmacists, and government or insurance company claims processors can all have access to patient prescription drug records.

We cannot claim that any automatic data processing system will guarantee the success of a drug insurance program. But without such a system, we can guarantee that any large program will be a disaster.

PATIENT COST-SHARING

It has already been pointed out that some form of cost-sharing by patients in a national drug insurance program will undoubtedly be demanded to minimize overutilization and to reduce program costs (see Chapter 7). Three approaches are usually considered:

- Co-payment, or the payment of a fixed dollar amount on each prescription.
- Co-insurance, or the payment of a fixed percentage of the

cost of each prescription, a method that might have particular appeal during a period of inflation.

- An annual deductible system, which would require the payment by the patient of a fixed amount of prescription drug expenditures per year.

All of these approaches have evident advantages and disadvantages.[20] Common to all three is the risk of setting the level of cost-sharing so high as to yield only false economies, resulting in significant underutilization and higher overall health care expenditures.[21] There is also the danger that a low level of cost-sharing might encourage overuse of prescription drugs.

> *We believe that the most equitable method of cost-sharing, even though it would involve administrative complexities, would be to use a deductible. The amount of the deductible should be set for individuals or for families.*
>
> *The deductible should be waived entirely for the poor and for those of any income level when their drug expenditures become a hardship. Proof of eligibility is now required under the Medicaid and food stamp programs, and should present no serious problem.*
>
> *Whatever the type of cost-sharing required, no pharmacy— community or chain—should be permitted to waive it as a means of attracting business.*

Unlike co-payment or co-insurance, using a deductible may mean that some patients who do not meet the deductible requirement will not present their claims, and some data will therefore not be entered into the computer. This would result in lower processing costs, but it would make it difficult to undertake comprehensive drug utilization review. We recognize that proof of eligibility may be subjected to gross abuse. As with Medicaid and food stamps, the amount of abuse can be somewhat controlled, but it probably cannot be completely prevented.

Ideally, as Allen Brands, now Assistant Surgeon General, has indicated, there should be a single deductible covering all health care. "I don't think a drug deductible should be viewed in isolation," said Brands. "If the deductible approach is going to be used, it should be applied in all health services—a single deductible for physician services, hospital bills, and drugs."[22]

We heartily agree but feel that this approach will become feasible only when national health insurance is implemented for essentially all health care services furnished to any covered group.

PATIENT INVOLVEMENT IN DECISIONS

We have already indicated our strong belief that patients are entitled to have a voice in any decisions involving their treatment with drugs—or, for that matter, with any other form of therapy. They have a right to accept treatment or to refuse it, to follow directions or to ignore them—even if this noncompliance may threaten their health or their lives (see Chapter 2).

All patients (or the parents of young children) are entitled to be informed on these points:

- The diagnosis, even if only tentative, and the nature of the illness.
- The nature of the proposed drug and its intended effects.
- The risks entailed in using the drug and the risks entailed in not using it.
- Precisely when and how the drug should be used and any precautions that should be taken in storing it.
- The nature of possible side effects and what to do if they occur.
- The probable duration of the treatment.
- What to do if treatment is skipped for a day or two.
- The probable cost of the product.

Whether such information should be given by the physician, the pharmacist, or both, and whether it can be provided more effectively in oral form or in a printed patient package insert is yet to be decided. Whatever the decision, it must be based on analyses of actual trials with the various approaches and not on any professional or territorial prerogatives.

We strongly endorse the present policy of FDA to proceed in this field with due caution, carefully testing all major approaches which have been proposed.

We support the policies of individual drug companies to voluntarily prepare patient information sheets for distribution by physicians or pharmacists, with prior approval of the text by FDA. This distribution should be monitored by both the companies and FDA to detect any adverse psychological effects on patients.

If any patients cannot obtain clear, intelligible answers to their questions about their drugs from their present physicians or pharmacists, they would be well advised to go elsewhere for their health care.

It has often been claimed that patients can easily obtain more information on how to operate a digital wristwatch, an electric toaster, or a pocket radio than they can get on a drug that may injure or kill them.

UTILIZATION REVIEW

One of the few major routes toward cost-containment and rational prescribing that is supported both by the brand-name drug industry and by organized medicine is drug utilization review.[23] (See Chapter 8.) The value of this review has been amply demonstrated in hospitals where the DUR committee has adequate authority to control irrational prescribers, first by using an educational approach, and then, if education fails, by instituting more direct controls on prescribing. We have serious doubts if similar programs can be quickly or effectively instituted in community practice, where essentially the sole weapon available to nongovernmental DUR committees is persuasion.

> In hospitals, DUR operations should be expanded and strengthened with the full participation of clinicians, clinical pharmacologists, and clinical pharmacists.
>
> Out of the hospital, DUR committees should be developed by county medical societies, Professional Standards Review Organizations, or other local groups, also with the participation of clinicians, clinical pharmacologists and clinical pharmacists.
>
> Acceptable prescribing standards should be developed and widely publicized within the health professions so that significant deviations may be determined.[24]
>
> The drug insurance program must expect to pay for the operating costs of DUR.
>
> Public representation on DUR committees[25] may be considered in the future, but there should be no such public members until the committees and practicing physicians have developed reasonably smooth working relations.

If voluntary efforts fail to prevent irrational prescribing or to cut down unnecessarily high drug expenditures, it would appear that the government would have no alternative but to refuse to pay.[26] There can be no valid reason for squandering taxpayer dollars on grossly irrational prescriptions.

CONCLUSION

Times have changed. Ten years ago, recommendations such as the ones we have presented in this chapter could not possibly have received dispassionate consideration by any of the interested parties. Those were the days when FDA officials frequently and publicly chastised the drug industry, and when leaders of the industry called for the firing of at least three successive FDA commissioners. The real or alleged sins of either FDA or the industry or both were repeatedly excoriated in congressional committee hearings. Both organized medicine and organized pharmacy denounced government interference (and also each other), and consumer advocates were angry at virtually every other interest group.

Recently, and for reasons that are not altogether clear, the situation has been altered. There are still differences of opinion on many issues, but these no longer lead inevitably to violent disputes. Top representatives of government, medicine, pharmacy, and industry now meet effectively and productively, with a growing mutual respect and a recognition that no group can have all of its demands accepted. During the past few years, congressional leaders have maintained their obligations as watchdogs over the public good, but their drug hearings have been somewhat less fiery than before. FDA continues to draw criticism, as do the Federal Trade Commission and virtually every other regulatory agency, but it may be safely assumed that any regulatory agency that does *not* receive criticism is simply not doing its job.

One noteworthy sign of the changed situation came early in 1980, when Lewis Engman, the new president of the Pharmaceutical Manufacturers Association, met with staff members of FDA's Bureau of Drugs. Earlier, some PMA members had indicated that they were willing to go along with a postmarketing surveillance program, provided that it would concern only new drugs. Let old drugs, like sleeping dogs, lie, they had insisted. Now, however, Richard Crout, director of the bureau, told Engman: "Our largest difficulties come from things already on the market. I think that if you look at what our biggest flaps have been through recent years, they are oral contraceptives, they are oral estrogens, they are the removal of certain drugs. . . ." Engman agreed that surveillance must cover both old approved drugs and new ones. The industry, he said, cannot "hide behind that NDA [New Drug Application] 'badge of approval.'"

There must be an adversary relationship between the PMA and

the FDA, the PMA president continued, in order to help the consumer. "We have the same goals," he emphasized. "I'm glad we have a vigilant FDA. We welcome it as a second-line defense that can only help us."[27]

Recently, FDA Commissioner Goyan gave us this view:

> The flowering of the pharmaceutical industry after World War II is one of the most amazing aftermaths of that conflict. One of the outcomes of those successes was that almost all of the pharmaceutical industry went from being relatively small family-owned businesses to being corporate giants. In a society where the "bottom line" is sacred, the stresses which are put upon corporate management have become immense. For example, in what other industry is it likely to be alleged that one might be selling too much of one's product? Furthermore, how often does other corporate management find itself being challenged to bring products on the market which clearly will never repay their research and development costs? Such difficulties are indeed the way of life in the pharmaceutical industry today.
>
> In the face of such difficulties, it is pleasant to note that many pharmaceutical manufacturers have responded by working with agencies such as ours to limit the improper use of their drugs, while others have volunteered to sponsor drugs for which there can be no direct economic advantage. I believe that such examples of cooperation will increase in the next few years as both the pharmaceutical manufacturers and we discover the long-term benefits accruing both to us and to the public health of such a cooperative spirit.[28]

It is largely because of these changes that many of the policy issues concerning national drug insurance have been examined calmly and responsibly in the last several years. There are still unresolved issues, but on some points there is broad agreement. There is, we believe, acceptance of the decision that the interests of the public—not those of government, of industry, of physicians, or of pharmacists—must come first.

Appendix

Key to Generic and Brand Names and Drug Class

Generic Name	Brand Name	Drug Class or Major Therapeutic Use
allopurinol	Zyloprim	Gout therapy
ampicillin	Amcill, Omnipen, Penbritten, Pensyn, Polycillin, Principen	Antibiotic
brompheniramine + decongestants	Dimetapp	Cold therapy
cephalexin	Keflex	Antibiotic
chloral hydrate	Kessodate, Noctec	Sedative
chloramphenicol	Chloromycetin, Chloromyxin	Antibiotic
chlordiazepoxide	Librium	Anti-anxiety
chlordiazepoxide + clidinium	Librax	Anti-anxiety, anti-intestinal spasm
chlorpromazine	Thorazine	Antipsychotic
cimetadine	Tagamet	Ulcer therapy
clindamycin	Cleocin	Antibiotic
*clioquinol	Enterovioform	Antidiarrhea
diazepam	Valium	Anti-anxiety
diethylstilbestrol (DES)	Stilphostrol, Tylosterone	Estrogen
diphenoxylate + atropine	Lomotil	Antidiarrhea
erythromycin	EES, Erythrocin, Ilosone, Pediamycin, Wyamycin	Antibiotic
ethambutol	Myambutol	Tuberculosis therapy
flurazepam	Dalmane	Sedative
ibuprofen	Motrin	Anti-arthritis
isoniazide (INH)	Nydrazid	Tuberculosis therapy
isoproterenol	Isuprel, Norisodrine, Proternol	Bronchial dilator
lincomycin	Lincocin	Antibiotic

Appendix (cont.)

meperidine	Demerol	Analgesic
meprobamate	Equanil, Miltown	Anti-anxiety
nitrofurantoin	Furadantin	Antibacterial
oxytetracycline + sulfamethizole + phenazopyridine	Urobiotic	Antibiotic, antibacterial
penicillin G	Pentids, Pfizerpen, Robicillin	Antibiotic
penicillin V	Betapen, Ledercillin, Pen-Vee K, Vee-Tids	
*phenformin	DBI, Meltrol	Antibiotic
phenobarbital	Luminal	Diabetes therapy
pilocarpine	—	Sedative
prednisone	Deltasone, Metacorten, Orasone, Sterapred	Glaucoma therapy
		Anti-inflammatory
propoxyphene	Darvon	Analgesic
pseudoephedrine	Sudafed	Bronchial dilator
reserpine	Serpasil	Antihypertensive
rifampin	Rifadin, Rimactine	Tuberculosis therapy
secobarbital	Seconal	Sedative
tetracycline	Achromycin, Panmycin, Sumycin	Antibiotic
†thalidomide	Kevadon	Sedative
*ticrynafen	Selacryn	Antihypertensive, diuretic
tolbutamide	Orinase	Diabetes therapy
trimethoprim + sulfamethoxazole	Bactrim, Septra	Antibacterial
valproate, sodium	Depakene	Epilepsy therapy

NOTE: Included in the brand names listed here are the original brand name together with selected branded generic names. Some of the products included here are marketed in a variety of salts and esters.

*No longer marketed in U.S.

†Never marketed in U.S.

Key to Abbreviations
Used in the References

In our research, much valuable material was obtained from the background papers and reports of the HEW Task Force on Prescription Drugs, the hearings conducted by Senators Estes Kefauver and Gaylord Nelson, the hearings conducted by the House of Representatives' Subcommittee on Science and Technology on FDA's drug approval process, the background monograph published by the National Center for Health Services Research (NCHSR) on policy options for drug coverage under national health insurance, and the NCHSR conferences on national and international drug insurance. In the following pages, these and other important sources are identified and abbreviated as follows:

RxTF, *Current Programs*
> U.S. Department of Health, Education, and Welfare, Office of the Secretary, Task Force on Prescription Drugs, *Current American and Foreign Programs* (Washington, D.C.: U.S. Government Printing Office, 1968).

RxTF, *Drug Makers and Distributors*
> Ibid., *The Drug Makers and the Drug Distributors* (Washington, D.C.: U.S. Government Printing Office, 1968).

RxTF, *Drug Prescribers*
> Ibid., *The Drug Prescribers* (Washington, D.C.: U.S. Government Printing Office, 1968).

RxTF, *Drug Users*
> Ibid., *The Drug Users* (Washington, D.C.: U.S. Government Printing Office, 1968).

RxTF, *Insurance Design*
> Ibid., *Approaches to Drug Insurance Design* (Washington, D.C.: U.S. Government Printing Office, 1969).

RxTF, *Final Report*
    Ibid., *Final Report* (Washington, D.C.: U.S. Government Printing Office, 1969).
U.S. House of Representatives, *FDA's Process*
    U.S. House of Representatives, Committee on Science and Technology, Subcommittee on Science, Research and Technology, *The Food and Drug Administration's Process for Approving New Drugs* (Washington, D.C.: U.S. Government Printing Office, 1979).
U.S. Senate, *Administered Prices*
    U.S. Senate, Committee on the Judiciary, Subcommittee on Antitrust and Monopoly (the Kefauver Committee), *Administered Prices in the Drug Industry* (Washington, D.C.: U.S. Government Printing Office, various years).
U.S. Senate, *Competitive Problems*
    U.S. Senate, Select Committee on Small Business, Subcommittee on Monopoly (the Nelson Committee), *Present Status of Competition in the Pharmaceutical Industry* (Washington, D.C.: U.S. Government Printing Office, various years).
Drugging of the Americas
    Milton Silverman, *The Drugging of the Americas* (Berkeley and Los Angeles: University of California Press, 1976).
Drug Insurance Options
    Milton Silverman and Mia Lydecker, *Drug Coverage Under National Health Insurance: The Policy Options* (Washington, D.C.: U.S. Department of Health, Education, and Welfare, National Center for Health Services Research, DHEW Publication No. [HRA] 77-3189, 1977).
International Drug Reimbursement
    Albert I. Wertheimer, ed., *Proceedings of the International Conference on Drug and Pharmaceutical Services Reimbursement* (Washington, D.C.: U.S. Department of Health, Education, and Welfare, National Center for Health Services Research, DHEW Publication No. [HRA] 77-3166, 1977).
National Drug Insurance Conference
    Milton Silverman and Mia Lydecker, eds., *Proceedings of the National Conference on Drug Coverage Under National Health Insurance* (Washington, D.C.: U.S. Department of Health, Education, and Welfare, National Center for Health Services Research, DHEW Publication No. [PHS] 78-3208, 1978).
Pills, Profits, and Politics
    Milton Silverman and Philip R. Lee, *Pills, Profits, and Politics* (Berkeley and Los Angeles: University of California Press, 1974).

References

No. 1. DRUGS AND THE DRUG INDUSTRY

1. Milton Silverman, "Drug Insurance: Who Needs It?" in *National Drug Insurance Conference*, p. 8.

2. *Annual Survey Report* (Washington, D.C.: Pharmaceutical Manufacturers Association, various years).

3. Vincent Gardner (Health Care Financing Administration and National Association of Chain Drug Stores) and Thomas Fulda (Health Care Financing Administration), personal communications, 1979 and 1980.

4. "The Top 200 Drugs," *Pharmacy Times* 46:31 (April 1980).

5. H. E. Simmons and Paul D. Stolley, "This Is Medical Progress? Trends and Consequences of Antibiotic Use in the United States." *Journal of the American Medical Association* 227:1023 (March 4, 1974).

6. Michael B. Balter and J. Levine, "The Nature and Extent of Psychotropic Drug Usage in the United States," *Psychopharmacology Bulletin* 5:3 (July 1969).

7. "The Top 200 Drugs."

8. RxTF, *Drug Users*, p. 21.

9. Ibid.

10. U.S. Department of Health, Education, and Welfare, National Center for Health Statistics, *The National Ambulatory Medical Care Survey*, 1975 Summary, Series 13, No. 33, 1978.

11. *Pills, Profits, and Politics*, p. 19.

12. RxTF, *Insurance Design*, p. 77.

13. Robert M. Gibson, "National Health Expenditures, 1978," *Health Care Financing Review* 1:1 (Summer 1979).

14. *Pills, Profits, and Politics*, Chapter 2.

15. Paul de Haen, "Compilation of New Drugs, 1940 Through 1975," *Pharmacy Times* 42:40 (March 1976).

16. Pharmaceutical Manufacturers Association, *Annual Survey Report*, various years.

17. David Ennals, "Address to Parliament," London, April 28, 1977.

18. *Pills Profits, and Politics*, Chapter 3.

19. "Undergraduate Medical Education," *Journal of the American Medical Association* 243:849 (March 7, 1980).

20. *Drugging of the Americas*.

21. John S. Yudkin, "Provision of Medicines in a Developing Country," *Lancet* 1:810 (April 15, 1978).

22. Ennals, "Address to Parliament."

23. *Pills, Profits, and Politics*, p. 35.

24. Ronald W. Hansen, "The Pharmaceutical Development Process: Estimates of Development Costs and Times and the Effects of Proposed Regulatory Changes," in Robert I. Chien, ed., *Issues in Pharmaceutical Economics* (Lexington, Mass.: D.C. Heath, 1979).

25. C. Joseph Stetler, paper presented before a meeting of the Food and Drug Law Institute, Washington, D.C., May 21, 1979.

26. Richard Emmitt, quoted in *F-D-C Reports*, March 13, 1978, p. 13.

27. "FDA Hastens Approval of 'Important' New Drugs," *American Pharmacist* NS19:182 (April 1979).

28. Drug Regulation Reform Act of 1978, S. 2755, H.R. 11611.

29. Drug Regulation Reform Act of 1979, S. 1075, H.R. 7035.

30. Sam Peltzman, *Regulation of Pharmaceutical Regulation* (Washington, D.C.: American Enterprise Institute for Public Policy Research, 1974); and "Frustrating Drug Advancement," *Newsweek*, January 8, 1973, p. 49.

31. *Pills, Profits, and Politics*, Chapters 4 and 5; *Drugging of the Americas*; Richard J. Barnet and Ronald Müller, *Global Reach: The Power of the Multinational Corporations* (New York: Simon and Schuster, 1974); Robert J. Ledogar, *Hungry for Profits* (New York: IDOC/North America, 1975); Yudkin, "Provision of Medicines"; Joseph A. Roman, "Mefenamic Acid—Classic Case of Misinformation," *American Pharmacist* NS19:48 (April 1979); Charles Medawar, *Insult or Injury* (London: Social Audit, 1979), pp. 111-124.

32. U.S. Department of Health, Education, and Welfare, Food and Drug Administration, *New Drug Evaluation Briefing Book* (Washington, D.C., various years).

33. William M. Wardell, "The Drug Lag Revisited: Comparison by Therapeutic Area of Patterns of Drugs Marketed in the United States and Great Britain from 1972 through 1976," *Clinical Pharmacology and Therapeutics* 24:499 (November 1978); and William M. Wardell, statement in U.S. House of Representatives, *FDA's Process*, pp. 79-91.

34. Barbara Moulton, statement in U.S. House of Representatives, *FDA's Process*, pp. 399-406.

35. *Pills, Profits, and Politics*, pp. 243-248; William M. Wardell, "A Close Inspection of the 'Calm Look,'" *Journal of the American Medical Association* 239:2004 (May 12, 1978); and Gregory J. Ahart, statement in U.S. House of Representatives, *FDA's Process*, pp. 29, 30, and 35.

36. M. N. Graham Dukes and Inge Lunde, personal communications, 1979 and 1980.

37. Donald Kennedy, statement in U.S. House of Representatives, *FDA's Process*, p. 154.

38. *Sunday Times of London*, Insight Team, *Suffer the Children: The Story of Thalidomide* (New York: Viking Press, 1979).

39. Donald Kennedy, statement in U.S. House of Representatives, *FDA's Process*, pp. 187, 188, and 201.

40. Frederick Suchy et al., "Acute Hepatic Failure Associated with the Use of Sodium Valproate," *New England Journal of Medicine* 300:962 (April 26, 1979).

41. Olle Hansson, *Arzneimittel-Multis und der SMON-Skandal* (Berlin: Arzneimittel-Informations-Dienst GmbH, 1979); and T. Soda, ed., *Drug-Induced Sufferings—Medical, Pharmaceutical and Legal Aspects* (Proceedings of the Kyoto International Conference Against Drug-Induced Sufferings, Kyoto, Japan, April 14-18, 1979) (Amsterdam-Oxford-Princeton: Excerpta Medica; New York: Elsevier North-Holland, 1980).

42. Review Panel on New Drug Regulation, *Final Report* ("The Dorsen Report") (Washington, D.C.: U.S. Department of Health, Education, and Welfare, May 1977), pp. 28 and 29.

43. Paul de Haen, "Is There a Drug Lag in Europe?" *Medical Marketing and Media* 14:15 (July 1979).

44. *Pills, Profits, and Politics*, Chapter 7.

45. Donald Kennedy, "FDA and Academic Medicine," a paper presented before a meeting of the Council of Academic Societies of the Association of American Colleges, Washington, D.C., November 7, 1977.

46. Leonard G. Schifrin, in *National Drug Insurance Conference*, pp. 43-46; Richard Shoemaker, in ibid., pp. 99-101; and T. Donald Rucker, in ibid., pp. 55, 56, and 122.

47. *Pills, Profits, and Politics*, pp. 166-168.

48. Vincent Gardner, "Drug Insurance and Cost Containment," in *National Drug Insurance Conference*, pp. 35-40.

49. Frank Markoe, Jr., in *National Drug Insurance Conference*, pp. 40-43.

50. *Pills, Profits, and Politics*, p. 260.

51. Kenneth L. Melmon, "Preventable Drug Reactions—Causes and Cures," *New England Journal of Medicine* 284:1361 (June 17, 1971).

52. *Pills, Profits, and Politics*, p. 265.

53. Editorial, "Blood Dyscrasia Following the Use of Chloramphenicol," *Journal of the American Medical Association* 149:840 (June 28, 1952).

54. Hershel Jick et al., "Replacement Estrogens and Endometrial Cancer," *New England Journal of Medicine* 300:218 (January 1, 1979); and Hershel Jick, Alexander M. Walker, and Claude Spriet-Pourra, "Postmarketing Follow-Up," *Journal of the American Medical Association* 242:2310 (November 23, 1979).

55. Fred Karch and Louis Lasagna, *Adverse Drug Reactions in the United States* (Washington, D.C.: Medicine in the Public Interest, 1970).

56. Hershel Jick et al., "Comprehensive Drug Surveillance," *Journal of the American Medical Association* 213:1455 (August 31, 1970).

57. Russell R. Miller, "Drug Surveillance Utilizing Epidemiologic Methods," *American Journal of Hospital Pharmacy* 30:584 (July 1973).

58. C. T. Dollery and M. D. Rawlins, "Monitoring Adverse Reactions to Drugs," *British Medical Journal* 1:96 (January 8, 1977); Editorial, "Side-Effects of Practolol," ibid. 1:577 (June 14, 1975).

59. L. E. Böttiger, "Adverse Drug Reactions: An Analysis of 310 Consecutive Reports to the Swedish Drug Reaction Committee," *Journal of Clinical Pharmacology* 13:373 (October 1973).

60. Karch and Lasagna, *Adverse Drug Reactions*; and Hershel Jick, "Drugs—Remarkably Non-Toxic," *New England Journal of Medicine* 291:824 (October 12, 1974).

61. Karch and Lasagna, *Adverse Drug Reactions*.

62. Brian L. Strom and Kenneth L. Melmon, "Can Postmarketing Surveillance Help to Effect Optimal Drug Therapy?" *Journal of the American Medical Association* 242:2420 (November 30, 1979).

63. *Final Report: Joint Commission on Prescription Drug Use* (Rockville, Md.: Joint Commission on Prescription Drug Use, 1980).

64. Eliot Marshall, "A Prescription for Monitoring Drugs," *Science* 207:853 (February 22, 1980).

65. *F-D-C Reports*, March 17, 1980, p. 9.

66. Ibid.

No. 2. PATIENTS

1. U.S. Department of Health, Education, and Welfare, National Center for Health Statistics, *The National Ambulatory Medical Care Survey*, 1975 Summary, Series 13, No. 33, 1978.

2. Ibid.

3. Jere E. Goyan, quoted in Joann S. Lublin, "What Should We Know About Prescription Drugs?" *Wall Street Journal*, January 25, 1980.

4. David L. Seckett and R. Brian Haynes, *Compliance with Therapeutic Regimens* (Baltimore: Johns Hopkins University Press, 1976).

5. Ronald B. Stewart and Leighton E. Cluff, "A Review of Medication Errors and Compliance in Ambulant Patients," *Clinical Pharmacology and Therapeutics* 13:463 (July-August 1972).

6. Sackett and Haynes, *Compliance with Therapeutic Regimens*; Bonnie L. Svarstad, "Physician-Patient Communication and Patient Conformity with Medical Advice," in David Mechanic, ed., *The Growth of Bureaucratic Medicine: An Inquiry into the Dynamics of Patient Behavior and the Organization of Medical Care* (New York: John Wiley, 1976).

7. Mickey C. Smith and David Knapp, *Pharmacy and Medical Care*, 2nd edit. (Baltimore: Williams and Wilkins, 1976).

8. *Pills, Profits, and Politics*, p. 249.

9. Pieter Joubert and Louis Lasagna, "Patient Package Inserts. I. Nature, Notions, and Needs," *Clinical Pharmacology and Therapeutics* 18:507 (November 1975).

10. Center for Law and Social Policy, "Petition to the FDA to Acquire More Adequate Patient Labelling of Prescription Drugs," Washington, D.C., 1975.

11. Irving S. Colcher and James W. Bass, "Penicillin Treatment of Streptococcal Pharnygitis," *Journal of the American Medical Association* 222: 657 (November 6, 1972); Edward E. Madden, "Evaluation of Outpatient Pharmacy Patient Counseling," *Journal of the American Pharmaceutical Association* NS13:437 (August 1973); Thomas R. Sharpe and Robert L. Mikeal, "Patient Compliance with Antibiotic Regimens," *American Journal of Hospital Pharmacy* 31:479 (May 1974); Joseph A. Linkewich, Robert B. Catalano, and Herbert L. Flack, "The Effect of Packaging and Instruction on Outpatient Compliance with Medication Regimens," *Drug Intelligence and Clinical Pharmacology* 8:10 (January 1974); and Mary E. Mattar, James Markello, and Sumner J. Yaffe, "Pharmaceutical Factors Affecting Patient Compliance," *Pediatrics* 55:101 (January 1975).

12. David E. Kanouse and Louis A. Morris, "Patient Package Inserts: Effects on Patient Knowledge, Attitudes and Behavior," a paper presented before a meeting of the American Public Health Association, Los Angeles, October 17, 1978; and David L. Sackett et al., "Randomised Clinical Trial of Strategies for Improving Medication Compliance in Primary Hypertension," *Lancet* 1:1205 (May 31, 1975).

13. *Evaluating Patient Package Inserts* (Washington, D.C.: National Academy of Sciences, Institute of Medicine, 1979).

14. Jere E. Goyan, quoted in Lublin, "What Should We Know?"

No. 3. PHYSICIANS

1. RxTF, *Final Report*, p. 22.

2. Ibid., p. x.

3. Mark Novitch, quoted here from *Pills, Profits, and Politics*, p. 283.

4. U.S. Department of Health, Education, and Welfare, National Center for Health Statistics, *The National Ambulatory Medical Care Survey*, 1975 Summary, Series 13, No. 33, 1978.

5. Henry L. Lennard, Leon J. Epstein, Arnold Bernstein, and Donald C. Ransom, *Mystification and Drug Misuse* (San Francisco: Jossey-Bass, 1971).

6. George E. Crane, "Clinical Psychopharmacology in its 20th Year," *Science* 181:124 (July 13, 1973).

7. Irving K. Zola, "Medicine as an Institution of Social Control," *Sociological Review* 20:487 (November 1972).

8. Barry Blackwell, "Psychotropic Drugs in Use Today," *Journal of the American Medical Association* 225:1637 (September 24, 1973); and Leo E. Hollister, "Valium: A Discussion of Recent Issues," *Psychosomatics* 18:1 (1977).

9. Sidney Zisook and Richard A. DeVaul, "Adverse Behavioral Effects of Benzodiazepines," *Journal of Family Practice* 5:963 (December 1977).

10. U.S. Department of Justice, Drug Enforcement Administration, and U.S. Department of Health, Education, and Welfare, National Institute on Drug Abuse, data from Project DAWN, 1977.

11. Blackwell, "Psychotropic Drugs"; Nathan S. Kline, "Antidepressant Medications: A More Effective Use by Family Physicians, Internists and Others," *Journal of the American Medical Association* 227:1158 (March 11, 1974); and Ingrid Waldron, "Increased Prescribing of Valium, Librium and Other Drugs—An Example of the Influence of Economic and Social Factors on the Practice of Medicine," *International Journal of Health Services* 7:37 (1977).

12. R. Jeffrey Smith, "Study Finds Sleeping Pills Overprescribed," *Science* 204:287 (April 20, 1979).

13. U.S. Department of Health, Education, and Welfare, National Institute on Drug Abuse, *Sedative-Hypnotic Drugs: Risks and Benefits* (Washington, D.C.: Alcohol, Drug Abuse, and Mental Health Administration, August 1977).

14. Robert duPont, quoted in "Sleeping Pill Study Cites Death, Abuse," *San Francisco Chronicle*, December 7, 1977.

15. Hugh J. Parry et al., "National Patterns of Psychotherapeutic Drug Use," *Archives of General Psychiatry* 28:769 (June 1973); Kline, "Antidepressant Medications"; Elmer A. Gardner, "Implications of Psychoactive Drug Therapy," *New England Journal of Medicine* 290:800 (April 4, 1974); and Leo E. Hollister, "Drugs for Emotional Disorders," *Journal of the American Medical Association* 234:942 (December 1, 1977).

16. Henry L. Lennard, Leon J. Epstein, Arnold Berstein, and Donald C. Ransom, "Hazards Implicit in Prescribing Psychoactive Drugs," *Science* 169:438 (July 31, 1970); Charlotte Muller, "The Overmedicated Society: Forces in the Marketplace for Medical Care," *Science* 176:488 (May 5, 1972); and David J. Greenblatt and Richard I. Shader, *Benzodiazepines in Clinical Practice* (New York: Raven Press, 1974).

17. Ronald L. Katz, "Drug Therapy: Sedatives and Tranquilizers," *New England Journal of Medicine* 286:757 (April 6, 1972).

18. *Pills, Profits, and Politics*, p. 283.

19. Ibid., pp. 121-135.

20. Andrew W. Roberts and James A. Visconti, "The Rational and Irrational Use of Systemic Antimicrobial Drugs," *American Journal of Hospital Pharmacy* 29:1054 (October 1972); Calvin M. Kunin, Thelma Tupasi, and William A. Craig, "Use of Antibiotics—A Brief Exposition of the Problem and Some Tentative Solutions," *Annals of Internal Medicine* 79:555 (October 1973); Franklin E. May, Ronald B. Stewart, and Leighton E. Cluff, "Drug Use in the Hospital: Evaluation of Determinants," *Clinical Pharmacology and Therapeutics* 16:834 (November 1974); Edward H. Kass, "Quality Assurance and the Use of Antimicrobial Drugs in General Hospitals: An Introduction," 1976 (unpublished); Mary Castle et al., "Antibiotic Use at Duke University Medical Center," *Journal of the American Medical Association* 237:2819 (June 27, 1977); Stephen R. Jones, "The Effect of an Education Program upon Hospital Antibiotic Use," *American Journal of Medical Sciences* 273:79 (January-February 1977); George W. Counts, "Review and Control of Antimicrobial Usage in Hospitalized Patients," *Journal of the American Medical Association* 238:2170 (November 14, 1977); and Gerald W. Chodak and Mar-

tin E. Plaut, "Use of Systemic Antibiotics for Prophylaxis in Surgery," *Archives of Surgery* 112:326 (March 1977).

21. Chodak and Plaut, "Use of Systemic Antibiotics."

22. Kass, "Quality Assurance."

23. J.S. Remington, "Trouble with Antibiotics," *Human Nature* 1:62 (June 1978).

24. John H. Dingle, George F. Badger, and William S. Jordan, Jr., *Illness in the Home* (Cleveland: Press of Western Reserve University, 1964).

25. *National Ambulatory Medical Care Survey.*

26. American Medical Association, Department of Drugs, *AMA Drug Evaluations*, 4th edit. (Chicago: American Medical Association, 1980), p. 69.

27. Kunin et al., "Use of Antibiotics."

28. Robert R. Brook and Kathleen N. Williams, "Effect of Medical Care Review on the Use of Injections," *Annals of Internal Medicine* 85:509 (October 1976).

29. *AMA Drug Evaluations*, p. 69.

30. *National Disease and Therapeutic Index* (Ambler, Penn.: IMS America, 1977).

31. Bryan S. Finkle et al., "A National Assessment of Propoxyphene in Postmortem Medicolegal Investigations," *Journal of Forensic Sciences* 21:706 (October 1976).

32. Harry K. Ziel and William D. Finkle, "Increased Risk of Endometrial Cancer among Users of Conjugated Estrogens," *New England Journal of Medicine* 293:1167 (December 4, 1975); Donald C. Smith et al., "Association of Exogenous Estrogen and Endometrial Carcinoma," *New England Journal of Medicine* 293:1164 (December 4, 1975); and Thomas M. Mack et al., "Estrogens and Endometrial Cancer in a Retirement Community," *New England Journal of Medicine* 294:1262 (June 3, 1976).

33. Robert Hoover, Laman A. Gray, and Joseph F. Fraumeni, Jr., "Stilbestrol (Diethylstilbestrol) and the Risk of Ovarian Cancer," *Lancet* 2:533 (September 10, 1977).

34. R. I. Pfeffer and S. Vanden Noort, "Estrogen Use and Stroke Risk in Postmenopausal Women," *American Journal of Epidemiology* 103:445 (May 1976).

35. L. N. Ajabor, "Effect of Exogenous Estrogen on Carbohydrate Metabolism in Postmenopausal Women," *American Journal of Obstetrics and Gynecology* 113:383 (June 1972).

36. Boston Collaborative Drug Surveillance Program, "Surgically Confirmed Gallbladder Disease, Venous Thromboembolism, and Breast Tumors in Relation to Postmenopausal Estrogen Therapy," *New England Journal of Medicine* 290:15 (January 3, 1974).

37. "Estrogen Warnings Ordered," *San Francisco Chronicle*, July 21, 1977; and Jane E. Brody, "Estrogen Therapy—Is the Cure Worth the Gamble?" *San Francisco Chronicle*, December 12, 1979.

38. RxTF, *Drug Prescribers.*

39. *Pills, Profits, and Politics*, Chapter 12.

40. *Guide to Prescription Drug Costs* (Baltimore: U.S. Department of

Health, Education, and Welfare, Health Care Financing Administration, HCFA—02104, April 1980).

41. *AMA Drug Evaluations.*

42. Brook and Williams, "Effect of Medical Care Review."

43. "MDs Curb Amphetamine Prescribing," *American Medical News*, March 27, 1978, p. 11.

No. 4. PHARMACISTS: PLIGHT OR PROMISE?

1. *Pills, Profits, and Politics*, pp. 190-205.

2. Ibid., pp. 310-312.

3. T. Donald Rucker (Ohio State University), personal communication, 1979.

4. *The Lilly Digest* (Indianapolis: Eli Lilly and Co., 1979), p. 7.

5. T. Donald Rucker, personal communication, 1979.

6. T. Donald Rucker, "Around and Beyond UCAS [Uniform Cost-Accounting Systems]—The Road to Economic Survival for Community Pharmacies," *Journal of the American Pharmaceutical Association* NS17:292 (May 1977).

7. William S. Apple, "Do You Know Your Professional Fee?" *Journal of the American Pharmaceutical Association* NS7:25 (January 1967).

8. Health Information Designs, *A Determination of the Range of Administrative Costs Associated with the Handling of Third-Party Prescriptions. Final Report* (Washington, D.C.: Health Information Designs, 1979).

9. Michael A. Riddiough, "A Pharmacy Service is not a Pharmacy Service is not a Pharmacy Service," *American Pharmacy* NS19:8 (July 1979).

10. *Pills, Profits, and Politics*, p. 298.

11. Robert P. Fudge and Peter H. Vlassos, "Third Party Reimbursement for Pharmacist Instruction about Antihemophilic Factor," *American Journal of Hospital Pharmacy* 34:831 (August 1977).

12. Michael A. Riddiough, in *National Drug Insurance Conference*, p. 69.

13. Riddiough, "A Pharmacy Service."

14. Robert C. Johnson, "Coverage of Full Pharmaceutical Services," in *National Drug Insurance Conference*, pp. 59 and 60.

15. Allen Brands (Public Health Service), personal communication, 1979.

16. David A. Knapp, in *National Drug Insurance Conference*, p. 65.

17. *Pills, Profits, and Politics*, p. 199; J. Edward Bell et al., "A New Approach to Delivering Information to the Physician through a Pharmacy Consultation Program. Part IV: Evaluation Results," *American Journal of Hospital Pharmacy* 30:300 (April 1973); J. Heyward Hull and Fred M. Eckel, "Evaluation of the Pharmacist as a Drug Therapy Advisor on Ward Rounds," *American Journal of Hospital Pharmacy* 30:687 (August 1973); Kenneth R. Dillard et al., "Appropriate Use of Antibiotics Improved by Use of Surveillance Program," *Hospitals* 51:81 (January 1977); P.H. Vance, "The Effect of a Pharmacist Drug Surveillance Program in an Acute Ward," *Canadian Journal of Hospital Pharmacy* 26:71 (March-April 1973); and Eric Herfindal and

Donald Kishi, "Medical Audits and Clinical Pharmacy," in Eppo van der Kleijn and J. R. Jonkers, eds., *Clinical Pharmacy* (Amsterdam: Elsevier/North-Holland Biomedical Press, 1977), pp. 249-258.

18. *Pills, Profits, and Politics*, pp. 202 and 203.

19. Harold L. Hirsh, "Legal Pitfalls for Today's Pharmacist," *Professional Pharmacy* 3:1 (Winter 1977).

20. George Archambault, in *National Drug Insurance Conference*, p. 106; and Alan R. Nelson, in ibid., p. 93.

21. Alan R. Nelson, ibid.

22. "CPhA Secures Pharmacist Prescribing in Health Manpower Pilot Projects," *California Pharmacist* 25:34 (January 1978).

23. "California Testing Plan to Broaden Prescribing Policy," *American Medical News*, February 3, 1979, p. 3.

PART III. COST-CONTAINMENT

1. RxTF, *Insurance Design*; and RxTF, *Final Report*.

2. Gordon R. Trapnell, *National Health Insurance Issues: The Cost of a National Prescription Program* (Nutley, N.J.: Roche Laboratories, 1979).

NO. 5. THE GREAT GENERIC CONTROVERSY

1. *National Drug Insurance Conference*, pp. 15-34.

2. Margaret Krieg, *Black Market Medicines* (Englewood Cliffs, N.J.: Prentice-Hall, 1967), p. 207.

3. *Pills, Profits, and Politics*, p. 142.

4. *PMA Newsletter*, November 3, 1975.

5. United States of America v. Jamieson-McKames Pharmaceutical, Inc., et al., United States District Court, Eastern District of Missouri, Eastern Division, No. 77-131 CR(3), March 29, 1979.

6. *Pills, Profits, and Politics*, p. 143.

7. Paul A. Brooke, *Resistant Prices: A Study of Competitive Prices in the Antibiotic Markets* (New York: Council on Economic Priorities, 1975), p. 87.

8. *F-D-C Reports*, April 16, 1979, p. 16.

9. Pharmaceutical Manufacturers Association, personal communication, 1979.

10. *Pills, Profits, and Politics*, pp. 145-147.

11. U.S. District Court, District of Maryland, Civil No. Y-78-2449, May 20, 1979.

12. RxTF, *Final Report*, p. x.

13. *Pills, Profits, and Politics*, p. 114.

14. Elmer B. Staats, statement in U.S. Senate, *Competitive Problems* 20:7996 (1971).

15. *Pills, Profits, and Politics*, pp. 140-145 and 147-151.

16. RxTF, *Final Report*, p. 31.

17. William S. Apple (American Pharmaceutical Association), personal communication, 1979.

18. *De Haen Nonproprietary Name Index* (New York: Paul de Haen, Inc., 1977), p. vii.

19. *F-D-C Reports*, January 15, 1979, pp. 7 and 8; and Theodore Goldberg et al., "Evaluation of Economic Effects of Drug Product Selection Legislation," *Medical Care* 17:418 (April 1979).

20. *F-D-C Reports*, January 15, 1979, pp. 7-9.

21. Ibid., p. 11.

22. Ibid., p. 6.

23. *Maximum Allowable Cost for Drugs* (Washington, D.C.: Department of Health, Education, and Welfare, Office of the Secretary, 1977).

24. Thomas Fulda (Health Care Financing Administration), personal communication, 1980.

25. Vincent Gardner, "Drug Insurance and Cost Containment," in *National Drug Insurance Conference*, p. 37.

26. William F. Haddad, statement in U.S. Senate, *Competitive Problems* 1:13 (1967).

27. *Approved Drug Products with Proposed Therapeutic Equivalence Evaluations* (Washington, D.C.: U.S. Department of Health, Education, and Welfare, Food and Drug Administration, Bureau of Drugs, January 1979).

28. *F-D-C Reports*, January 30, 1978, p. 33.

29. Ibid., January 15, 1979, p. 9.

30. Ibid., June 11, 1979, p. 7.

31. Ibid., January 15, 1979, p. 15.

32. "FDA Endorses New York Equivalent Drug List," *FDA Consumer* 12(1):19 (February 1978).

33. *F-D-C Reports*, January 30, 1979, p. 35.

34. Ibid., January 15, 1979, p. 14.

35. RxTF, *Final Report*, pp. 36 and 37.

36. U.S. Senate, *Administered Prices*.

37. U.S. Senate, *Competitive Problems*.

38. RxTF, *Final Report*, p. 31.

39. U.S. Congress, Office of Technology Assessment, Drug Bioequivalence Panel, *Drug Bioequivalence* (Washington, D.C.: U.S. Government Printing Office, 1974).

40. M.C. Meyer, R.E. Dann, P.L. Whyatt, and G.W.A. Slywka, "The Bioavailability of Sixteen Tetracycline Products," *Journal of Pharmacokinetics and Biopharmaceutics* 2:287 (1974); M.C. Meyer, G.W.A. Slywka, R.E. Dann, and P.L. Whyatt, "Bioavailability of 14 Nitrofurantoin Products," *Journal of Pharmaceutical Sciences* 63:1693 (November 1974); Marvin C. Meyer, Armen P. Melikian, Philip L. Whyatt, and Gerald W.A. Slywka, "Hydrochlorothiazide Bioavailability: An Evaluation of Thirteen Products," *Current Therapeutic Research* 17:570 (June 1975); Gerald W.A. Slywka, Armen F. Melikian, Philip L. Whyatt, and Marvin C. Meyer, "Propoxyphene Bioavailability: An Evaluation of Ten Products," *Journal of Clinical Pharmacology* 15:598 (August-September 1975); Gerald W.A. Slywka, Armen P. Melikian, Arthur B. Straughn, Philip L. Whyatt, and Marvin C. Meyer, "Bioavailability of 11 Sulfisoxazole Products in Humans," *Journal of Pharmaceutical Sciences* 65:1494 (October 1976); Philip L. Whyatt, Gerald W.A. Slywka, Armen P. Melikian, and Marvin C. Meyer, "Bioavailability of 17 Ampicillin Products," *Journal of Pharmaceutical Sciences* 65:652 (May 1976); Armen P. Melikian,

Arthur B. Straughn, Gerald W. A. Slywka, Philip L. Whyatt, and Marvin C. Meyer, "Bioavailability of 11 Phenytoin Products," *Journal of Pharmacokinetics and Biopharmaceutics* 5:133 (1977); Marvin C. Meyer, Armen P. Melikian, and Arthur B. Straughn, "Relative Bioavailability of Meprobamate Tablets in Humans," *Journal of Pharmaceutical Sciences* 67:1290 (September 1978); and Marvin C. Meyer, Arthur B. Straughn, Gollamudi Ramachander, Jerry C. Cavagnol, and A. F. Biola Mabadeje, "Bioavailability of Sulfadiazine Solutions, Suspensions, and Tablets in Humans," *Journal of Pharmaceutical Sciences* 67:1659 (December 1978).

41. "Some Manufacturers Disclose Sources of Supply," *California Pharmacist* 21:7 (October 1973) and subsequent issues.

42. Brooke, *Resistant Prices*.

43. *F-D-C Reports*, January 15, 1979, p. 8.

44. Ibid., January 30, 1978, p. 33.

45. "The Drugmakers' Rx for Living with Generics," *Business Week*, November 6, 1978, p. 205; and Anthony J. Vetrano, "Implications of the Lannett and Pharmadyne Decisions," *American Journal of Hospital Pharmacy* 37:537 (April 1980).

No. 6. FORMULARIES

1. RxTF, *Drug Prescribers*, p. 12.

2. RxTF, *Final Report*, p. 38.

3. Stephen G. Sudovar, Jr., and Susan D. Rein, *Managing Medicaid Drug Expenditures—An Analysis of Divergent Approaches* (Nutley, N.J.: Roche Laboratories, 1978); and Marvin C. Meyer, Herbert Bates, Jr., and Robert G. Swift, "The Role of State Formularies," *Journal of the American Pharmaceutical Association* NS14:63 (December 1974).

4. Mickey C. Smith and Darego W. Maclayton, "The Effect of Closing a Medicaid Formulary on the Prescription of Analgesic Drugs," *Hospital Formulary* 12:37 (January 1977).

5. RxTF, *Final Report*, p. 40.

6. T. Donald Rucker and James A. Visconti, *How Effective Are Drug Formularies? A Descriptive and Normative Study* (Washington, D.C.: American Society of Hospital Pharmacists, 1978); and T. Donald Rucker, "Drug Formularies: Do They Work?" *American Pharmacy* NS19:31 (January 1979).

7. *Pills, Profits, and Politics*, pp. 121-133.

8. *The Selection of Essential Drugs. Report of a WHO Expert Committee.* WHO Technical Report Series 615. (Geneva, Switzerland: World Health Organization, 1977).

9. Antonio Ruas, cited in Joseph Hanlon, "Are 300 Drugs Enough?" *New Scientist* 79:708 (September 7, 1978).

10. Aida A. LeRoy (Health Information Designs, Washington, D.C.), personal communication, 1979.

No. 7. PATIENT COST-SHARING

1. RxTF, *Current Programs*.

2. Surendra K. Mansinghka, *National Health Insurance Issues—Viability of the Cost-Sharing Concept* (Nutley, N.J.: Roche Laboratories, 1978).

3. Allen J. Brands (Public Health Service), in *National Drug Insurance Conference*, p. 108.

4. RxTF, *Current Programs*, pp. 137, 140, 143, 171, 178, and 196.

5. Milton I. Roemer, Carl E. Hopkins, Lockwood Carr, and Foline Gartside, "Copayments for Ambulatory Care: Penny-Wise and Pound-Foolish," *Medical Care* 13(6):457 (June 1975).

6. Dennis Hefner and William Duwe, *Ambulatory Pharmaceutical Services for Medicare Recipients: A Pilot Project* (Springfield, Va.: National Technical Information Service, PB-289232, 1977).

7. Vincent Gardner, in *National Drug Insurance Conference*, p. 38.

8. Dennis Hefner, in ibid., p. 46.

9. T. Donald Rucker, in ibid., p. 55.

No. 8. DRUG UTILIZATION REVIEW

1. RxTF, *Final Report*, p. 48; and RxTF, *Insurance Design*, p. 64.

2. Donald C. Brodie, "Drug Utilization Review/Planning," *American Journal of Public Health* 46:103 (1972).

3. Frank F. Furstenberg, M. Taback, Harry Goldberg, et al., "Prescribing as an Index to Quality of Medical Care: A Study at the Baltimore City Medical Care Program," *American Journal of Public Health* 43:1299 (1953).

4. Charlotte Muller, "Medical Review of Prescribing," *Journal of Chronic Diseases* 18:689 (1965).

5. Leighton E. Cluff, "The Prescribing Habits of Physicians," *Hospital Practice* 2:100 (1967).

6. Paul D. Stolley and Louis Lasagna, "Prescribing Patterns of Physicians," *Hospital Practice* 2:100 (1967).

7. Robert F. Maronde, Peter V. Lee, Margaret M. McCarron, and Stanley Seibert, "A Study of Prescribing Habits," *Medical Care* 9:383 (September-October 1971); Robert F. Maronde, Stanley Seibert, Jack Katzoff, and Milton Silverman, "Prescription Data Processing: Its Role in the Control of Drug Abuse," *California Medicine* 117:22 (September 1972); and Robert F. Maronde, "Drug Utilization Review," in Albert I. Wertheimer and Patricia J. Bush, eds., *Perspectives on Medicines in Society* (Hamilton, Ill.: Drug Intelligence Publications, 1977), p. 169.

8. Fred Wegner, in *National Drug Insurance Conference*, pp. 102 and 103.

9. Robert F. Maronde (University of Southern California), personal communication, 1979.

10. Paid Prescriptions, *Pharmacy Inventory Systems*, Segments 3 and 7, LAC-USC Medical Center (Burlingame, Calif.: Paid Prescriptions, September-December 1974).

11. Maronde, "Drug Utilization Review."

12. Sue Madsen, in *National Drug Insurance Conference*, p. 81.

13. Sheila A. West et al., "Drug Utilization Review in an HMO: I. Introduction and Examples of Methodology," *Medical Care* 15:505 (June 1977).

14. "Tranquilizers—Largest Drug Category in Nursing Homes,"

Congressional Record (Senate), September 13, 1971, p. 14170; A.B. Magnus, "Tranquilizers in Nursing Homes? A Question of Use, Abuse, or Misuse," *Nursing Homes* 21:31 (July 1972); A.B. Magnus, "Are Tranquilizers Used as 'Chemical Straitjackets'? Do Adequate Safeguards Exist?" *Nursing Homes* 21:24 (March 1972); "Medicaid Drugs in Nursing Homes," *Congressional Record* (Senate), April 27, 1972, p. 6855; and Donald C. Brodie, Paul Lofholm, and Roger A. Benson, "A Model for Drug Utilization Review in a Skilled Nursing Facility," in Donald C. Brodie and Roger A. Benson, eds., *Drug Utilization Review and Drug Usage as a Determinant of the Quality of Health Care* (Rockville, Md.: U.S. Department of Health, Education, and Welfare, National Center for Health Services Research, 1976), p. 126.

15. Wayne A. Ray, "A Study of Antipsychotic Drug Use in Nursing Homes: Epidemiological Evidence Suggesting Misuse," *American Journal of Public Health* 70:485 (May 1980).

16. *Continuing Problems in Providing Nursing Home Care and Prescribed Drugs Under the Medicaid Program in California* (Washington, D.C.: General Accounting Office, 1970), p. 19.

17. Aida A. LeRoy and M. Lee Morse, *A Study of the Impact of Inappropriate Ambulatory Drug Therapy on Hospitalization* (Washington, D.C.: U.S. Department of Health, Education, and Welfare, Health Care Financing Administration, 1977).

18. U.S. Senate, Subcommittee on Long Term Care of the Special Committee on Aging, *Drugs in Nursing Homes: Misuse, High Costs, and Kickbacks* (Washington, D.C.: U.S. Government Printing Office, 1975).

19. U.S. Department of Health, Education, and Welfare, Social and Rehabilitation Service, Social Security Administration, *Federal Register* (January 17, 1974), p. 2238.

20. Alan Cheung and Ronald Kayne, "An Application of Clinical Pharmacy Services in Extended Care Facilities," *California Pharmacist* 23:22 (September 1975).

21. Samuel W. Kidder, "Saving Cost, Quality and People: Drug Reviews in Long-Term Care," *American Pharmacy* NS18(7):18 (July 1978).

22. Cited in Kidder, ibid.

23. Donald C. Brodie and William E. Smith, Jr., "A Conceptual Model for Drug Utilization Review," in Brodie and Benson, eds., *Drug Utilization Review*, p. 107.

24. Joseph D. McEvilla, "A Computerized Prescription Recording System," *Journal of the American Pharmaceutical Association* NS7:636 (1967).

25. San Joaquin County Medical Society, Foundation for Medical Care, *Progress in Prepayment* (Stockton, Calif.: Foundation for Medical Care, 1969).

26. Aida A. LeRoy, M. Lee Morse, and W.C. McCormick, *Physicians' Responses to Peer Review and Drug Utilization Review of a Medicaid Drug Program* (Jacksonville, Fla.: Paid Prescriptions, 1976).

27. R. Lee Morse (Health Information Designs, Washington, D.C.), personal communication, 1978.

28. Alan R. Nelson, in *National Drug Insurance Conference*, p. 92.

29. Robert R. Brook and Kathleen N. Williams, "Effect of Medical Care Review on the Use of Injections," *Annals of Internal Medicine* 85:509 (October 1976).

30. David A. Knapp, Brenda M. Brandon, Sheila West, and Dean E. Leavitt, "Drug Use Review—A Manual System," *Journal of the American Pharmaceutical Association* NS13(5):417 (August 1973); and David A. Knapp and Francis B. Palumbo, "Dollar Costs of Conducting Drug Use Review," *Journal of the American Pharmaceutical Association* NS17(4):231 (April 1977).

NO. 9. DRUGS AND COST-SAVING

1. Edward P. Cohen, "Basic Medical Research—Where Spending Money Saves Money," *American Medical News,* July 27, 1979.

2. R.Y. Keers, *Pulmonary Tuberculosis: A Journey Down the Centuries* (London: Baillière Tindall, 1978), pp. 209-250.

3. *Pills, Profits, and Politics,* pp. 8 and 9.

4. Philip Hopewell (San Francisco General Hospital), personal communication, 1980.

5. Evan D. Riehl, George Bereznicki, George Rogers, Robert Reza, and Joseph Eagan, "An Integrated Approach to Tuberculosis Care in the Commonwealth of Pennsylvania," *American Journal of Public Health* 67:162 (February 1977).

6. Donald R. Roden, "A Study to Determine the Prevalence and Cost of Glaucoma," a paper presented before the National Conference on Glaucoma Detection and Treatment, Tarpon Springs, Florida, January 10-11, 1980.

7. American Medical Association, Department of Drugs, *AMA Drug Evaluations,* 4th edition (Chicago, Ill.: American Medical Association, 1980), p. 353.

8. Robert L. Levy, statement before a press conference at the National Heart, Lung, and Blood Institute, Bethesda, Maryland, November 27, 1979.

9. Levy, ibid.

10. "Five-Year Findings of the Hypertension Detection and Follow-Up Program: I. Reduction in Mortality of Persons with High Blood Pressure, Including Mild Hypertension," *Journal of the American Medical Association* 242:2562 (December 7, 1979).

11. This last point is made in ibid.: "II. Mortality by Race, Sex and Age," *Journal of the American Medical Association* 242:2572 (December 7, 1979).

12. Levy, statement.

13. R. Reader et al., "The Australian Therapeutic Trial in Mild Hypertension," *Lancet* 1:1261 (June 14, 1980).

14. Robert F. Dee, quoted in Scott A. Baris, "SmithKline's Revival," *New York Times,* September 16, 1979, section 3, p. 1.

15. Warren Finkelstein and Kurt J. Isselbacher, "Cimetidine," *New England Journal of Medicine* 299:992 (November 2, 1978).

16. Richard S. Jacobs, "Possible Overutilization of Cimetidine," *Drug Intelligence and Clinical Pharmacy* 13(1):43 (January 1979); and Sam K. Shi-

momura, "Current Antacid Prescribing," *UCSF Pharmacy and Therapeutics Forum* 27(3):1 (May/June 1979).

17. SmithKline News Release, April 24, 1980.

18. George von Haunalter and Virginia V. Chandler, *Cost of Ulcer Disease in the United States* (Menlo Park, Calif.: Stanford Research Institute, 1977).

19. *Present Cost of Peptic Ulceration to the Dutch Economy and Possible Impact of Cimetidine on this Cost* (Rotterdam: Netherlands Economic Institute, 1977).

20. *The Impact of Cimetidine on the National Cost of Duodenal Ulcers* (Bryn Mawr, Penn.: Robinson Associates, 1978).

21. John Geweke and Burton A. Weisbrod, "Some Economic Consequences of Technological Advance in Medical Care: A Case of a New Drug," Discussion Paper 602-80, Institute for Research on Poverty, University of Wisconsin, April 1980.

22. Anthony Culyer and John Maynard, "Treating Ulcers with Cimetidine Can Be More Cost Effective than Surgery," *Medeconomics*, April 11, 1980.

23. Most of the material in this section is based on the elegant analysis published in 1979 by the Congressional Office of Technology Assessment. See Congress of the United States, Office of Technology Assessment, *A Review of Selected Federal Vaccine and Immunization Policies* (Washington, D.C.: U.S. Government Printing Office, September 1979). Information was also provided by Michael A. Riddiough (of the OTA), personal communications, 1979, 1980.

24. Cohen, "Basic Medical Research."

25. Donald R. Roden and W. Gerald Platt, *A Study to Estimate the Prevalence and Costs of Pneumonia* (Washington, D.C.: Pracon, Inc., February 1978).

26. Ibid.

No. 10. PROLOGUES TO NATIONAL DRUG INSURANCE: THE FOREIGN EXPERIENCE

1. This discussion updates and greatly expands material previously published by Simanis and by Silverman and Lydecker. See J. G. Simanis, *National Health Systems in Eight Countries*, U.S. Department of Health, Education, and Welfare, Social Security Administration, DHEW Publication No. (SSA) 75-11924 (Washington, D.C.: U.S. Government Printing Office, 1975); and Milton Silverman and Mia Lydecker, *Drug Insurance Options*, p. 37.

2. M. N. Graham Dukes and Inga Lunde, "Controls, Common Sense, and Communities," *Pharmaceutish Weekblad* 114:1283 (1979); and M. N. Graham Dukes and Inga Lunde, "Measuring the Effects of Drug Control— An Emerging Challenge," *Pharmaceutical Journal* (London) 223:511 (November 17, 1979).

3. Dukes and Lunde, "Controls, Common Sense, and Communities" and "Measuring the Effects of Drug Control."

4. This section is greatly indebted to Arthur Shields, "Report from

Australia," in *International Drug Reimbursement*, p. 37; and Arthur Shields (Australian Department of Health), personal communication, 1979.

5. This section is greatly indebted to Benjamin Huyghe (Belgian Ministry of Public Health and Family), personal communication, 1980.

6. Cited in *Le Soir* (Brussels), June 15, 1979.

7. Association Générale de l'Industrie du Médicament (AGIM), Brussels, Document 8822, September 28, 1979.

8. This section is greatly indebted to John A. Bachynsky, "Report from Canada," in *International Drug Reimbursement*, p. 73; John A. Bachynsky (Canadian Department of National Health and Welfare), personal communication, 1979; Thomas R. Fulda and Paul F. Dickens, III, "Controlling the Cost of Drugs," *Health Care Financing Review* 1(2):55 (Fall 1979); Patrick Tidball (Pharmacare, Government of British Columbia), personal communication; and Ken Brown (Manitoba Department of Health), personal communication, 1980.

9. This section is greatly indebted to Gunner Harder Andersen (Danish National Social Security Office), personal communication, 1980.

10. This section is greatly indebted to Simone Sandier and Thérèse Lecomte (Centre de recherche pour l'étude et l'observation des conditions de vie—CREDOC), personal communication, 1979.

11. This section is greatly indebted to Spyros Doxiadis, Meropi Violaki-Paraskeva, and Spyros Marketos (Greek Ministry of Social Services), personal communication, 1979.

12. This section is based largely on the Italian Ministry of Health, "Revisione del prontuario terapeutico per l'assistenza farmaceutica I.N.A.M.," *Gazzetta Ufficiale della Repubblica Italiana*, Supplement 328 (December 10, 1976); the Italian Ministry of Health, ibid., Supplement 238, Part 1 (August 26, 1979); "Istituzione del servizio, sanitario Nazionale. Legge 833," ibid., Supplement 360, Part 1 (December 28, 1978); and the Italian Ministry of Health, personal communication, 1980.

13. This section is greatly indebted to Tetsuo Nakano and Toru Ebihara (Japanese Ministry of Health and Welfare), personal communications, 1979 and 1980; and Chikataro Kawasaki (School of Pharmacy, Kobe-Gakuin University), personal communication, 1979.

14. This section is greatly indebted to Poppe Siderius and M.N. Graham Dukes (Dutch Ministry of Public Health and Environment), personal communication, 1979.

15. This section is greatly indebted to James L. Mauger (Chemists' Guild of New Zealand) and John S. Phillips (New Zealand Department of Health), personal communication, 1979.

16. This section is greatly indebted to Bjørn Jøldal, "Report from Norway," *International Drug Reimbursement*, p. 105; and Bjørn Jøldal (Royal Norwegian Ministry of Social Affairs), personal communication, 1979.

17. This section is greatly indebted to Rune Lönngren, "Report from Sweden," in *International Drug Reimbursement*, p. 61; Birgitta Davidson, Ake Nohrlander, and Hans Sarv (Apoteksbolaget), personal communication, 1979; Sven Strom, Birgitta Davidson, and Jan-Olof Brånstad, *Medical Care and Pharmaceutical Service in Sweden* (Stockholm: Apoteksbolaget, 1979); and Olle Hansson (University of Göteborg), personal communication, 1979.

18. This section is greatly indebted to Reinhard Kämpf (Swiss Federal Office of Social Security), personal communication, 1980.

19. This section is greatly indebted to T.D. Whittet, "Report from the United Kingdom," in *International Drug Reimbursement*, p. 85; and Brian Wills (United Kingdom Department of Health and Social Security), personal communication, 1979.

20. This section is greatly indebted to Irmela Helmer, "Report from West Germany," in *International Drug Reimbursement*, p. 29; Irmela Helmer (West German Federal Ministry for Youth, Family Affairs, and Health), personal communication, 1979; Robert Maronde (University of Southern California), personal communication, 1979; and Werner Schwarz (University of California, San Francisco), personal communications, 1979 and 1980.

21. Albert I. Wertheimer, *Drug Delivery Systems and Pharmacy Services in Eastern Europe* (prepared for the Fogarty International Center of the National Institutes of Health, Bethesda, Maryland, and reproduced by the U.S. Department of Commerce, National Technical Information Service, Springfield, Virginia, NTIS PB-299 499, 1979).

No. 11. THE AMERICAN EXPERIENCE

1. This section is largely based upon information in *Drug Insurance Options*, p. 25; and James C. Crutcher (Veterans Administration), personal communication, 1979.

2. This section is largely based upon information in *Drug Insurance Options*, p. 24; and Leslie V. Leversee (CHAMPUS), personal communication, 1979.

3. This section is largely based upon information in *Drug Insurance Options*, p. 24; and Allen J. Brands (U.S. Public Health Service), personal communication, 1979.

4. This section is largely based upon information in Thomas Fulda (Health Care Financing Administration), personal communications, 1979 and 1980.

5. RxTF, *Final Report*, p. 2.

6. U.S. Congress, Office of Technology Assessment, *A Review of Selected Federal Vaccine and Immunization Policies* (Washington, D.C.: U.S. Government Printing Office, 1979).

7. This section is largely based upon information in *Drug Insurance Options*, p. 25; and the National Pharmaceutical Council, *Pharmaceutical Benefits Under State Medical Assistance Programs* (Washington, D.C.: National Pharmaceutical Council, 1979).

8. William S. Apple, in *National Drug Insurance Conference*, p. 88.

9. National Pharmaceutical Council, *Pharmaceutical Benefits*.

10. This section is largely based upon information in *Drug Insurance Options*, p. 23; Sheila K. Touquan (Blue Cross Association, Blue Shield Association), personal communication, 1979; Vincent Gardner (National Association of Chain Drug Stores), personal communication, 1979; and William D. Thompson (Blue Shield of California), personal communication, 1979.

11. This section is largely based upon information in *Drug Insurance Options*, p. 21; Sue Madsen, in *National Drug Insurance Conference*, p. 81;

and Sue Madsen (Group Health Cooperative of Puget Sound), personal communication, 1979.

12. This section is largely based upon information in Julian Weiss and Nina Auger (Kaiser Foundation Health Plan), personal communication, 1980.

13. This section is largely based upon information in *Drug Insurance Options*, p. 22; and Patrick F. Killeen (United Auto Workers), personal communication, 1979.

No. 12. THE POLICY DECISIONS

1. The recommendations presented in this chapter are based in considerable part on the background monograph prepared for the 1977 National Conference on Drug Coverage Under National Health Insurance, and on the Proceedings of that conference. See Silverman and Lydecker, *Drug Insurance Options*; and Silverman and Lydecker, eds., *National Drug Insurance Conference*.

2. Robert M. Ball, personal communication, 1980.

3. RxTF, *Insurance Design*; and T. Donald Rucker, in *National Drug Insurance Conference*, p. 121.

4. *Drug Insurance Options*, p. 71.

5. Ibid.; and Vincent Gardner, in *National Drug Insurance Conference*, p. 30.

6. Irwin Lerner, in *National Drug Insurance Conference*, p. 97.

7. Donald F. Beste, Jr., in ibid., p. 23.

8. *Drug Insurance Options*, p. 75.

9. Alan R. Nelson, in *National Drug Insurance Conference*, p. 92.

10. Monroe E. Trout, in ibid., p. 27.

11. Robert C. Johnson, in ibid., p. 13.

12. *Guide to Prescription Drug Costs* (Baltimore: U.S. Department of Health, Education, and Welfare, Health Care Financing Administration, HCFA-02104, April 1980).

13. *Drug Insurance Options*, p. 81.

14. Ibid.

15. *National Drug Insurance Conference*, pp. 57-73.

16. *Drug Insurance Options*, p. 88.

17. Ibid., p. 86.

18. Richard F. deLeon, in *National Drug Insurance Conference*, p. 75.

19. *Drug Insurance Options*, p. 90; Richard F. deLeon, in *National Drug Insurance Conference*, pp. 76-78; Sue Madsen, in *National Drug Insurance Conference*, p. 81; and Bruce Siecker, "Computers for Pharmacy (Survival Technology)," *American Pharmacy* NS20(3):19 (March 1980).

20. *Drug Insurance Options*, p. 78.

21. Vincent Gardner, in *National Drug Insurance Conference*, p. 38; and Dennis Hefner, in *National Drug Insurance Conference*, pp. 46 and 47.

22. Allen J. Brands, in ibid., p. 108.

23. *Drug Insurance Options*, p. 92.

24. Donald F. Beste, Jr., in *National Drug Insurance Conference*, p. 111.

25. Fred Wegner, in ibid., p. 102.

26. Vincent Gardner, in ibid., p. 38.

27. *F-D-C Reports*, February 25, 1980, p. 14.

28. Jere E. Goyan (Food and Drug Administration), personal communication, 1980.

Index

Acquisition cost of drugs, for pharmacies, 61-62, 175, 189-190

Adverse drug reactions, 15, 19, 22, 30-35, 85, 140; detection by pharmacists, 68, 69, 116; and number of drug products available, 141; in nursing homes, 115-117; and post-marketing surveillance of new drugs, 33-35, 129-130; reporting of, by patients, 41; reporting of, by physicians, 32-33

Advertising, 14, 15, 16, 27, 28, 161. *See also* Drug companies, promotional activities of

Alaska, 175

Alberta, 148

Alcohol, use of, in combination with drugs, 41, 69, 114

Alcoholism, 48

Allergies: to drugs, recorded in patient medication records, 69, 110-111, 113, 179, 191; to penicillin, 33; treatment of, 47, 71

Alles, Gordon, 50

American Home Products Co., 95

American Hospital Formulary Service, 171

American Medical Association (AMA): and adverse drug reactions, 32; *Drug Evaluations*, 54, 57; and drug utilization review systems, 120; and generic vs. brand-name drugs, 82; and patient package inserts, 43; and Pharmaceutical Manufacturers Association, 16

American Pharmaceutical Association (APhA), 16, 90; and generic vs. brand-name drugs, 85; uniform cost-accounting system, 63, 64

American Public Health Association, 16

American Society of Hospital Pharmacists, 99

Aminopyrine, 22

Amphetamines, 33, 50, 58-59

Ampicillin, 79, 111

Analgesics, 33, 54-55, 98, 140, 149

Anemia, pernicious, 47, 67, 174

Angina, 70, 155

Antacids, 155

Anti-anemia drugs, 155

Anti-arthritis drugs, 23, 185

Antibiotics, 3, 19, 61, 71, 140; adverse reactions to, 33; cost, of different types, 54; cost-effectiveness of, 122-125, 131; foreign reimbursement policies for, 144, 149, 154; injected vs. oral, 119; and patient compliance, 41, 44; questionable prescribing of, 7, 47, 51-54, 109, 111. *See also* specific drug names

Anticancer drugs, 33, 144, 150, 154, 185

Anticoagulants, 33, 85, 155

Antidepressants, 3, 8, 33, 144

Antidiabetic drugs, 33, 70, 95, 149

Antidiarrhea drugs, 34

Antiexpectorants, 95

Antihistamines, 19, 52, 140, 144

Antihypertensive drugs, 3, 33, 34, 126-128, 149, 154-155, 185

Anti-infectives, cost-effectiveness of, 121-122

Anti-obesity drugs, 185, 187

Antisubstitution laws: in foreign countries, 142, 144, 149; state, 78, 79, 82, 83, 86, 93, 96. *See also* Generic vs. brand-name drug products

188; and generic vs. brand-name drugs, 84, 91-92

France, 14, 21, 22, 23; national drug insurance program, 139, 149-152, 192

Friedman, Milton, 25

Furadantin, 80

Furness, Betty, 91

Furstenberg, Frank, 109

Gallbladder disease, as adverse reaction to estrogens, 55

Ganellin, Roger, 128

Gardner, Vincent, 29, 88, 107

Gastrointestinal complaints, 49

General Accounting Office, U.S., 115

Generic-name drugs, 8; as cost-containment measure, use of, 120; manufacture by brand-name companies, 86

Generic vs. brand-name drug products, 16, 17, 69; and antisubstitution laws, 79, 83; and co-insurance, 104-105; comparative frequency in prescriptions, 83, 93; and existing health programs, 172, 173, 177, 178, 180, 181; and government policy in proposed insurance program, 28-29, 78, 186; and hospital pharmacy committee policy, 58; and market shares of competing products, 26; Paid Prescriptions study of Medicaid patients, 118; and pharmacists' recommendations, 64, 69; pharmacy policies on, 85; price differences, 26, 80, 92-93, 95-96. See also Antisubstitution laws; Prescribing patterns; Substitution laws

Generic vs. brand-name products, foreign drug insurance policies on: Australia, 142; Belgium, 145; Canada, 146, 147; Denmark, 149; France, 151; Great Britain, 166; Greece, 154; Italy, 156; Netherlands, 158; New Zealand, 159; Norway, 161; Sweden, 163; Switzerland, 165; West Germany, 168

Generix Co., 80

Germany. See West Germany

Glaucoma, 125-126

Glucose intolerance, as adverse reaction to estrogens, 55

Gonorrhea, 53, 71, 122

Gout, 70

Government drug reimbursement programs, 77, 78; and formularies, 97; and generic vs. brand-name drugs, 82-83, 86-88, 93; restrictions on reimbursement amounts, 61-62, 86-88. See also Federal agencies; Medicaid; Medicare

Goyan, Jere, 40, 45, 73, 198

Great Britain, 23; adverse drug reaction reporting program, 33; American drug company sales in, 14, 129; government

regulation of drug profits, 12; national drug insurance program, 137-141 passim, 166-167; number of drugs on market, 21, 139; regulation of drug promotion, 15-16, 28

Greece, 139, 152-154

Group Health Cooperative of Puget Sound, 113-114, 178-179

Guatemala, 102

Guide to Prescription Drug Costs, 57, 80, 189

Haddad, William, 88

Hawaii, 179

Hay fever, 47

Haynes, Brian, 41

Headache remedies, 22, 55

Health and Human Services, U.S. Department of. See Health, Education, and Welfare

Health Care Financing Administration (HCFA), 57, 80, 88, 107, 189

Health, Education, and Welfare, U.S. Department of (HEW): and cost-accounting guidelines for pharmacies, 64; drug utilization review requirement for nursing homes, 116; Maximum Allowable Cost (MAC) program, 86-88, 173, 175, 190; and model substitution law, 91-92; and proposed capitation system, 192; Review Panel on New Drugs, 23; Task Force on Prescription Drugs, 39, 46-47, 56, 57, 75, 83, 92, 94, 108-109

Health Information Designs, Washington, D.C., 63

Health Maintenance Organizations, 60, 83, 113-114, 178, 192

Heart disease: coverage under national health insurance, 184; treatment, 3, 18, 21, 39, 47-48, 126-128

Hefner, Dennis, 107

Hemorrhage, as adverse drug reaction, 33

Herdman, Paul, 90

Hinshaw, Corwin, 123

Hirsh, Harold, 70

Histamine-blockers, 3

Hormones, 71; and adverse drug reactions, 33, 55

Hospitalization, use of drugs to reduce need for, 121-133 passim

Hospitals, 36; and drug utilization review systems, 108-112, 120, 196; formularies in, 97, 99-101, 110; generic-name drugs, use in, 58; questionable use of antibiotics in, 52-53; and training of physicians about drugs, 57-58

Huck, John, 90

Hungary, 169

Designer: Randall Goodall
Compositor: In-House Composition
Printer: Vail-Ballou Press
Binder: Vail-Ballou Press
Text: 11/13 Garamond
Display: Typewriter